The Big Red Suitcase

The Big Red Suitcase

Margot Stornelli

ARPress
ILLUMINATING IDEAS.
EMPOWERING VOICES

ARPress
45 Dan Road Suite 15
Canton MA 02021
 Hotline: 1(888) 821-0229
 Fax: 1(508) 545-7580

Ordering Information:
Quantity sales. Special discounts are available on quantity purchases by corporations, associations, and others. For details, contact the publisher at the address above.

Printed in the United States of America.

 ISBN-13:   Softcover   979-8-89676-689-6
             eBook   979-8-89676-690-2

Library of Congress Control Number: 2025924880

Contents

Dedication

In memory of my Dutch sister, Jeannet, whose life ended too soon. I miss you every day.

My sincere gratitude to my parents, June and Leo, who gave me opportunities to travel and live internationally, experiences that shaped the course of my life.

To my adult children, Jessica and Andrew, and their families, imagine life in a time before technology ruled the world. Discover your (grand)mother's heritage, what makes her tick!

Disclaimer

This memoir reflects the author's recollections of experiences during her life with some details altered for clarity and privacy. Some names and characteristics have been changed, some events have been compressed, and dialogue may be supplemented. All people within are actual individuals; there are no composite characters. There are some sensitive traumatic events that may be disturbing. The content presented herein is based on the author's perspective and interpretation of the subject matter. Neither the publisher nor any associated parties shall be held responsible for any consequences arising from the opinions or interpretations expressed within this book.

Introduction

Born and raised in the middle of the twentieth century in western New York State, imagine growing up in the sixties and seventies, a time marked by war, civil unrest, and racial inequality, alongside the rise of pop culture. During these turbulent decades, I enjoyed the privilege of exploring the world on two continents with my family and independently. My senior year abroad living in a small village in Europe immersed in the language and culture of that country opened my eyes to what life was like in a land resurrected from the devastation of World War II.

My debut memoir, *The Big Red Suitcase: how my love for travel and adventure led to a student exchange program across the pond and marriage across the border,* is a true story composed from a lifetime of memories, some fictionalized to create this narrative. There are sensitive issues describing physical and mental challenges that played a key role in shaping my character. This autobiography reveals my heritage and life changing moments for my children, grandchildren, and future generations.

Returning to America was difficult while my heart remained in a dreamy fairytale. Entering adulthood in the eighties and nineties, weekend journeys across the border to a large metropolis, I married and experienced more culture shock, adapting to life in a multi-cultural society where diversity was encouraged not suppressed.

Toronto, Ontario, Canada became my forever home to live, work, play, and raise my children. Embracing Canadiana after witnessing the terrorism of September 11, 2001, in the USA, convinced me to pursue citizenship in my new homeland. Adapting to the evolving technological landscape of the new millennium ignited my curiosity, lifelong learning, and online communication skills, necessary to stay current with the changing societal norms.

Holding on to my American heritage was vital for survival as my life evolved into new experiences and nurturing family relationships. Maintaining dual citizenship had pros and cons but having spent more than half of my life in Canada, I felt more Canadian every day. Cultural immersion in Europe and Canada developed my character along with learning opportunities beyond the internet and classrooms. Adapting to rapidly changing technological advancement required resilience to remain relevant in the twenty-first century.

Living in a variety of different environments, from small villages to large cities and small apartments to large homes in four countries on two continents, opened doors for opportunities beyond my wildest dreams…

Welcome to my world!

Prologue

Graduation Day -Tuesday June 28, 1973
Bus to the Airport

My high school graduation day! While four hundred fellow classmates donned caps and gowns to celebrate this monumental achievement, I was beyond excited to board a Greyhound bus in the high school parking lot at 8:30 a.m. along with fifty other students from across the region on an adventure of a lifetime.

We travelled to Detroit Metropolitan Wayne County Airport to join three hundred students from across the nation in the Youth for Understanding Exchange Program on a flight across the ocean to Copenhagen, Denmark. We were going to spend a year in Europe, residing with host families while attending school. A life-changing adventure making new friends, experiencing new cultures, and learning through travel, discovery and exploration in foreign countries for high school graduates.

Youth for Understanding (YFU) had mailed a notice with my family assignment and travel instructions in the middle of May, stating

"The date of departure and night flight to Europe from Detroit was Tuesday, June 28, 1973. Further information from your regional representatives regarding specific travel arrangements from your home to the Detroit Airport would follow."

John, a young new teacher in the district and the Western New York travel coordinator for YFU, sent a separate letter a week later with the details of the bus ride to Detroit from Irondequoit High School (IHS) in Rochester. A former exchange student himself, he assisted the organization as an ambassador during the summer, escorting students to and from their destinations. He had to arrange those details before notifying his group of students who came from the west and central corners of the state including Buffalo, Rochester, Syracuse, and Binghamton. It was nice that the pickup point was at my school. He mentioned to Doug, the Greyhound Coach driver, that he graduated from IHS seven years earlier, and thought it would be a central location to pick up a group of students. He received permission from the school board administration to use the extra-large high school parking lot shared with Dake Middle School next door. Classes finished for the school year and only families that dropped off students for the bus gathered in the parking lot that morning, before the graduating students arrived later in the afternoon.

His letter had read,

"My name is John, and I will be your YFU guide as you embark on your year abroad to Europe from Rochester, New York. Please meet me at the parking lot of Irondequoit High School on Cooper Road at eight o'clock in the morning on Tuesday, June 28, 1973, to travel in an air-conditioned coach bus to Detroit. The bus will depart from the school at 9:00 a.m. Please arrive on time to get instructions, your airline tickets, and load your luggage on the coach. I will accompany you, along with fifty-two students, on both the bus ride and the flight to Copenhagen. Upon arrival in Copenhagen, everyone will receive further information from the European representatives regarding transportation to their destinations across the continent."

Mom and I hugged and kissed goodbye on one cheek. She smiled and whispered in my ear, "This is my third time sending a child to Europe. Enjoy the adventure, an experience you will remember for the rest of your life!"

"I love you. I will miss you." I whispered back. She knew how to relieve my anxiety.

In a few months' time, I would discover that at that moment she was already planning a surprise visit to see me at Christmas. I had said goodbye to Dad the night before because he always left the house at 6:00 a.m. to make his hospital rounds before the secretaries opened the office in the morning. Greg called at 10 p.m. (7 p.m. Pacific Coast Time) on Sunday evening to wish me "bon voyage."

Other parents shed tears of both sadness and joy as their children loaded their bags into the luggage compartment and rushed to the window seats on the bus. The students, all strangers, arrived from various schools around central and western New York state. I found a window seat on the bus about five rows behind the driver. A tall, young woman was sitting in the aisle seat when I approached, and she pointed to the empty seat by the window.

"I would like you to sit with me," she said as she got up so I could slide into the window seat.

"Don't you want to sit by the window?" I queried.

"No, I prefer to stretch my legs in the aisle," she yawned.

"My name is Margot," I introduced myself smiling, "What is yours?"

"Mary." Appearing nervous, she added, "I couldn't sleep last night. What about you?"

"I have been looking forward to this adventure for a long time." I smiled, "I am super exited that it is finally happening,"

She stared at me wide-eyed as though she could hardly believe I wasn't as nervous as she was and then said, "This is my first time flying to Europe. I have never traveled alone."

"You're not alone, everyone on this bus is traveling to the same place. This reminds me of a class field trip," I assured her. "We can stick together if that makes you feel better."

Her eyes lit up smiling, "That would be nice, if you don't mind."

I looked around, "Nobody else from my school is on this bus," I said. I was relieved there were no familiar faces.

"I don't recognize anyone from my school in Webster here either," Mary claimed as she stood up glancing behind her nervously.

"Good, we can become new friends." I remarked. "When we return home next year, we can get together as we live across the bay from each other."

"Yeah, it will be nice to reconnect after our adventure finishes," she agreed.

We got comfortable, fastened our seat belts, and reclined our seats. It was going to be a long day with the overnight flight to Europe. We chatted while the bus cruised on the thruway.

In Buffalo, we were a little confused when the bus turned off the thruway. A tall guy with glasses and a mustache, rose from his seat in the back of the coach and spoke loudly grabbing everyone's attention, "Hey, why are we in the lane pointing to Canada? I thought we were going to Michigan!"

"It is more direct to travel along the north side of Lake Erie through Canada instead of the south side of the lake through the United States to Michigan" beamed John, our YFU leader, at the front of the coach. He grabbed the folded paper road map on the driver's console and pivoted to face the group of curious students as he traced the route with his fingers while he talked, to show everyone the shorter distance crossing the border.

We heard another voice mumbled behind us, "Hmmm, a geography lesson. Can't get away from school this summer." It got everyone talking about the road trip as no one was prepared for the long drive to Detroit.

John continued addressing the students, "As you boarded the bus, I asked everyone to keep their passports with their wallets, not in their luggage. You have them to enter Europe and will need them at the USA/Canada border stations."

Pointing towards the driver, John said, "Doug says it'll be faster to travel through Ontario if everyone had their travel documents in hand to present to Customs."

Everyone started arguing about the bus route, not really knowing what they were talking about.

"Calm down please!" John shouted. "He's driven this route for years; we should trust his judgement."

The bus continued onto the Peace Bridge, a mile long bridge stretching across the Niagara River connecting the USA to Canada, one of three such bridges between Buffalo and Niagara Falls, a popular tourist area on both sides of the border. At the customs booth entering Fort Erie, Ontario, Canada, John told the border agent through the open door, "The bus took a shortcut from New York state through Canada to the Detroit Airport for an international flight tonight."

Doug cleared the booth and parked the bus next to the building. John stood up to face the students and announced, "Please sit still, obey the Canadian agent, and don't leave the bus. When he leaves, you can use the restroom inside the building entrance."

A tall middle-aged man dressed in a security uniform with a baton and holster attached to his belt, boarded the bus to make his inspection. He was not used to a busload of teenagers, as most days he dealt with seniors on day trips to the Falls and festivals in Ontario. As the agent walked down the aisle on the bus, each student handed him their passport for a quick glance and it was given back to them. He looked at me to ensure my picture matched my face and said, "You are not wearing eyeglasses in the picture."

Smiling I replied, "I wore contact lenses and eyeglasses interchangeably, Sir." I wore my glasses that day knowing it would be a long time before I could remove my contacts and did not want to lose them.

He moved to the next row of seats and occasionally made comments about hair styles, eyeglasses, mustaches, wide and long sideburns, and beards on other students. We all chuckled as he was curious how teenagers' appearances changed drastically from the time their passports were issued in the past five years as facial features mature rapidly during their high school years. Teenagers' appearances reflected the trends of the season. Shoulder length hair was very common on both boys and girls at that time.

The agent finished his inspection in forty minutes. When he left, we stepped outside and lined up to use the restroom for a five-minute break. After the students returned to the bus, John took a head count and the bus continued the journey, crossing back into the USA on the Ambassador Bridge to Detroit four hours later. It felt like a long drive following the 401 to Windsor, Ontario, a route I had never traveled before, unlike the urban landscapes I saw on shopping trips to Toronto with my mother and sister. The bus traveled fast without delays at the borders. It would get busier later in the week with two holidays in both countries; Canada Day was celebrated on Friday, July 1 and Independence Day in the USA followed on Monday, July 4. Doug was pleased that there were no accidents or construction to slow down, arriving at the airport before 3 p.m., thirty minutes ahead of his scheduled 3:30 p.m. arrival.

The American border guard waved the coach through the gate without another inspection when John told him through the opened door pointing to his YFU badge pinned to the breast pocket of his shirt, "We are all Americans, and the driver took a short cut through Canada from Buffalo to reach the Detroit Airport for an international flight this evening." John, an experienced traveler representing YFU, was trained to be confident and consistent in his explanations to the border agents. We arrived at the airport in the middle of the afternoon, five hours before our scheduled flight time.

Doug stepped outside to stretch, opened the two luggage doors, and assisted students down the three steps to the curb. As I exited the bus, I thanked him for the smooth ride. He smiled as everyone said goodbye. Sitting close to the front of the bus, Mary and I overheard the conversations between our driver and our guide. We both felt more confident about the ride listening to them talk about their travels. Doug lived in Detroit and was happy to come home to his family after a week of driving through the Appalachian Mountains near the East Coast. He enjoyed long-distance coach driving as an opportunity to see the country. He always requested the YFU routes during the summer months to mingle with students and listen to their stories as it would bring him home for a few days. He sent his oldest child to Brazil last year and had plans to send two more children overseas in the future. His children loved listening to his stories about bus trips.

We collected our bags from the luggage compartment and walked into the terminal. It was hot when we left the bus. I did not need the sweatshirt wrapped around my waist. I wore my navy-blue and gold sweatshirt with the school logos on the front and back:

Irondequoit Indians Class of '73

The school teams were known as the "Indians" since 1924 when the school was founded, honoring the indigenous roots of the area. However, the district voted to change the mascot to "Eagles" in 2001 to create a more inclusive and respectful school environment.

Waiting in line at the Trans World Airlines (TWA) ticket counter to check my bag, I felt lighter without my sweatshirt wrapped around my body, so I stuffed it into my big red suitcase to have one less thing to carry through the airport and on the airplane. Surprisingly, my big red suitcase was under the forty-four-pound weight limit, weighing only forty-two pounds. I slipped my boarding pass inside my passport stored in a zipper pocket of my purse so that I would not lose it.

On the weekend, Mom had suggested that she would send my winter jacket and boots via United Parcel Service (UPS) in the fall like she sent items to Aunt Toni when she lived in Japan. It was a dependable courier service for items too large for the regular mail service and had been in business since the beginning of the twentieth century, operating around the world. I left my white fur hat, scarf, and gloves on my bed next to my red winter jacket and knee-high suede boots for her to mail in October. I also left my electric hair dryer behind, because Europe uses 220 voltages not 120 volts, the standard in North America. I was aware that Europe used Metric, not Imperial measurements, so I would be adapting to a lot of new ideologies, like temperature, distance, and weight. As much as I anticipated Europeans being like Americans, these subtle differences reminded me that I was stepping into a new and unknown world, an ocean away from home.

John reminded all students, "Please stick together and pay attention. Don't lose your boarding pass, go through customs, and follow the signs to Gate A16 in Terminal 2. I will meet you there before we board the plane."

A guide leading the group to Europe helped ease students' anxieties. John planned to meet his cousin who was hitchhiking through Scandinavia before returning to the USA. He enjoyed this assignment; every summer, he would explore a different region of the continent for two weeks before escorting students from the previous year's exchange program back home. It was a great summer job to help fund his college education with free travel. He also signed up for the trips at the end of August to bring students home from the summer program before the start of the school year in September. He hinted to our group that we might meet him again on our return trip home next year.

As Mary and I stepped off the bus and collected our suitcases, we took in the sight of the huge international airport in front of us, anticipating our journey that would define our future lives.

Overnight Flight

Mary anxiously asked me questions as we walked through the terminal. I saw the restroom sign and nudged her to join the line outside the entrance when we approached it. She smiled five minutes later when we emerged outside the door. I was relieved as the red light above the lavatory on the bus always flickered indicating it was "*OCCUPIED*". We found a water fountain and filled our thermoses. With no snacks in her purse, I waited at the snack bar where she bought chips, then we hustled down the long hallway to gate A16.

By five o'clock in the afternoon, all students gathered at the gate lobby with their carry-on bags and snacks. John sat with us by the windows to watch our luggage load onto the plane. He took attendance calling our names on his clipboard to ensure everyone was accounted for. The students clapped when their bag lifted into the cargo hold. It was their first overseas flight and there was a mix of bewilderment and excitement; but having travelled to Europe previously with my family, I was confident that it would be safe. It was my first international adventure alone, an exciting but scary thought.

Mary sat beside me facing the window so she could see the activity of the other planes on the tarmac. I showed her how they taxied over to a runway then turned to gain speed to ascend into the sky. She smiled and opened her bag of chips while I grabbed my granola bar and apple from my purse. We pulled out our boarding passes and noticed that we would be sitting together in row 19B and 19C. We smiled, knowing we were spending the night together.

At seven o'clock, the gate agent announced, "Please line up to board the eight o'clock flight to Copenhagen. A night flight over the Atlantic Ocean, crossing six time zones, it will be morning when you land."

We walked on the tarmac to climb the stairs to board the aircraft, found our assigned seats, and tossed our hand luggage into the storage bin above our heads. There were no covered skybridges to walk to the airplane at that time. It was dusk, the sun was setting, and the moon was rising without a cloud in the sky. When the plane taxied down the runway, we listened to the safety check and buckled our seatbelts. It was a smooth ride with no turbulence, and the stars were bright as I looked out my window. Joanne, seated on the other side of the aisle, said excitedly, "The full moon shone brightly to guide us on our journey!"

Danny sitting next to her chuckled, "I saw the cow jumping over the moon."

We all laughed at the nursery rhyme reference. After spending the day together on the bus, in the airport, and switching to the plane, the group became more comfortable traveling together, cracking jokes, and relieving their anxiety.

At cruising level, dinner was served. As two flight attendants rolled a cart down the aisle, everyone lowered the table latched to the seat in front of them. They worked quickly to serve the food. One angry passenger, it sounded like Bill yelling, the guy who complained about the detour to Canada on the bus, rang the buzzer and when a third flight attendant answered the call, he complained of hunger.

That flight attendant walked to her station, grabbed the microphone, and calmly responded so everyone could hear, "Please stay in your seats while we distribute the trays. Everyone will receive the same dinner and be served in row number order. We can't honor special requests. Be patient and you will get your meal momentarily." I was amused by this announcement having traveled on long flights in the past, but many students had no idea what to expect as first time passengers.

A small, covered tray with breaded fried chicken, mashed potatoes, peas, and vanilla pudding for dessert was placed on my table. The food was cold, chicken was hard, and the vegetables were mushy, but everyone was hungry late in the evening. The clatter of forks and knives drummed melodies as we ate our food. When we finished the meal, the flight attendants rolled two carts down the aisle, to collect the trays and serve beverages. The dirty dishes, silverware, and glasses were removed from the aircraft to be washed between flights; paper napkins and straws were collected in trash bags. We had a choice of sodas, juice, water, or lemonade. I chose lemonade and Mary had apple juice.

After dinner, the pilot dimmed the lights and reminded everyone, "Please raise the tables back into position and pull the shade down on the windows." The signal above our heads indicated that we could recline our seats to sleep. The flight attendants rolled a cart down the aisle, handing out pillows to all passengers.

After a long day of travel, I dozed off as soon as my head rested on the pillow against the window. The cabin became quiet, as snoring whistled through the aisle. Resting in a semi-reclined position surrounded by hundreds of people gave me some comfort. It was a light sleep as I was conscious of the engine noise in the cabin while dreaming about this new adventure. *"Daniel"* by Elton John (1973), a ballad about traveling on a jet plane, a popular song on the radio that summer was playing on rewind in my head.

Hours later, the pilot announced, "The plane will land in Malmo, Sweden. The flight plan changed to divert traffic away from an accident in Denmark." Jolted awake in shock, everyone was relieved that we were safe. The flight attendants rolled two carts down the aisle, first to collect the pillows and second to serve a continental breakfast consisting of a croissant with a choice of apple or orange juice. Mary and I chose apple juice. We printed our names, addresses, and phone numbers on scraps of paper napkins to call each other next summer. I stuffed the napkin with "***Mary Jenkins, Holt Rd., 789-0392***" into the zipper pocket of my purse to keep it in a safe place.

As the plane landed, John, the leader on our bus, stood in the aisle as our group sat directly behind him, bellowing, "Your host families' representatives have been notified of our delay," and barked sharply "Please stick together and don't step out of line upon entering the terminal." We roared at this comment; he sounded like a drill sergeant. It startled everyone to attention as we yawned after a restless night on the airplane.

When the plane taxied to stop, we descended the stairs onto the tarmac, walked into the terminal in an orderly fashion, collected our luggage at the baggage claim counter, and marched through customs to get our passports stamped. Our European hosts watched in awe as the young American students respectfully lined up with their passports and bags for inspection. We were so tired and bewildered that we were quiet and well behaved. Led into a room where signs indicated our destinations, Mary and I hugged goodbye. She was going to Switzerland for the year.

Twenty-Four Hour Coach to Belgium

I found the sign for Belgium with Germany and The Netherlands listed above it. It would be another long drive, the last stop on the bus. I walked over to the far corner of the room where students lined up to board the motor coaches outside the terminal. My coach was the last one at the far end of the sidewalk and Mary went to her coach at the front of the line. She waved as I dragged my big red suitcase past her bus. The driver loaded my big red suitcase into the assigned luggage compartment for each stop the bus would make along the route, a sign for "Germany" above the first door, "The Netherlands / Belgium" on the last door.

As I boarded the coach, the new YFU leader, "Franz" embossed on the name badge pinned to his lapel, welcomed weary students in perfect English. A tall handsome guy with chin length blonde locks and a bushy beard and mustache, he grabbed my arm to help me step up and politely asked, "What is your name and where are you going, young lady?"

"Margot, Belgium." I whispered, yawning.

He gave me a brochure with an orange border from the bottom of the stack in his hand and checked my name on the list on his clipboard.

Each passenger received a color-coded brochure that identified the different regions. The orange border represented the Benelux region of Belgium, The Netherlands, and Luxemburg. I sat next to Linda, who had a brochure with a red border, travelled to Hamburg, Germany. She sat in the aisle seat so she could leave the bus before me. When Franz sat down at the front of the bus across from the driver, he nodded his head that everyone boarded. The driver started the engine and waited his turn to move into traffic.

I liked sitting by the window to rest my head and view the scenery. The air-conditioned bus drove onto a ferry to cross the North Sea to Denmark. A short ferry crossing, signs read in large bold red letters, "**STAY IN YOUR VEHICLE.**" There was no observation deck for people to walk about. All the buses from my flight took this ferry because our arrival destination changed and then cruised the highways of Europe.

There were no passport checks at the border points from Sweden, into Denmark, and later into Germany, The Netherlands, and last to Belgium. The border guard communicated in German with Franz, who explained that we had already passed through customs at the airport in Sweden and proceeded through the gates. Bilingual in at least two languages, the YFU leaders were trained to work with teenagers promoting the program and relieved any anxiety students had about travel and staying in the countries they visited. The trusted advisors ensured our journeys were safe and our lived experiences memorable. When I joined, the program operated in forty countries for twenty years and remained popular for student travel half a century later, creating fabulous memories across generations.

Driving through Germany, I marveled at the scenery. The roads traversed beautiful landscapes as they roamed through the countryside, reminding me of the family road trip through Southern Europe six years earlier. The bus traveled south to Hamburg and Hanover to drop off students holding the red border brochures, then turned west towards The Netherlands to stop in Amsterdam to drop off more students, and finally south into Belgium for its last stop, a twenty-four-hour journey from start to finish. Three different drivers wore the same uniform with a red tie and blazer. They changed shifts when the bus dropped off students. When Linda left the bus, I lifted the arm rest in the middle of our seats to rest my weary legs.

Although these stops took an hour each time for students to depart and collect their luggage, the remaining passengers were told to stay on the bus so that there was no confusion with wayward teenagers wondering inside the bus stations. At the second stop, Franz took a head count of the remaining passengers and stepped inside the station to purchase drinks and bratwurst sandwiches for us. Bratwurst tasted like the white hots I ate back home in Rochester; a German sausage, made from pork and veal, and seasoned with ginger, nutmeg, coriander, or caraway. It was too greasy and spicy for me, but I was hungry. The croissant I ate for breakfast on the airplane was a long time ago. I devoured it, a sample of new foods and flavors introduced to me that year. We could stand, stretch, and walk in the coach aisle. There was a small lavatory at the back for bathroom breaks.

In Amsterdam, Franz asked the remaining seven students to sit together at the front of the bus. As the bus travelled the final leg of the journey, it took approximately two hours to reach Antwerp. We had a lively discussion about our adventure, as we came from different corners of the USA. Holding up the postcard, he asked, "Do you have a brochure with an orange border? Orange was specific to The Netherlands and Belgium region. Keep this card in a safe place with your passport." The contact information became useful to me two months later.

He also explained, "All of these countries belonged to the European Union (EU); therefore, the passport checks only happened at the airports for international travelers. It was not necessary to check the passports when driving between countries. On trains, conductors will check for tickets. However, bring your passports whenever you travel with your families to be prepared for random checks." He had similar discussions with students as they left the bus inside each station.

On the final leg of the bus ride, Franz became friendly with the remaining passengers. He explained that he lived in Belgium and planned a two-week break before taking American students on the previous year's program via coach bus back to Copenhagen for their return home. He would then travel to North America to escort those students back home for the summer with John. He was visiting his cousins in Canada, his first vacation to Montreal before returning in August with European students on the summer program in America and then start his final school year at the University of Groningen, The Netherlands. He was excited about the road trip driving across Canada from Halifax on the east coast to Vancouver on west coast.

I was a bit stunned that the journey took so long, so I pulled the letter from YFU that I received in Rochester out of my purse to review it before the arrival in Antwerp. It did not mention the twenty-four coach ride.

The letter stated, "All students will meet in Detroit for an overnight flight to Copenhagen. Regional representatives in the USA (*John*) and Europe (*Franz*) will coordinate your connecting transportation to your destination."

I was not aware that another day of bus travel was on the agenda upon arrival in Europe. There was no communication regarding how long this bus ride would take.

When the bus arrived at the station in Antwerp, Belgium, I adjusted my watch to 10:30, displayed on the large wall clock with a short arrow pointing up between the X and XI and the long arrow pointing down at the VI above the arrival and departure screens. One had to learn Roman numerals to read analog clocks correctly, there were no digital devices at that time. It was Thursday morning, fifty hours after I kissed my mother goodbye in America. The driver placed our luggage on the sidewalk when we left the bus.

Another YFU leader at the station, Annemieke, greeted the seven students and welcomed us to Belgium in English. She explained that she studied at the university in Brugge and coordinated all YFU arrivals and departures into the country from Antwerp and Brussels, remaining local to care for her young children. After we collected our luggage, she led us to the room where our host families gathered. I learned who my host family would be six weeks earlier. I took the photographs out of my purse and found the Van Leet family in the middle of the crowded room.

An incredible journey for a teenaged girl was just beginning as she arrived in Europe to live with a family and attend school in a foreign country to learn an unfamiliar language, immersing herself into the culture, totally different from her previous European vacations with her family as a tourist. Those memories flashed in front of me igniting my fierce desire to embark on this new adventure. But first, let's take a short trip down memory lane to learn about my childhood and understand the excitement that led to this event before we continue this journey of a lifetime!

PART I

GROWTH AND PRIVILEGE

Born and Raised

in the USA

(1956 – 1973)

Chapter 1

Flashback: Growing Up in Irondequoit

The Office

As the third child in a middle-class family, I entered the world on the first day of spring during the Eisenhower administration, in the middle of the twentieth century.

My father, a family physician, opened his practice in Irondequoit, a suburb north of the city overlooking Lake Ontario, a year before I was born. Another brother was also born eighteen months after my birth in this home. The corner of St Paul Boulevard and Cooper Road was a busy intersection to raise a young family with four children of two girls and two boys, aged five years apart from oldest to youngest. A fenced enclosure in the front yard provided a play space outside with a screen door leading into the kitchen where my mother could watch us from inside the house.

The office had three examination rooms attached to the back of the house with the waiting room in the front by the entrance door overlooking Cooper Road. The beige stucco building, an old two-storey home where we lived for five years, had three huge bedrooms with large walk-in closets on the second floor. We played tag and hide and seek upstairs on rainy days roaming through the tunnels among the hanging clothes.

There was a large yard with a patio and bushes on the opposite side of the house facing St. Paul Blvd. Mrs. Tarrant, an older woman whose family moved to Texas, lived alone in a large white house on St Paul next door to the office. She liked to give us her homemade treats of delicious cookies and cakes. Large older homes lined the boulevard that stretched a few miles north towards the lake and a direct route with buses to downtown Rochester to the south. We were not allowed to play in the yard on that side of the house due to the traffic that travelled at high speed on that four-lane road.

One day when my younger brother, Paul and I were playing outside in the fenced enclosure facing Cooper Road while my older siblings, Mark and Jan, attended Briarwood Elementary School, we saw the family car sitting in the driveway. It was always parked in the garage. We played one of our favorite games. I grinned, "Paul, do you want to go shopping?"

He replied, "Yeah, Marg, we need bread and butter from Wegmans. Mom will take us shopping after school." She waited until Mark and Jan arrived home, so we would drive to Wegmans together as a family.

I pointed to the car, and said, "Let's pretend we are driving to the grocery store." We walked across the yard to the driveway and found the gate on the sidewalk ajar. The passenger door was unlocked; we climbed into the front seat and buckled the seatbelts. I sat in the driver's seat pretending to drive to Wegmans. As I grasped the steering wheel, I noticed a lever behind it with **P R N D L** on the handle. Paul and I did not know what the letters meant but our curiosity soared. When I touched it, the car moved backward. Suddenly, we rolled down the hill, across the street into the neighbor's garage door.

"CRASH!"

One of his patients, Jane Smith, walked along the sidewalk and down the three steps to her car parked in the small lot parallel to the street, noticed the moving car and ran back inside to alert my dad of the incident. "Marie, where is the doctor?"

He came out of his study that was across from the entrance door next to the waiting room and raised his voice, "What is the matter, Jane?" as she was huffing and puffing short of breath.

She was waving her arms frantically pointing out the door to the street and said, "Look out the window, your car is rolling!" He saw the car across the street in the neighbor's driveway and rushed outside.

Looking through the screen door to the kitchen, he yelled, "June come outside, the kids are in the car!" They ran across the street together to fetch me and my brother.

When the car stopped abruptly, in front of the neighbor's garage door, Paul and I screamed in horror. At three and four years old, in shock, we didn't know what happened. Mom and Dad opened the doors, applied the emergency brake, unbuckled our seatbelts, and picked us up to comfort us. They carried us across the street back into our house and quickly checked that we were not bruised or injured. Mom sat with us on the couch and read our favorite Mother Goose book to calm us down. I loved her animated expressions when she read stories to us, a tradition that continued for years when we came home for lunch during the school day. She read the entire series of Freddy the Pig books by Walter Brooks (c.1927- 1958) while we attended Listwood Elementary School in our new childhood home.

Dad went back across the street and saw Mrs. Wilson wandering around the car in her sundress, wondering what happened. He apologized for our mischief and promised to speak to her husband about repairs and reimbursement after he finished in the office later that day.

After dinner, Mr. Wilson knocked on the kitchen door, furious but understanding when he talked to my dad. Standing near the bedroom window overlooking the driveway, Mark saw the red flashing lights on the Irondequoit Police car that pulled into the driveway and called mom over to the window. She ran downstairs to meet the officer as he knocked on the door, showed him where my dad was sitting with Mr. Wilson, and then returned upstairs to the children.

The gentlemen shook hands and sat down at the table. Dad started the conversation looking at the police officer, "Good evening, Sir. This is Mr. Wilson, who lives across the street where the garage door broke. We are negotiating a settlement to get it replaced."

The car was towed away an hour earlier for repairs. Officer Dean introduced himself pointing to his badge, "Doc and Mr. Wilson, my name is Officer Dean." He coughed and continued, "I am not here to press charges, Doc, but we need to file an accident report. Your patient, Jane Smith, reported to the police station after her appointment at your office today. Mr. Wilson arranged for me to meet here at seven o'clock to assess the damage."

Dad replied, "Yes, Jane witnessed the car moving when she left and came back inside to alert me immediately. I was grateful that she acted quickly."

Mr. Wilson looked up from his insurance policy on the table disgusted and said, "Nice to meet you, Officer." He puffed on his cigarette then said, "The doctor's children were outside playing and found the car unlocked. Then all hell broke loose!" Mark sat at the top of the stairs in his pajamas out of sight, laughing quietly.

Dad recounted the story to the gentlemen that I told my mother about our game. As soon as it happened, he ran outside to rescue his children, surveyed the damage, and informed Mrs. Wilson that he would talk to her husband later.

Seated around the dining room table, the men negotiated a cash deal to avoid auto and home insurance claims. Mr. Wilson and my dad signed the police report, and they were handed a carbon copy of the five-page mimeographed document (two for the claimants, three for the police department). The gentlemen shook hands and left the house. Dad came upstairs and told mom that everything was resolved peacefully. Mom never left the car in the driveway again, always parked it in the garage. Back at his bedroom window, Mark watched the policeman walk across the street with Mr. Wilson who photographed the damaged garage door.

Few cars had seatbelts, but my parents ordered them when they bought the green AMC Nash two years earlier to keep their children secure when driving. We clasped the seat belts as soon as we sat in the front seat, a habit we learned when we graduated from our booster chairs. We had to buckle up each time we went for a ride in the car. Mom locked the car and set the emergency brake when it was sitting in the driveway after that dreadful day. I don't remember the accident; my father recounted it repeatedly throughout my life, making it more dramatic every time. After this accident, my parents decided it was time to move to a new safer neighborhood.

I often wondered later in life if this trauma contributed to my anxiety when driving. I always buckled my seatbelt as a driver and as a passenger. I reminded my passengers to buckle up before I drove anywhere. Decades later, it became the law with stiff penalties and fines where cars stopped at RIDE (Reduce Impaired Driving Everywhere) checkpoints. The seat belt saved my life in three automobile accidents as an adult; skidding into a snowbank on the highway at age 20, rearended in a school parking lot twenty years later in Canada and colliding with a pickup truck while making a left turn visiting an old friend in New York a decade after that. I paid high automobile insurance rates most of my life due to these accidents.

Dad worked at this office for forty years before he joined a group practice on Ridge Road. An older couple moved into the office house as caretakers when we moved to our new home, cleaning the office after hours. A private practice, he was on call every day of the week from morning until night every day of the year.

When he booked vacation time, there were two other doctors who took his calls, and they rotated on weekends so that Dad also took their calls. Prior to answering machines and voice mail, patients were instructed to call an answering service, later known as a call center at the University of Rochester Medical Center (URMC) if the doctor did not answer the phone, and the switchboard operators contacted one of the other doctors on call. This call center serviced all doctors in the city. The Doctors Exchange phone number was listed below my father's office phone number on his appointment and drug prescription pads, as well as in the annual telephone book; a one-inch-thick magazine of white and yellow pages updated, reprinted, and delivered to each house every year. The white pages listed all the residents, and the yellow pages listed the businesses in alphabetical order. All residents who owned a telephone were published in the phone book. One paid a fee for an unlisted number if they did not want their name published. There were no business cards to give to patients.

With four children soon attending school, the family outgrew the house attached to the office. Irondequoit was a nice town to raise the family and new subdivisions were emerging around the schools. It was necessary to move to a larger home in a safer neighborhood after five years living at the cramped office on a busy intersection. Mom enjoyed managing a new project, designing a new home for her growing family.

Childhood Home

Upon moving to our new house on Old North Hill in July 1960, the children transferred to Listwood Elementary and then Dake Middle School in the fifth grade for four years before entering Irondequoit High School in the ninth grade on Cooper Road. The three schools were situated in a rectangle between List Ave and Cooper Road where they shared the sports fields in the middle and students could walk or bike across the fields to fetch their siblings to travel home together. All three schools were a ten-minute walk from our new home off List Avenue and from the office on Cooper Road. Our childhood home was a ten-minute walk or bike ride along Dake Avenue to the office; the neighborhood formed a triangle between the two homes and the three schools.

I was excited to start kindergarten in the fall, walking to school with my sister and new neighbors. Mom and I walked to Listwood Elementary School together on the first day of school to meet my teacher, Miss York, for an orientation session. Mr. Stacy, the Principal, welcomed new students and parents to the school community. At that time, kindergarten was a half day every day with one teacher for twenty students. All the students lived within a ten-minute walk to the school from Pinegrove Avenue to Titus Avenue on the east side of Cooper Rd. and St. Paul. The boundary included a mixture of older homes and new subdivisions of single family detached houses. All streets were safe secondary roads with sidewalks, crosswalks, and stop signs with a posted school speed limit.

Old North Hill was situated in a new subdivision with twenty custom-built homes occupied by young families. Each homeowner designed their own property, resulting in unique styles from bungalows to side and back splits; although most were two-storey colonial homes with a central staircase, three or four bedrooms, a full bathroom upstairs, and a powder room near the kitchen on the main floor. All homes had an attached two car garage on the front of the house and inside the garage, an entry door into a laundry / mud room that led to the kitchen.

Our house near the top of the street sat on two lots, with twenty-five hundred square feet of living space. A two-storey "Cape Cod" style home where all the bedrooms faced the back of the house and a large attic tucked into the roof on the front, became our family home for more than three decades.

The basement stairs led to a large playroom with a bumper pool table and a ping-pong table where we held tournaments. A chalk board hung on the wall to keep score and I played school with my friends. We took turns being the teacher and the student. A large storage room on the opposite side of the stairs had a long hallway wrapped behind the staircase styled like a "bomb shelter" as the Cold War between the USA and Soviet Union was a constant threat to our society. Shelves contained canned goods, alongside seasonal tools and equipment. In the winter, there were bicycles, a lawn mower, rakes, and a sailboat in the storage room, while in the summer, toboggans, skis including boots and poles, and snow shovels were placed there. We played tag and hide and seek in the basement when we could not go outside.

All the children helped with the chores to make the switch between seasons. We also shared the yard maintenance; cut the grass, weeded the lawn in the spring, raked the leaves in the fall, and shoveled the snow in the winter. When the inground cement pool was installed, we learned how to measure the chlorine, vacuum the walls, and clean the tiles that bordered the cement sidewalk wrapped around the pool. Cleaning the pool was my favorite outdoor chore wearing a bathing suit to suntan on those days. A large pool cover was stretched across the top of the water in September and removed in May to protect it from storms, wind, leaves, and snow. The whole family assisted my dad with the opening and closing of the pool each year. We rolled up and moved the cover over to the grass outside the gate to hose and clean off the accumulated debris, a job that lasted an entire day. Preparing the pool for swimming took another day to vacuum, treat, and heat the water.

All chores were appropriate for our age. With everyone pitching in, it became a labor of love that we were proud of and prepared us for the responsibility of home ownership later in our lives.

On Saturday mornings when Dad worked at the office and Mom shopped or took one of the children to an appointment, Mark supervised his younger siblings with an enthusiastic sense of humor. He often teased me, "Marg, you won't get your allowance if you don't dust the furniture to my satisfaction."

I reminded him, "Mom is the judge not you!"

He vacuumed the floors. Sometimes I spilled salt and pepper on the floor under the table so that he had to vacuum again before mom came home. The large wood table that sat six people, sat against the wall with the staircases leading to the basement and second floor behind it. Dad and Mark sat at the head and foot of the table, Jan and I sat on a bench against the wall facing the television, and Paul and my mom sat across from us.

In the sitting area was a round card table with two chairs, a loveseat and rocking chair facing the twenty-inch television placed on a built-in counter with cupboards below and shelves above so we could watch the news when we sat down for meals. The news broadcasted three times during the day with updates during morning talk shows every thirty minutes from 7 – 9 a.m., local and national news from 6 – 7 p.m. and a recap of local news at 11 p.m. The television stations started their programs at seven o'clock in the morning and shut down at midnight, playing the national anthem at the beginning and end of the day.

The cupboards stored puzzles and board games, and the shelves housed World Book and Britannica Encyclopedias, our vinyl record collection, and my parents' literature volumes from college. We were well prepared for family game days and to research school assignments. Dad had a typewriter in his study behind the garage where we could type our school essays. Most of the time, he volunteered to type our assignments in the evening while we worked on other homework. Dad learned speed typing in college. He enjoyed analyzing our research and writing skills and discussing what we learned in school.

The open concept kitchen and family room sat to the right of the front door foyer and the combined dining / living room on the left side accommodated our guests. There was a long counter under the windows facing the street with drawers and cupboards filled with glasses, dishes, silverware, and linens used for special occasions in the dining room. The counter was set up as a buffet for guests to serve themselves during these weekend events, with delicious quiches and strawberry crepes for brunch and a variety of meat and vegetable casseroles for dinners. The dining room table had an extension to seat twelve guests. When there were more than twelve, the children ate at a separate table.

My mother, a good cook, loved to entertain guests with home-cooked meals. Often my sister and I baked cookies and desserts. As we got older, we prepared salads and appetizers. Jan and I always set and cleared the table and washed the dishes. Guests included relatives and family friends.

My late maternal grandmother, Jean, was a seamstress and mom taught me how to sew. There was a large hall closet with a white Singer Sewing Machine set inside a table across from my bedroom where she spent hours mending old clothes or sewing new creations for the family using Vogue and Singer paper patterns in different shapes and sizes. In middle school Home Economics class, girls learned cooking in seventh grade and sewing in eighth grade to prepare us for our future roles as homemakers. Everyone cleaned up the mess before class finished. I made a jelly roll log one weekend when I missed that class. It was full of strawberry jam and tasted delicious. The sewing class staged a contest to see who could sew the most clothes in a year. A classmate, Peggy, and I tied for first place, each sewed forty outfits, approximately one per week. Miss Clarke gave us gift certificates to redeem at the local fabric store for prizes. I continued sewing my own clothes for years but eventually resorted to simple mending projects like repairing rips, reattaching buttons, and altering hem lines.

The boys attended Industrial Arts, learning basic home maintenance, and woodworking in the seventh and eighth grades to prepare them as future homeowners. Mark made a wooden bird house that hung on a tree in our yard filled with seeds that attracted birds in the spring and summer months before flying south for the winter. Paul made a small bench that became his chair on the porch.

My father enjoyed playing a Steinway baby grand piano in the corner of the living room surrounded by large windows overlooking the backyard. One of his favorite songs was *Moon River*, made popular in the movie, *Breakfast at Tiffany's*, (1961) an American romantic comedy starring Audrey Hepburn and George Pepperd as well as classical music. When I heard him play, I snuck into the living room, sat beside him on the bench, turned the pages, and sang the lyrics. There was sheet music inside the piano bench of classical musicians, movie themed music scores, and later our favorite rock bands.

All the children took piano lessons from Mrs. Vick. Dad drove us to her home at seven o'clock in the morning before school on Thursdays. She held annual recitals at her home where all her young pianists memorized a song to perform in front of their parents. We took turns practicing scales and assigned songs every day before and after school for thirty minutes with the timer ticking while attending elementary school. We stopped the lessons before we reached high school. Playing the piano resonated with me my entire life; taking classical lessons in college and purchasing an upright piano in my future home. Mom saved the sheet music I bought as a teenager to play those songs when we visited and later in my future home.

A large, screened porch in the middle of the rear of the home housed two large picnic tables with benches for summer barbeques and picnics. There was a stone path from the porch door to the pool at the bottom of the hill. The lot on the side of the house was a steep hill with a volleyball net, baseball diamond, and a tall swing set at the end of the property. We spent years tobogganing in winter, swinging high above the trees in summer, and playing baseball and volleyball with friends and relatives. My future children loved visiting their grandparents at this house, playing in the yard and swimming in the pool.

We hosted parties with friends and relatives during the summer and staged a "country fair" for the neighborhood. We charged twenty-five cents admission per person. Dressed in my black Halloween witch's costume, I served witches brew in a pop-up tent. Each year I mixed a different flavor of delicious Kool-Aid. My brothers fooled their audience with cards and magic tricks, and my sister read a Ouija Board to amuse the neighborhood children. Everyone enjoyed themselves. We donated our funds to Lollipop Farm, a local charity where we adopted dogs and cats for family pets.

Kris lived across the street with her older sister and their parents, whose father worked at Kodak and her mother worked weekends at Sibley's Department Store in Irondequoit Plaza. We often rode our bikes to the store on Saturdays and enjoyed a treat at the soda fountain. We walked to school together, played outside until dinnertime, and shared weekend sleepovers watching movies and playing board games.

Our friendship lasted a lifetime after we both moved out of our parents' homes.

I made new friends in our neighborhood at school. I often played at my classmates' homes until dinnertime. At that time, the mother stayed home during the day with younger children, running errands, cooking, and cleaning. They welcomed the neighborhood children in their homes and yards. It was safe to walk or ride a bike around the neighborhood and residents did not mind all the youngsters running around outside. At that time, outdoor play included tag, hide and seek, hopscotch, and jump rope; friendly games engaging two or more children in cooperative play situations. Parents did not call to arrange play dates in advance. If our friends were not outside, we moved on to another friend's home. I learned how to tell time in kindergarten and wore a Minnie Mouse watch to make sure I returned home by half past five in the afternoon. Although digital watches and future cell phones have clock apps, an analog watch was the one piece of jewelry I have worn my entire life.

During our summer vacations, we took swimming lessons in an outdoor pool at Carolyn's home on another street in the neighborhood. We rode our bikes to her house dressed in our bathing suits and flip flops and carried a rolled-up towel attached to the rack above the rear tire on our bikes. It was fun to learn to swim with other neighbors outside on a quiet street. She was the captain of the high school swimming team with lifeguard certification. Teaching swimming to neighborhood youngsters was her summer job earning money for college. There were no community centers nearby. Classes were cancelled on rainy days, and we stayed home. Swimming became my favorite exercise throughout my life in future homes and gym memberships.

The town Parks Department ran a day camp for children every summer outside behind the town hall surrounded by woods. For two summers when I was seven and eight years old, Mom arranged for my sister, my cousin, and I to attend this camp together. During a two-week session, we learned how to build a lean-to (a small one room hut) with pre-cut wood logs and rope. It was a co-ed day camp for school-aged boys and girls where we brought lunch from home each day. Mom made a large batch of tuna fish for sandwiches and packed juice thermos, fruit, and crackers for snacks. The camp counselors, high school and college students, gathered the group around picnic tables in the morning and gave us instructions on how to build the lean-to. They tied the rope around the logs to make it sturdy.

As the youngest of the three girls, I let Jan and Sandy design our project. It was fun and the weather cooperated with sunny days. No rain enabled us to complete the project without getting wet or muddy and the logs were dry, not soggy. Every day, a handsome dark haired teenage counselor, Gary, came over to our site to view our progress.

He smiled as he sat on the grass in front of us, "Girls, this looks great. It is taking shape. It looks like a teepee."

Jan replied, "We followed your instructions. It should not fall."

Sandy added, "With three of us, we made the base a little wider and the opening a little bigger."

Gary nodded in agreement and said, "Keep up the excellent work girls. You will be proud when finished." He looked at me smiling, "I watched you carry the logs; your sisters needed a helper."

"They are doing the hard work," I replied, "but I hold it while they put it together." He winked at Sandy and moved on to the next group.

On the last day, everyone celebrated in the evening. The counsellors grilled hotdogs and hamburgers and lit a campfire where everyone shared stories and sang songs. We brought sleeping bags that day to spend the night in our handmade shelters under the stars. It was our first camping experience sleeping outside without our parents. The three of us were proud of our craftmanship; the lean-to didn't fall on top of us as we slept. The parks staff dismantled the structures after camp finished in time for the next session. This day camp experience prepared us for the love of nature when the family embarked on camping, hiking, and road trips.

My sister and I attended a two-week overnight summer camp, called Camp Onandaga on Long Lake near Syracuse, New York, a ninety-minute drive from our home. It was our first time living away from home without our parents. We stayed in a cabin with five other girls and a camp counselor. They divided up the girls according to their age. I was in a group with nine-year-olds, and my sister was in a group with eleven-year-olds. There were ten cabins at this camp and a main lodge for meals and large group activities.

When we arrived on the first day, a Sunday afternoon, we gathered in groups in the main building with our assigned counselors to listen to an orientation outlining the camp rules, activities, and protocols. We enjoyed our first arts and crafts session making name tags. Each counselor prepared different colored animal cutouts for their campers who then printed their names on the tag and colored it. My group had pink cats called the "Pink Panthers." My sister's group had blue birds called the "Blue Jays." We attached the name tags to our white camp T-shirts with safety pins.

At dinner on the first evening, the counsellors introduced themselves. Susan told us, "You can talk to your sisters in the other cabins during the large group activities, but we want you to always sit together with your cabin mates during mealtimes. That is how all the counselors keep track of their groups."

Sara remarked, "My mother told me to eat with my sister."

"You are eating together, but at a separate table," Chris replied, "The menu changes daily, but everyone eats the same meal at the same time in the cafeteria."

Linda added, "The camp director discussed the rules with all parents at registration. They are aware that the girls are grouped together by their age and sisters would be separated."

We brought our own sleeping bag, pillow, towel, and toiletries along with our clothes in a duffle bag. There was a separate bathhouse that everyone shared for showers and toilets. Outdoor activities during the day included swimming, archery, boating, waterskiing, shuffleboard, arts, and crafts. In the evenings, everyone gathered around a campfire to roast marshmallows and sing songs. On cool rainy days, we played board games and jigsaw puzzles in the main lodge.

Organized for girls ranging in age from eight to fourteen years old, the counselors were high school and college students, working a summer job to earn money for the school year. The camp hired a nurse to monitor girls with allergies, colds, headaches, and menstrual cycles. The nurse's office contained aspirin, first aid kits, inhalers, and sanitary pads for campers and counselors. We enjoyed it so much that we returned the following summer for another two-week session. Our very first experience living independently away from home prepared us to leave home after graduating high school.

Family Roots

My paternal grandparents immigrated to America from Italy and my maternal grandparents came from Russia through England. Learning more about my heritage inspired my desire to travel and immerse myself in foreign cultures to discover the world.

In the sixties, my parents joined the Civil Rights Movement. A non-profit organization, FIGHT (Freedom, Integration, God, Honor, Today), was established by local churches and Black leaders that pressured local industries like Kodak to integrate their workforces. The family attended the famous March on Washington led by Martin Luther King, Jr., during the summer of 1963. We joined the crowd at the Washington Monument that week documented by national news broadcasts. My parents were ambitious taking four young children to this massive rally, our first time participating in a crowded outdoor event, to support nationwide civil rights activism.

Marvin, the first Black student to attend Irondequoit High School, lived with us for two years (1962 - 1964) arranged through the FIGHT organization. He was the star of the basketball team, where we sat in the bleachers to watch his games and cheered for our home team, the Irondequoit Indians, wearing blue and gold uniforms. Our family enjoyed a lifelong bond with Marvin and his wife and daughter, as they returned to Rochester for high school reunions and family weddings and I met them a few times on vacation in Florida with my future husband and children.

A few months later, on Friday, November 22, 1963, a chilly November day, President Kennedy's trip to Dallas, Texas was broadcast live on the three national television networks. When the motorcade drove through Daley Plaza, three gunshots were heard and the President's body slumped over as he was hit in the head, killing him instantly. I was seven years old in the second grade at Listwood Elementary School. The principal entered each classroom to report the sad news and dismissed all classes so everyone could go home. Mark walked across the field from Dake Middle School to meet Jan, Paul, and I at the playground to walk home together. When we arrived, Mom gave us each a hug with tears flowing down our cheeks as we entered the house. The twenty-inch black and white television in the family room tuned into CBS News as Walter Cronkite recounted the events that led to the assassination that morning. All regular programming was suspended for the rest of the week to provide real time coverage of the events surrounding the President's assassination, funeral and burial. It was a sad time for my family and the entire nation.

The assassination that shocked the world was documented in history books, libraries, and museums. Clint Hill (1932 – 2025), who was the Secret Service agent in charge of First Lady Jacqueline Kennedy, stood on the back of the President's car when the bullets blasted the motorcade, and he lunged towards the President and First Lady sitting in the back seat of the open car. He worked for several presidents during his career but this event haunted him for the rest of his life as he was in his early thirties with a young family at that time. He penned a memoir, "*Five Days in November*" (Gallery Books, 2013), describing the events as he witnessed it up close and personal. Paul Landis, a fellow agent riding in the car behind the President, (1935 -) authored "*The Final Witness*" (Chicago Review Press, 2023). He was the youngest bachelor agent on the team, and resigned from the Secret Service a year later, haunted by that experience. It took a lot of courage to break their silence to document the assassination that they witnessed decades after the event. They wrote diaries of their daily work experiences as official records for the government agency.

A week later, we celebrated the annual Thanksgiving holiday with my dad's twin sister's family, a somber occasion that year. Aunt Julie always helped with the cooking, making delicious side dishes and desserts to serve with the turkey that Mom prepared. It was an all-day affair to prepare and roast the bird in the oven. Mom reciprocated when my aunt hosted the holiday. The three girls, my cousin, my sister, and

I, always set and cleared the table, and washed and dried the dishes together. I enjoyed helping my mother make pumpkin pies. Whenever I helped with baking, I stood on a stool to reach the counter and used the electric mixer, licking the beaters and the bowls while the pies were baked in the oven.

My family attended Lake Avenue Baptist Church located near my paternal grandfather's home. Every Sunday morning, we attended the service led by Reverend Hill, who preached about the political and social issues of the day. My mother supervised the nursery, and I often joined her to help care for the toddlers on Sunday mornings. There was a story time, crafts table and play table with donated toys and games.

My father went on hiking and canoe trips with the men's group from the church. One of these trips to the Canadian wilderness of Algonquin Park in northern Ontario, occurred when Senator Robert F. Kennedy was assassinated at the Ambassador Hotel in Los Angeles, California in June 1968. He celebrated his victory of the California state primary as he followed in his brother's footsteps to run for President. My dad and his friends didn't hear the news until they drove home two days later.

We attended church until my teenage years when Reverend Hill retired. I enjoyed dressing up every Sunday as a young girl and socializing with peers in the youth group activities apart from my school friends. It was an enriching age-appropriate spiritual experience in a calm social environment without the social justice activism and community service expectations of future generations of young adults.

After Church, we picked up my paternal grandfather at his home on Dewey Avenue to join us for Sunday lunch and visit at our home for the day. Pop made a huge pot of sauce with his home-grown tomatoes to bring to our house and mom cooked spaghetti and meatballs for the meal. He grew vegetables in his backyard and grape vines hung along the top of the fence where he made red wine for our weekend dinners. He was my only living grandparent when I was a child. Due to his advanced age, we didn't have a close relationship with him; it resembled a caregiving situation when we were young children.

Fidel immigrated to Ellis Island in 1907 from Italy, aged twenty-two years with his five brothers and sister who settled in western New York State. He worked as a janitor at the church to support his family through two World Wars and the Great Depression. His first wife and firstborn son died in childbirth. In the mid-1920s, he married a second time. Elisabetta, ten years younger than him, an Italian immigrant from Boston, who gave birth to my father and two daughters. She was determined to integrate her children into the American way of life and instilled the values of education and hard work.

My father and his sisters spoke Italian at home and learned English at school. Sadly, she passed away before witnessing her children's achievements, as all three excelled in their higher education and careers. Elisabetta died of cancer at age fifty when they were teenagers at the end of World War II. Dad served as a clerk at Fort Benning, Georgia for eighteen months during the war. That experience inspired him to become a doctor. He pursued ten years of university and medical school education at the University of Rochester where he met my mother, a research scientist at the U of R Medical School. They got married in June 1951.

Pop lived alone until he suffered a stroke, paralyzed for a few years until his death in November 1970, at eighty-five years old. When he could no longer care for himself, he lived at our house and my aunt's homes. There was a sofa bed in my dad's study and a bathroom next to the laundry room behind the garage so that he had privacy and did not climb the stairs. His favorite television show on weekend evenings, *Lawrence Welk Variety Show*, featured an orchestra, singers, and dancers. I enjoyed watching it with him on the twenty-inch color TV in the family room. Color televisions replaced black and white TVs in everyone's homes in the mid-sixties.

I met my grandfather's sibling's families at a reunion in Medina, New York, as a young teenager, and we attended each other's weddings over the next decade. These were lively events with dozens of distant cousins, tons of Italian food, and joyous merriment in the backyards of our homes. Decades later, I reconnected with my Medina cousins on Facebook searching for my surname, remembering their first names, and we met once more in Buffalo before the Pandemic renewing our familial bond through social media.

We had a close relationship with my dad's sisters' families, celebrating holidays and family birthdays together. It was heartbreaking when they moved away from Rochester in the 1970s. Aunt Toni's family lived in Japan as missionaries for two decades after the war. They shared fascinating stories about life in Japan. When they returned to America, they settled in the Midwest to pursue academic teaching careers and then retired to a senior's residence in California near Aunt Julie's home. Every summer, for a quarter century, they drove their motorhome across the continent visiting friends and relatives in Canada and the USA.

Aunt Julie's family moved to southern California so that Uncle Arnie could pursue a career in horticulture. Sandy and I flew back and forth during the summers of our high school years to visit each other's families. It was fun to explore the Laguna and Redondo beaches along the Pacific coast, Hollywood and Disneyland. That was the first time I flew across the country alone, an exciting adventure for a fifteen-year-old girl. It was so much fun that I returned the following summer on another solo adventure for two weeks visiting my California cousins. Throughout our lives, we visited each other many times whenever they visited my parents in Rochester. Sadly, both Uncle Arnie and Aunt Julie passed away in their seventies at the turn of the century, but their legacy lived on in their children. The distance did not end the family ties; it simply strengthened the family bonds.

My mother's family emigrated from Latvia to England and later to America in the early twentieth century. My maternal grandmother passed away from diabetes at forty-nine years old shortly after my parents' marriage before I was born. My mother's brother, Uncle Norman, served in the Navy during World War II in the Pacific Ocean. He gave my mother two Japanese dolls after the war that were passed on to me to display on my bookshelves. He moved his family from Rochester to the east coast to pursue his business interests. We stopped by their home on our vacations and they visited Rochester frequently.

I cherished a special lifelong bond with my relatives although years passed without contact. I maintained connections through annual Christmas letters, social media, and occasional visits at each other's homes or meeting them at my parent's home in Rochester. As our family tree expanded from one generation to the next, the bonds loosened to focus on our careers, children and grandchildren, but the love never died for my blood relatives. Attending family weddings and funerals decades later strengthened the family bonds while creating memorable vacations.

Chapter 2

Family Vacations – childhood flashback continues

Exploring North America

The family enjoyed travelling on school breaks exploring the USA and Canada. We piled into the family station wagon at dawn to embark on road trips throughout the continent, often taking a full day to arrive at our destination. Mom packed a picnic lunch of sandwiches, fruit, snacks, and drinks that we ate at rest stops along the route. We took turns sitting in the middle of the front bench seat to hold the colorful paper road maps. AAA (American Automobile Association) travel agents created a "triptik," a detailed route of a journey to allow drivers to track mileage, gas stations and construction zones, like a GPS (global position system) today. As AAA members, a travel planning service was available in addition to the emergency roadside assistance. I became a lifelong member to its sister organization in Canada (CAA). The privilege and love of travel became rooted in my soul at an early age. Our vacations ranged from outdoor adventures to cultural tours of museums and historic sites at home and abroad.

In my preschool years, we took road trips to the east coast exploring Cape Cod, Massachusetts and Myrtle Beach, South Carolina. I don't remember these vacations but have viewed them on films and slides that Dad recorded of our early years. He often set up the movie and slide projectors in the living room when our cousins visited to recall the "good old days" and treated his future daughters- and sons-in-law to these films when our engagements were announced.

As a Pisces drawn to water, I once wandered off and got lost on a beach, prompting lifeguards to look for me. After that, my older sister always stayed with me during future beach holidays. This story was often retold, becoming more dramatic over time.

During the school year, we had a five-day break for Thanksgiving from Wednesday to Sunday as the holiday is always celebrated on the fourth Thursday of November. The next vacation was a week off between Christmas and New Years, usually from December 24 to January 2. A four-day weekend in February to celebrate Presidents Lincoln's and Washington's birthdays; later referred to as Presidents Day, became a three-day weekend celebrated on the third Monday of that month.

At Easter, the school closed for a week whenever it occurred as it was celebrated on a different Sunday each year in March and April. Dad often booked time off that week to take the family on a road trip. On those vacations, we explored historical sites such as Mount Vernon, Williamsburg, Gettysburg, and Philadelphia. Seeing these sites in person emphasized what I learned in school and deepened my pride and understanding of my American cultural heritage.

One of the family's favorite destinations was hiking in the White Mountains of New Hampshire carrying backpacks for a three-day journey across the Presidential range where fully staffed huts, the size of a lodge, were situated at the tops of the mountain peaks. The huts housed one hundred people, with two bunk rooms, one for men and one for women. My sister and I claimed a top bunk while my mother slept on the bottom bed. The staff served hot meals for dinner and breakfast, and packed bag lunches of sandwiches, fruit, and drinks that the hikers took on their journeys the next day. The meals and bagged lunches were the same for everyone. We did not carry sleeping bags, pillows, bath towels, or kitchen utensils, just our personal items in our backpacks that weighed ten pounds. In the evenings, the hikers gathered around a campfire, played cards and board games, and told stories of their adventures. We met families from across the USA and Canada.

All trails were marked to ensure safety that led us to the destination. We climbed to a summit on day one, hiked across the top of the range on the second day, and descended back to the lodge at the base of the mountain where the car was parked on the last day, averaging five to ten miles and hiking six to eight hours each day. The huts at the top of each mountain peak were named after Presidents. The highest peak, Mt. Washington, had a cog railway leading up to the summit where a fancy hotel for tourists stood.

On our first mountain trip, we were lost in a hailstorm at the summit with other hikers. We were half a mile away from the hut but could not see it. Suddenly, flashing lights were seen in the distance. Two gentlemen in our group gathered sticks to light a fire as a signal. Mom pulled me and my siblings away from the fire to keep us safe. The hut staff sensed danger as seats were empty when dinner was served. They sent out a search party to rescue the missing people and spotted the flames with their search lights. They counted fourteen people around our campfire; the number of people missing on the roster and led us back to the hut. They brought a toboggan to transport the children. It was scary for this five-year-old girl and my siblings.

This vacation became an annual family tradition through my teenage years. After the hiking expedition we explored other parts of New England on our way home, visiting friends, cousins, and beach towns along the North Atlantic Coast. I loved the culture of these small towns and the fresh air of the ocean breeze. A great way to unwind after a grueling hike on mountainous terrain. This annual tradition at the end of summer was a nice retreat away from home and the hustle and bustle of Rochester before returning to another year of school in the fall.

In the winter, we learned to snow ski at resorts in New York and Vermont. The first time, when I was five years old, we drove to Snow Ridge Ski Resort near Turin, NY in the Adirondack Mountains. We were outfitted with skis, poles, and boots from Murphy's Ski Haus in Irondequoit before the trip. Mom and I wanted to quit after the first day.

As we sat down for dinner Dad asked everyone, "How do you like snow skiing?"

Mom said, "Even though I am bundled up with warm gloves on, it is too cold. My boots were uncomfortable." I nodded in agreement.

The boys laughed and said, "It was a lot of fun, flying through the snow."

Dad remarked, "It is great exercise, but we need to take lessons tomorrow to learn the proper techniques for turning, gliding, stopping, and traversing the hill from top to bottom. I almost hit skiers at times." At that time, helmets did not exist and were not mandatory on the ski slopes until decades later to prevent head injuries during falls.

After dinner, we left the dining room and sat in the lobby while mom and dad visited the ski reception desk. They bought lift tickets for the next day and arranged a family group lesson at 10 a.m. the next morning. Mom and I agreed to try one more day with the lessons paid for.

After a five-year hiatus, I resumed skiing at Hunt Hollow, a ski club in Naples, New York, a one-hour drive south of Rochester where we had a family membership. The two hills were marked, one for beginners and the other for expert skiers with a chair lift in the middle to transport skiers up to the top of the hill. I skied on the beginner trails. I did not cause any mischief in the cold snow and followed the arrows on the trail. The chalet was comfortable with benches and tables to change our boots and eat a bag lunch from home. There was no snack bar or dining facility when it first opened. A fireplace was situated in the middle of the lounge with chairs wrapped around it for weary skiers to sit and warm up their frozen hands and feet.

Twenty years passed before dad broke his leg skiing and was forced into retirement from the sport. He took my brothers on weekend ski trips to ski resorts in the Adirondacks, New England, and Canada. My sister and I skied for about a decade until marriage. My brothers introduced it to their future spouses and children. The sport evolved into snowboarding, a sport my future son liked in high school, and cross-country skiing, hiking on flat surfaces; popular Olympic sports that I enjoyed watching on television.

In the summer of 1965, when I was nine years old, the family embarked on our first cross country adventure. We flew to San Francisco and then rented a car to explore national parks and cities in the southwest region of the USA from San Francisco, California to Denver, Colorado for three weeks. We drove down the Pacific Coast Highway through Monterrey to Los Angeles and San Diego, visiting national parks, Disneyland, and the San Diego Zoo. Then we headed east to the Hoover Dam, Grand Canyon and national parks in Arizona, New Mexico, and Utah. We finished the journey in Denver at Rocky Mountain National Park before flying back home. My brother, Paul, eventually relocated to Denver for university and his future career. This family adventure happened five years prior to my cousin's relocation to California, becoming a favorite destination for many more family visits as an adult.

The national parks had hiking trails and visitor centers displaying their local history including the settlement of the west in the nineteenth century as well as the history and culture of the Indian tribes in the region. We purchased artifacts of pottery, jewelry, and blankets woven by the native people. We stayed in cabins and lodges in these parks; there were no hotels nearby. It was exciting to see the region in person, to enhance what I learned in Social Studies at school and experience the reality of the wild west that was portrayed in movies and television.

Three years later, in the summer of 1968, at age twelve, Dad shipped the family station wagon from Toronto, Ontario to Edmonton, Alberta and we embarked on a three-day train ride across Canada through Ontario and the Prairies to Alberta. It was my first overnight train trip and visit to Canada.

It was nice that we could view the scenery from the moving train and walk through the train cars to the dining car. We did not have to sit still, and wear seat belts like in an airplane or an automobile. We packed books, cards, and board games to keep us entertained. We slept on the train as the trip took three days and two nights to reach Edmonton. The train car had "cabins" with doors like miniature hotel rooms with bench seats facing each other that lowered into beds when we went to sleep. A drop leaf table attached to the wall under the window in between the seats was used for eating, reading, and playing games. Each train car had a bathroom with a toilet and sink, but no shower.

The train stopped in Sudbury and Thunder Bay (Ontario), Winnipeg (Manitoba), and Saskatoon (Saskatchewan) to pick up and drop off passengers. We could not leave the train at these stops.

The road trip began in Edmonton, Alberta where we drove south to Calgary to see a rodeo, Banff and Lake Louise, and then crossed the border into Glacier National Park, (Montana) Yellowstone, the Grand Tetons, (Wyoming) and Denver (Colorado) before heading east to return home to New York. Like the road trip in the southwest three years earlier, we visited national parks to hike trails and learn about the culture of the Indians and northwestern states and provinces. The station wagon had bench seats with three pairs of seatbelts. We took turns sitting in the middle of the front seat to navigate with the road map in hand. On this adventure, my baby brother, David, joined us while my oldest brother, Mark, spent the summer in Israel working on a Kibbutz. I fell in love with Canada, my future home a dozen years later.

It took three days to drive home from Denver; we stopped in Iowa and Indiana to spend the night in motels near the highway. On the third day as we entered New York, I turned on a Buffalo radio station in the car, when the news came on. There was chatter in the car, but I heard "Antonio Stornelli of Oakfield, was killed in a car accident yesterday." Dad yelled for everyone to be quiet. His Uncle Tony, one of Pop's brothers, passed away. He attended the funeral with his sisters and cousins. Pop did not attend the funeral of his younger brother; due to mobility issues he suffered after his stroke. He spent the summer months with his daughters, my aunts, when we embarked on our family adventures.

Discover Europe

My parents enjoyed a second honeymoon in Italy with their friends Rita and Dick for two weeks in the spring of 1963, celebrating twelve years of marriage. As it was during the school year, the children stayed home. Mom and Dad arranged their flights on separate days, to ensure one would be alive to care for the family if the other perished in a plane crash. Air travel was safe but risky with accidents happening often, so flying separately was a practice they adhered to keep the family safe.

Their itinerary began in Milan and traveled through Pisa, Florence, Venice, Rome, and Naples on a guided coach tour. They visited the Leaning Tower of Pisa, museums, art galleries, and cathedrals as well as the Vatican, Pompeii, and Mt. Vesuvius. They enjoyed a romantic gondola ride through the canals of Venice. It was their first trip to Europe with more to come, planting the seeds for a love of international travel in our family genes.

The children were placed with two neighbors to distribute caregiving responsibilities more effectively. The boys stayed with a neighbor who had five boys, and the girls stayed with a family friend on the next street. All the children attended the same schools, Listwood and Dake. We walked to school together each day. We missed our piano lessons because it was too far to ride our bikes, and we could not practice our lessons. My brother was exposed to mumps, so we stayed home from school for a week after our parents returned as a precaution to prevent the spread of the disease. Mom picked up our schoolwork so we would not fall behind in class. We were safe because we were vaccinated.

Four years later, in the summer of 1967, the children enjoyed their first overseas adventure. Our family traveled to Europe on a four-week holiday, visiting various countries when I was eleven years old. We flew to Zurich, Switzerland and hopped on the train to Stuttgart, Germany to purchase a beautiful maroon Mercedes, big enough for a family of six that Dad pre-ordered before the trip.

Relying on the travel guide, "Europe on $5 a Day" updated annually by Arthur Frommer (1929-2024), Mom determined where to go, what landmarks, hotels, guesthouses, and restaurants to visit. We drove through Switzerland, Austria, the former Yugoslavia (now Croatia), and Italy for a month, and returned to Geneva, Switzerland to fly home. We toured palaces, museums, the Matterhorn, Leaning Tower of Pisa, the Vatican, and other famous landmarks on our route. It was beautiful to see the vistas of Austria filmed in the Sound of Music in person. We retraced the route my parents traveled in Italy on their second honeymoon and witnessed the devastation of towns in Croatia bombed during the war and not rebuilt. The sights and sounds of Switzerland reminded me of the fairytales I read in library books. I often dreamt about returning to these countries in Europe, but it never happened. I was old enough to enjoy the culture, history, and beauty of these countries, creating memories I have cherished forever.

Mom spoke French and German, and Dad spoke Italian to merchants, but they always replied in English. We chuckled on a sweltering day in Italy when Dad asked an ice cream vendor riding a bicycle through a town square with huge thermal bags cradling the back wheel, "Quanto costa uno di questi?" (What does one of these costs?) and the gentleman laughed, "Sir, I give your children a vanilla cone," he replied in English.

Dad pulled out a bill and gave him a tip. The vendor smiled, thanking him and continued his ride. We found a bench by a fountain and enjoyed our treat in the middle of the square before entering a museum.

We reminisced about this holiday often at family reunions. It was an exciting time for the whole family as the four children, aged ten to fifteen years old, experienced the diverse cultures and history of Europe that we learned about in school. Mom was six months pregnant with her fifth child. She was exhausted, needing assistance walking up hills and stairs, but enjoyed herself without getting sick. At the end of the vacation, Dad shipped the Mercedes back home to America.

On the second European adventure two years later in the summer of 1969, age thirteen, we flew to London, England where my mom, baby brother, and I stayed in a guesthouse for three weeks while my dad, brothers and sister embarked on a guided bus tour of Scandinavia and Russia. Every day, mom and I walked with the baby in the stroller exploring the city. We visited Trafalgar Square, Picadilly Circus, Kensington Gardens, Big Ben, and 10 Downing Street as well as other famous landmarks.

I stayed in London to help my mom with the baby. I liked the idea of staying in one spot instead of traveling by bus to a different city every day. I was fascinated by the British culture portrayed in children's films, *Mary Poppins* and My Fair Lady as well as the *"British Invasion"* of popular music in America including the Beatles, Rolling Stones, and other British bands of the era. I loved London, it was the only time I ever visited the city; on future vacations, it served as a layover to another destination.

Mom called her cousin, Jack, in London, and we went to his home for a visit. They were related through my mother's grandparents, Alice and Barnet, who immigrated to America from England in the early

20th century. Jack and Selma had a son, Lawrence, who was four years younger than me. We met them a second time a week later when they came to our guesthouse. When my dad and siblings returned to London from their tour, we visited Stonehenge and Buckingham Palace together before the flight home to start school. I would love to return to London some day to explore the British Isles on a guided tour by train or bus.

These vacations were my fondest memories of my childhood. I enjoyed the privilege to travel in my youth, a unique learning experience that I recommend to everyone. If you are unable to make the journey in person, there are free books in your public library (hint: library cards are free, look in the 900s) as well as free travel documentaries on the Internet to take you on a fabulous journey in the comfort of your home. There are places I have yet to explore when the time is right.

Returning home from London, I was entering high school, the decisive step towards my adventure of a lifetime was taking shape!

Chapter 3

My Teenage Years

Nurturing Arts, Sports, and Culture

My parents introduced me to films, musicals, live theatre, and concert performances in Rochester at an early age. I loved Mary Poppins, Sound of Music, Annie, King and I, and My Fair Lady, popular musicals in the 1960s. I enjoyed dressing up to attend theatre productions at the George Eastman Theatre. I never tired of these films when they were later released on television. I watched the four-hour production of the Sound of Music annually during the Christmas season immersed in the culture and history of Austria during World War II.

Situated on the southern shore of Lake Ontario at the mouth of the Genesee River, between Buffalo and Syracuse, Rochester, the third largest city in New York state, that served as a significant economic, historical, and cultural center in western New York throughout the twentieth century. Surrounded by water with the Great Lakes to the north, the Erie Canal to the south and the Genesee River flowing through the middle of the city to the southern tier of the state, it was a hub for manufacturing and trade. The major employers in the region from the late nineteenth to the twenty-first century were Eastman Kodak, a developer of cameras and films, Bausch & Lomb, a manufacturer of contact lenses and eyeglasses, and Xerox, a producer of photocopiers and printers. A diverse community with a population of over 200,000 residents of all races and nationalities, it was also well known for its healthcare and educational institutions, the University of Rochester (UR) and Rochester Institute of Technology (RIT).

Historically, it was a stop for the Underground Railroad moving slaves to freedom in the nineteenth century as well as a meeting place for suffragettes securing the right to vote for women at the start of the twentieth century. Kodak, founded in the late nineteenth century, employed city residents for more than one hundred years in the region. Frederick Douglas, Susan B. Anthony, and George Eastman were famous residents with their homes designated as historical sites. Statues and museums were erected in their honor. In the twenty-first century, the city welcomed refugees from around the world; it was declared a sanctuary city during the Trump Administration to protect the immigrant population from deportation.

Focused on arts and culture with museums, art galleries, and post-secondary institutions that promoted the arts in all formats, the city was also famous for the annual Lilac Festival at Highland Park in May and the International Jazz Festival in June. The Eastman School of Music, named after the founder of Kodak, was renowned as one of the most prestigious music conservatories in the world.

In the early sixties, folk music and rock and roll were featured on "The Ed Sullivan Show," where the Beatles made their world debut in February 1964, just before my eighth birthday. I became a lifelong fan of the Beatles, the Bee Gees, Elton John, Bob Dylan, Carly Simon, Carole King, and other musicians.

I attended my first rock music concert with my sister and father at the War Memorial in downtown Rochester when I was nine years old to hear Simon & Garfunkel. I loved the melodies of their hit song, *"Sounds of Silence."* Dad loved the music but hated the rowdy crowds of teenagers, jumping and screaming in their seats surrounding us throughout the evening. I learned to play my favorite songs on the piano at home.

Rochester was not a popular stop for famous musicians; one had to travel to New York City or Toronto to view concerts. I wanted to travel to Toronto to hear the Beatles in 1964 but was too young. It would be another thirty years when I attended a Paul McCartney concert at the Air Canada Center in Toronto with my future husband. Hearing my favorite musician live in a stadium with twenty thousand Beatles fans was a dream come true. I sang and danced to his music in the aisle throughout the evening. While writing this narrative, the famous popular British musician is still touring the world in his golden years performing in smaller stadiums in smaller cities.

My weekly allowance and babysitting earnings paid for vinyl LPs (long playing records) of my favorite musicians at House of Guitars on Titus Avenue, where we biked to find records and sheet music. I spent hours on Saturday afternoons combing through the stacks of albums filed alphabetically by artist and band name. I purchased the sheet music of my favorite songs to practice on the piano at home. I learned "Hey Jude" by the Beatles, "Sounds of Silence" by Simon and Garfunkel, "Your Song" by Elton John, as well as hits from the Mary Poppins and the Sound of Music songbooks.

Playing these songs on the piano reminded me of my piano lessons, shaping a lifelong appreciation for music, the rhythm, lyrics, and melodies that evolved into the pop music era of the twentieth century. I never learned to play music by ear or memorized the notes of these masterpieces; I always referred to the music scores laid out in front of me on the piano. I realized the value of practicing scales during those lessons as I played the chords of these songs stretching my fingers over the black and white piano keys.

It was always a crowded music store as teens and local musicians searched for their favorite bands and purchased guitars. The store took over Grange Hall in 1964, a community gathering place where I took ballet lessons a few years earlier. It expanded operations to include all types of instruments and entertained musicians in the same location for decades through the twenty-first century.

At the end of that first decade in our new home, neighbors who lived at the end of our street played at a coffee house on Ridge Road. Bat and Don often played basketball with my brothers on our driveway. They invited us to listen to their music on weekends. One of my favorite songs was Don's presentation of "*Somewhere Over the Rainbow*," made popular by Dorothy in the Wizard of Oz (1939). They released an album, called "*Introducing Don Potter and Bat McGrath*," (1969) and moved to Nashville, Tennessee to pursue their careers in country and gospel music.

The family also enjoyed local sports events. There were no major league sports teams in Rochester. We attended baseball games at Silver Stadium, an outdoor venue with rows of bleachers when the Rochester Red Wings played. Dad would take the children to these games on Saturday afternoons where we ate white hot dogs, ice cream cones, and popcorn at our seats while cheering for our home team. It was nothing like the World Series winners, Toronto Blue Jays, that my future children enjoyed as avid sports fans and spectators.

The Hike for Hope, a well-attended annual charity event in Rochester, featured a twenty-five-mile route around downtown and the University of Rochester. I raised fifty dollars canvassing the neighborhood and teachers at school. Everyone I approached donated twenty-five cents per mile walked. Volunteer organizers at the finish line validated our sponsor sheets and congratulated hikers. I walked this route three times with different friends each year.

Promoted on the school announcements, everyone was encouraged to participate in the worthy cause as good exercise. Held across the country, Project Hope provided medical care to underdeveloped countries through the ship, "SS HOPE." Rochester, one of the leaders in the funding, raised over $2.5 million during the seven-year project.

Scheduled for a Sunday in the spring, the downtown route was closed to traffic for the day. Participants received a T-shirt promoting the event and were advised to wear comfortable sneakers or walking shoes. The route took about five hours to complete from start to finish. The streets were crowded with teens and adults of all ages supporting the cause. Police and paramedics were stationed at various points and volunteers offered water bottles to participants. Not aware that I should have trained for the event, I came home with sore feet but enjoyed the day socializing with friends. This twenty-five-mile hike around the downtown streets of Rochester was my introduction to community charity fundraisers, which would continue throughout my life.

My family life in the sixties and early seventies was happy and fun, full of adventures, and a variety of travel experiences. As I entered high school in 1970, my life changed dramatically as I prepared for my senior year abroad in Europe.

High School (1970 -1973)

Upon entering high school, it was my turn to attend an exchange program. My older brother and sister enjoyed summer programs in Israel and France. I wanted to go for a full year to immerse myself in the culture of another country. A summer program felt more like a vacation rather than a living or learning experience. My parents hosted another student in our home, Louisa from Brazil, when I was in ninth grade. She was fun to live with and taught me Portuguese, but I lost contact with her after her departure. Her time with our family was too short, as soon as we got to know each other, it was time to say goodbye.

I babysat two family friends with young children for five years on weekends in junior and senior high school. At that time, I earned fifty cents per hour, and a dollar after midnight, averaging $3 - $5 a week. I managed bottle feeding, changing diapers, reading stories, and putting babies and young children to bed for the night. The parents prepared their meals before I arrived and informed me not to bathe them as a safety precaution. There were no mandatory or certified babysitting courses for teenagers at that time. These parents trusted me to entertain and take care of their children before bedtime.

For the rest of the evening, I read books, listened to music, watched television, and tackled my school assignments, always on alert for cries from their bedrooms. I cherished lifelong friendships with these families watching the youngsters grow into mature adults via annual Christmas cards with photographs and later via Facebook and Instagram posts.

Tim and Nan had two girls, ages 7 and 9, who were fun to play games with. I always enjoyed caring for the girls before my trip to Europe. They lived in a large older home in the city near the hospital where I was employed at my first full time job a few years later. They stayed out late, asked me to spend the night at their home, and they drove me home the next morning. Caring for school-aged children was easier than babies as they were more independent with their bedtime routines. Playing board games, jigsaw puzzles and reading books with them encouraged learning and critical thinking skills for the three of us. Their parents joked that the girls would ask for a night with Margot, so they enjoyed a date night while I played with the girls.

I fell into the other babysitting job by accident. At school, Debbie asked me if I was available to sit one weekend in December before Christmas break in grade nine. She was committed to a family holiday party. She gave my name and number to Anna and told her I lived near the high school.

Anna dialed the house one evening after dinner and my mother answered the phone, "Hello, is Margot there? This is Anna. One of her friends gave me her name to babysit."

Mom replied, "Margot told me about that. Hold on, I will call her to the phone."

I picked up the line upstairs in my parent's bedroom, "Hello Anna, this is Margot. I understand you need a sitter on Saturday evening?"

"I have a twenty-month-old daughter, and I am pregnant, due in January," she sighed. "My husband and I like to go for dinner and to the movies on weekends."

"That is great," I replied, "What time should I be ready?"

"Tom can pick you up at seven o'clock and we would be home by midnight. Is that good for you?" she asked.

Mom came into her room and read my scribbled notes with their address, phone, date, and time on the notepad that Dad always kept by the phone. She nodded in agreement while I was talking. "I am looking forward to meeting you. Bye," I ended the call.

Tom picked me up on Saturday and drove me to their home, in the neighborhood past Pinegrove school. I was not allowed to walk or bike past Pinegrove, but I became more familiar with it as I got older. Looking after their daughter was fun, she was a year younger than my baby brother, so I knew how to entertain her and take care of a toddler. I put the baby to bed around half past eight and spent the rest of the evening watching television.

At that time, I enjoyed Saturday evening sitcoms of *Green Acres* with Buddy Ebsen and Eva Gabor and *Petticoat Junction*, a series featuring a widow with her three teenaged daughters, Bobbie Jo, Billie Jo, and Bettie Jo, who ran the Shady Rest Hotel, a small-town inn. These shows were hilarious romantic comedies set in rural America, that I enjoyed following when I was too young to date or go out with friends. The parents came home around eleven, paid me three dollars. I thanked Anna and then Tom drove me home.

In the car, he mentioned, "My wife is due to have a baby soon, so we won't be going out for a month or two. Would you like to come again?"

I replied, "Yes, I have a baby brother a year older than Laura, so I am used to the feeding and diaper routine."

"That's great, when we are ready in the new year, we will call you," He smiled.

I was surprised that they were looking for a new sitter. When he arrived at my driveway, he got out and opened the car door for me and waited until I unlocked and walked inside the front door before he left. Mom always left the front porch light on at night until the children came home. I turned it off before I went to bed.

When I saw Debbie in class on Monday, I told her about the evening. She admitted that she did not want to babysit a newborn and was happy that I agreed to take over the job. Anna called again in March, a bit scary, but they were confident I could manage their newborn baby boy. I looked after their babies on weekends for the next three years until I left for Europe. Babysitting prepared me for motherhood later in my life.

In grade nine, I registered for gymnastics with Lynn at the Rochester YWCA (Young Woman's Christian Association). They did not have a gymnastics team at my high school. Our parents shared the drive to the Y in downtown Rochester each week. It was fun to learn cartwheels, head, and handstands, walk on the balance beam, jump over the vault and swing on the uneven parallel bars. We participated in a recreational program, no regional competitions. I also joined their swimming classes to earn lifesaving certification. I did not join team sports at school, so the Y programs were a suitable alternative to staying active and improving my athletic skills.

In the first week of Grade ten, I scheduled a meeting after school with Mrs. Roberts, my four-year guidance counselor, on Monday afternoon. It was the one and only time I spoke with a guidance counselor during my high school years. I wanted to inquire about the student exchange program where my sister had traveled to France in the summer.

When I arrived after school that day, Mr. Shaw took me into his office and closed the door halfway. "I can't close the door because people will become suspicious, but we can still have a conversation.

Mrs. Roberts had an emergency at home," he explained. "The school pairs the girls with female counselors and the boys with male counselors so that students are more comfortable speaking with advisors of the same sex."

I was not aware of that policy but pleased that he explained it to me. He knew it was the first time I had spoken to a guidance counselor. I asked him, "Should I reschedule next Monday with Mrs. Roberts, when I don't have to work after school?"

"I read her note why you are here, so that I could answer your questions," he remarked. "It is fine for you to talk with me if you feel comfortable doing so."

I smiled, "Thank you for seeing me because I need to decide what to do and realized the application needs to be completed in a few weeks if I pursue this."

He showed me the brochures about the summer programs as well as the year programs abroad. He asked me, "Where would you like to go, I see you have taken both French and Spanish in school and did you learn Italian at home, your family's heritage?"

"I took Spanish at Dake, but my French is more current, having studied it in high school," I choked. "My dad spoke Italian with my grandfather when he was alive, not to his children."

"I looked up your older brother and sister's records who also took French, I assume that is what your parents would prefer," he grumbled.

"Do you want to go to Europe or explore other French speaking countries around the world?"

Excited, I answered, "Only Europe, there is France, Belgium and Switzerland where I have traveled previously." After I cleared my throat, I spoke in a serious tone, "Mr. Shaw, I want to go on the year program, a summer program is too short. I want to experience living abroad, getting to know a family and immersing myself in the culture. Would it be possible to do it in my senior year? Or do I have to wait, until after I graduate in Grade twelve?"

He paused for a moment and looked at my transcript on his desk. He then straightened his blue and gold tie with the gold Indian Chief, our school mascot, in front of his chest and positioned his chair to face me, commenting, "Margot, I know the history of your family in this community. Your father is well known with his medical practice. Your parents have supported our school board for a long time, bringing Marvin here when you were a young child and Louisa last year. I bet there will be more students in the future?"

I said, "Yes, there are two more brothers behind me to go through the system."

He said, "I know Paul, who is the second one?"

I chuckled and said, "David will be here in ten more years." He laughed, "I hope I am still around to meet him!" We sponsored Guillame from France when David was in high school.

He glanced at my transcript again, and explained, "You have good grades and two Advanced Placement courses from Grade eight in Math and Science. We can fast track your progress if you are willing to take an extra course each semester or at summer school and graduate a year early with the minimum requirement of thirty-two credits. That means there will be no additional Advanced Placement courses to submit to colleges in grade twelve if you graduate in grade eleven. You can also apply to colleges next year and request a deferred admission for one year."

Beaming ear to ear, "That is precisely why I wanted to meet with you today," I sighed. "I would prefer to go to Europe in grade twelve and then enter college when I return home at age eighteen instead of a year later."

"Have you discussed this with your parents?" he asked cautiously. "What are their thoughts?"

"I will discuss it with them now that you have confirmed graduating a year early," I replied, smiling and excited.

Handing me the programs, he continued, "Mrs. Roberts left applications for both programs in your file for me to give to you. Please go home and think about it and talk to your parents. The applications for both programs are due at the end of the month."

I rose from my chair, shook his hand, and grabbed my books. He handed me a large yellow envelope that contained the brochures and applications. "Mr. Shaw, thank you for taking the time to see me today to expedite the application," I remarked. Twenty-one months later, I graduated a year ahead of schedule and received advanced acceptance into college before leaving on the exchange program.

French became my favorite subject with Mr. Korytko as my favorite teacher. He was a handsome gentleman with chin length hair and wide sideburns who spoke French fluently that sounded authentic. He was aware of my desire to go on the student exchange program and encouraged me to join the French Club after school.

The club met every Wednesday after school with another French teacher, Mrs. McMahon. Members spoke French and experienced a variety of field trips to a French café, a French movie, and a French restaurant via bus. Each week the students shared treats from home inspired by French cuisine, croissants, and desserts.

In the spring, a four-day weekend bus trip drove all the club members to Montreal and Quebec City in Canada. It was a six-hour bus ride travelling along the south side of Lake Ontario to Canada. I had my passport in hand for the Canadian customs agent who stepped on the bus to check everyone's identification. I enjoyed traveling with likeminded students from all grades who spoke French and toured the museums, historical sites and battlefields of the War of 1812. We ate delicious meals in French restaurants and walked the streets near our hotel in the evening, arriving before the ten o'clock curfew in our assigned hotel room for roll call. In Quebec City, we stayed at the Chateau Frontenac, a majestic castle perched on top of the hill overlooking the city.

During the evening room check, Mrs. McMahon knocked on our door and yelled "What is all the noise in here?" Jeanne opened the door, and the teacher noticed the two boys who were absent from their room down the hall. The teacher led them back to their room. The following week at school the four troublemakers had to report to Mr. Stacy's office (he was the principal at Listwood years earlier before his promotion to high school). The boys received a two-day suspension while Jeanne and I had to get signed notes with a formal apology from our parents. My parents suspended my social activities after school for the rest of that week. High school administrators called home as I later learned with the mischief of my future children and teenagers in my future career.

Denise invited me to attend a religion club with her after school. I joined as my family no longer attended Lake Avenue Baptist Church. The Way Ministry, an international non-denominational Bible teaching and fellowship group, had a large following with students from all grades. The group met on Thursday afternoons after school. Having religious teaching with schoolmates was peaceful in a spiritual environment. When I met her years later at a school reunion, she described how the ministry had shaped her life with her pastor spouse. Would this be a premonition to my future career in a catholic school board...hmmm?

I worked in my father's office two afternoons a week so that the receptionists could leave early to spend time with their children after school. Irene and Lucille both worked two days during the week, so I covered Tuesdays for Irene and Fridays for Lucille. I answered the phone, scheduled appointments, showed patients to their examining room, and processed their bills and payments after the appointment.

In the summer, I worked every afternoon so that they received time off with their children. It was a part time job during my high school and college years, but I never included it on future resumes or job applications because it was a family business. The experience was beneficial and rewarding, preparing me for the business world in customer service / interpersonal relations including my future position at the hospital in the Patient Admissions Office and future career in Canada.

For years, Dad brought home a box of all the unpaid bills at the end of each month. The family gathered around the dining room table to fold, stuff and stamp more than five hundred envelopes before credit cards, electronic and third-party insurance payments became available. He treated us to dinner at Don & Bob's Burgers afterward, thanking us for our dedication and hard work. Was he preparing his children for the future business world, self-employment and accounting practices?

During the summers after the ninth and tenth grades, I flew alone to California for a two-week visit with Aunt Julie's family. I made the airline reservations and paid for them myself, from my babysitting and office earnings. It was the first time I was allowed to travel across the country by myself at age 15 years, a dress rehearsal for my European adventure of a lifetime. Each flight had a stop in Chicago, a large international airport where I changed planes. I nervously learned how to navigate my way through the busy terminal to catch my connecting flights, finding the gate locations on the huge arrival and departure screens, and walking through the terminal from one end to the other to make the connections on time.

The airports were busy during the summer, but I had my boarding passes in my hand from my first check in and found the departure gates with ease. I loved the responsibility and independence travelling alone on these vacations. My big red suitcase enjoyed a trial run for a lifetime of future vacations and adventures.

It was fun beach hopping at Laguna and Redondo beaches with my cousins, and we visited Disneyland, Beverley Hills, and Hollywood studios. One day, Sandy and I took the bus to downtown Los Angeles and strolled through Rodeo Drive, one of the most expensive shopping districts in the entire country. We enjoyed people watching and searching for Hollywood stars.

I also met their neighbor, Audrey, who lived across the street and her friends. When I returned the second summer, age sweet sixteen, she introduced me to Greg. We were chaperoned by my cousin, Sandy, and her boyfriend, Steve, who later married after graduation from college and celebrated their fiftieth anniversary at the time of writing. We went to the beach, to the movies, and shopped in local malls. We stayed in contact via phone calls and letter writing when I returned home to finish my last year of high school.

He visited me in Rochester the following Christmas for a week. He was eighteen with a driver's license, so we were allowed to use the family car on a date night to see a movie when he visited. My first love, we had made plans to meet when I returned home from Europe when I was eighteen years old. Sadly, those plans never happened, he found someone else as soon as I left the country.

When the four older children became teenagers, we had a five-minute time limit to use the phone as there was only one telephone line with three extensions. You could listen in on conversations from the other extensions; there was no privacy when talking on the telephone in a large home with seven people. Short spiral cords attached the head set to the base and a short telephone wire in the back of the base attached to wall outlets in the kitchen, my parent's bedroom, and my dad's study behind the garage. You could not walk and talk or go outside with the phone in your hand. A rotary dialer progressed to push buttons years later. If you made a mistake when dialing, you had to hang up to disengage the call and then pick up the receiver to start over, no backspace or cancel buttons to correct the error. Telephone numbers had seven digits; three letters followed by four numbers. A three-digit area code was required for long-distance calls but not for local ones.

In grade eleven, my last year of high school, I became ill with mononucleosis, confined to my bedroom for a month. This occurred after my second summer vacation in Los Angeles. Referred to as "the kissing disease," it was a viral infection with fever, fatigue, sore throat, and swollen lymph nodes in my neck. I felt weak and tired with no appetite, drinking liquids and soups. I completed school assignments at home during that time. When I returned to school, I was absent from gym class and barred from after-school activities and office work until my symptoms disappeared. No masks at that time, but my teachers moved my desk to a corner in the back of the room to prevent the spread of germs until I presented a doctor's note to the school nurse. After Thanksgiving, I rejoined my classmates in my assigned seat.

I put both French and Spanish on the exchange program application. I checked off the European countries that appealed to me.

I crossed out South America, Africa, and Asia; I was not interested in those continents that I had never visited previously. I received my host family assignment in the spring about six weeks before school finished for the summer. I was not going to a French or Spanish speaking country! I would be learning Dutch! Another foreign language to add to my repertoire. This became a new and exciting cultural experience!

YFU matched me to a family in Antwerp, Belgium where Flanders, a dialect of Dutch was spoken. I preferred Brussels to speak French, but the organization assigned students to families according to other factors, not just language. I exchanged letters with the family to introduce myself and to learn more about them. They were a middle-class family with three teenaged daughters, and the father was a dentist. They had a summer home in Ostende, a village by the North Sea. I would attend a Catholic high school wearing a school uniform. They had a three-week vacation planned in North America in July and arranged for me to stay with their friends at the seashore. It seemed like a good match except for the catholic school, but their vacation soon after my arrival was disturbing.

It was finally happening! Celebrating my senior year of high school abroad, a dream held close to my heart for a long time. The departure was scheduled for graduation day. I would not be walking across the stage to receive my diploma that evening. It arrived in the mail after I left the country!

PART II

ADVENTURE OF A LIFETIME

My Senior Year Abroad

(1973 – 1974)

Chapter 4

Arrival in Belgium

Antwerp

On Thursday morning, the thirtieth of June 1973, I arrived by coach bus in Antwerp, Belgium, fifty hours after I kissed my mother goodbye in America.

"Hallo Margot" Mevrouw Van Leet approached me with a hug and kiss on each cheek three times.

"Hello, Mevrouw Van Leet," I replied.

She said, "Please call me Mama and this is your Papa," nodding to her husband, who also hugged and kissed me on each cheek three times.

Pointing to her daughters, "And your sisters, Kathleen, Mineke, and Bette." The three girls exchanged hugs and kisses with me and Bette grabbed my big red suitcase as we walked outside to their car.

Driving through the city, Papa asked "How was your flight?"

"It was long," I yawned. "Pardon me, I am exhausted from two full days of travelling and little sleep."

The family was pleasantly pointing to churches, the school, and government buildings as we drove to their home. But I was not paying attention due to my exhaustion and nodded in agreement without talking.

Mama turned to look at the four girls squeezed into the back seat, "Of course, we will show you our home so you can settle into your room and lay down." The Peugeot was designed for five passengers not six; family outings were going to be cramped.

The car pulled onto a cobblestone street with large two-storey brick homes and beautiful flower gardens lined the verandas along the street. The Van Leet home had a structure on the side of the house with a "**Tandarts**" sign that pointed to the father's dental office on a small driveway with two parking spots.

Everyone removed their shoes at the front door. Mama entered the kitchen to make tea and grabbed a tray of sandwiches that she prepared earlier. The girls took me upstairs to show me the bathroom, separate toilet, and the bedrooms. Each bedroom had a large wash basin with a mirror and shelf above for toothbrushes, cosmetics, and combs. The girls had their own bedrooms with an extra bed and bureau in Mineke's room for me.

We returned downstairs for tea and sandwiches. I was not a tea or coffee drinker. My parents did not serve tea or coffee to the children back home. I noticed a knife and fork on my plate to cut the sandwiches.

As I picked one up with my hand, I saw the girls cutting theirs in bite size pieces and using the fork to lift the sandwich into their mouths. I dropped the sandwich from my hand and wiped it on my napkin on the table. Everyone had napkins in their laps. I adapted to the eating and drinking habits of Europeans quickly.

Culture shock as soon as I arrived in Belgium. Kissing three cheeks and removing shoes off your feet at the door never happened back home. Eating sandwiches with utensils, not with your hands. Placing the serviette (napkin) in your lap or on your chest, not leaving it on the table. The bathroom had a tub and shower with a small "WC" (water closet) for the toilet in the hall and wash basins in each bedroom. The entire family spoke (British) English as a second language. How did the girls learn the language so perfectly as my foreign language skills learned in school did not compare? There would be much more for this naive seventeen-year-old girl from America to grow accustomed to over the next year.

After lunch, I went to my room. Mineke came upstairs to show me the school uniform and gave me towels for bathing. It felt good to remove the jeans and tee shirt I wore for the past two days of travel and put on a nightgown for my nap. As soon as I laid down, I slept for the next twenty-four hours. The girls tried to wake me up for dinner, but I did not budge, so they let me sleep.

On Friday morning, three days after I left Rochester, I awoke at noon in a sunny bedroom in Antwerp, refreshed after the forty-eight-hour journey. I wrote two short notes to send home to America to assure Mom and Dad as well as Greg that I arrived safely. I showered and dressed in shorts and a tank top for a summer day. I went downstairs, placed my sandals by the door, and brought my sneakers that I wore on the trip upstairs. The family sat in the parlor, read the newspaper, and watched television. The three girls were also dressed in shorts and tank tops, so I felt comfortable in my choice of clothing.

As I entered the room, I said, "Good morning, it looks like a beautiful day outside." Mama spoke first and said, "Good morning, Margot, how did you sleep?"

"I slept well; the bed was comfortable." I said, smiling.

"You slept a long time; it is Friday afternoon now. We tried to wake you for dinner and breakfast," she replied, angry that I slept late. "But we also understood you had a long trip, so we did not disturb you."

"Thank you, I needed the rest after a long day of sitting on a noisy, crowded bus." I replied. I was also fighting jet lag crossing six time zones during the flight across the ocean.

"I hope I was quiet in the bedroom; I did not want to disturb you," Mineke remarked. "You appeared serene while sleeping."

I said, "I never heard a sound."

"Do you drink tea or coffee?" Bette asked, "Do you take it with cream and sugar?"

I answered, "I am used to milk or juice but I will try the coffee with milk."

"We have biscuits and croissants on the counter," Kathleen chimed in. "Would you like butter, jam, or honey on it?"

I smiled, "I would like a croissant with jam." And she rose to get one ready for me. I remembered from my family vacations that a continental breakfast of tea or coffee with biscuits was common throughout Europe.

We moved to the dining room table while I ate my breakfast where one place setting was untouched. There was no eating allowed in the kitchen, just food preparation. Mama put her newspaper down and sat across from me. Clasping her hands together, she said sternly, "Margot, we are leaving on our vacation in two weeks, so we will be busy preparing for this holiday as you get acquainted with our life here."

I took a sip of coffee and nodded, "What would you like me to do?"

Mineke turned to her mother and said, "We should walk into town and show Margot our school and get her uniform ready." The girls nodded in agreement.

Mama suggested, "Are you up to that today and then we don't have to worry about it in August?"

Appearing agreeable, I said, "Sure, I would like to prepare for school while we have the time." It felt like they planned this while I was sleeping.

We cleared the dishes and put sandals on to go for a walk. It took about fifteen minutes to walk to the school. The girls pointed out the bakery, butcher, and produce market that we passed along the way, sharing, "This is where Mama does most of her grocery shopping." Sometimes, she asks us to buy things for her." We also passed a post office so I could buy stamps to mail my letters.

When we arrived at the Institute Saint Mary, Kathleen rang the bell as the door was locked, and a nun dressed in her brown robe appeared. Recognizing the three sisters, she spoke with a hint of sarcasm, "Hello ladies, is this your American friend who will join us in the fall?"

"Hello, my name is Margot," I answered shyly. "I am looking forward to attending school here in September."

"Sister Agnes, we would like to show Margot the school," Bette eased the tension, "Mama spoke to you last week that she would be arriving this week."

"Yes, it is Friday, I have patiently waited for her arrival," Sister Agnes answered with scorn in her voice and a frown on her face.

"Sister, Margot had a long journey to come here, she arrived yesterday," Mineke replied confidently. "We want to get her acquainted with the school right away before we depart on our vacation."

Sister Agnes opened the door wider and motioned for us to enter the building. As we shuffled past her, she said, "Don't take too long and stop by my office before you leave."

We spent twenty minutes roaming through the corridors and the girls showed me the brightly lit gymnasium, auditorium, chapel filled with the glow of candles, and the cafeteria, in the center of the building and explained that each wing with long dark hallways and locked classrooms were assigned to different subject areas, one for math and science, one for history and religion, and the third hall to the right was for arts and languages. There were crucifixes on every classroom door and a statue of the Virgin Mary in the chapel. The girls took turns talking, no one dominated the conversation.

When we finished, we stopped at the office. Sister Agnes said, "Margot please come back a week before school starts so I can set up a schedule for you."

Kathleen replied, "We will return around the fifteenth of August after our vacation in America and our summer holiday in Ostende ends." I was not aware that school would start in August, I assumed it would begin after Labor Day in September, same as back home. I never saw that school again.

We walked home and Mama was outside watering the garden while she waited to drive us to the uniform store. Mineke showed me her uniform yesterday before I laid down for my twenty-four-hour snooze. It was a long brown skirt that hung below the knee, a white blouse, and a long brown sleeve sweater or a brown sleeveless vest, both open with buttons on the front. Everyone wore black loafers for shoes with brown or white knee-high stockings. She had three sets to change during the week but Mama, concerned about the laundry with three girls in uniforms, insisted that the girls wear the same outfit through the week and remove it as soon as they came home after school; change only if it was stained or smelled. I changed my school outfits every day. I never wore the same thing twice a week.

Mama and Kathleen sat in the front seat as she drove to the store. I sat in the middle of the back seat wedged between Bette and Mineke. It was located on a street with shops and restaurants about a ten-minute drive from their home. I did not notice any shopping malls driving home from the bus station like you see all over America. All the cars were parked along the street, no driveways or parking lots nearby. Mama told the salesclerk in Dutch, "Margot is an American attending the Institute Saint Mary for the year and needs two uniforms."

The clerk turned towards me, shook my hand, and spoke English, "Welcome, come over here so I can measure your size."

She took her tape measure from a drawer at a counter where she was working on alterations and wrapped it around my bust, waist and hips and recorded the centimeters on a notepad. I said, "I wear a size twelve at home." She looked at her measuring chart and said, "Oh that is a size forty in Europe. You will find that on the wall to your left."

I went to that rack, found my size, and placed it in front of my body. I asked her, "Do you have a fitting room so I can try it on?" She pointed to the door behind her cash register. I changed into a skirt and blouse that fit perfectly. I stepped out of the room to look in the mirror.

Mama approached me and with a peck on my cheek, said, "You look great, pick out another set so you have a spare during the week before I do the laundry." Hmm, she hates laundry!

I found a vest and a sweater so that I could wear one on cold and the other on warm days. She turned and stepped up to the counter, paid for it and the clerk wrapped the clothes carefully into a large shopping bag.

On the same city block, we walked to the shoe store. I picked out two pairs of white and three pairs of brown knee-high stockings, one for each school day during the week. The skirt hung below the knee so that I would not need full length stockings which I despised wearing, an accessory saved for special occasions when I dressed up.

The gentleman pointed to the chair to measure my foot size. He went into the back room and brought out two styles of loafers allowed at that school. I chose the shoes with the brass buckle on the front. Mama paid for it, and we drove home. While driving home, she winked in the rearview mirror, satisfied that her mission was accomplished.

As it was Friday, Catholic families traditionally ate fish for dinner. I offered to set the table as I always did back home, and she showed me where to find the dishes, glasses, silverware, and linen napkins. Europeans did not use paper napkins, a wasteful disposable item in America.

When Papa emerged from his office, Mama showed him the bags with the uniforms and shoes. I took the garment bags upstairs to hang the uniform in the closet so it would not get soiled or wrinkled for six weeks before the school year began. I never saw that uniform again. I wondered if they returned it or if the girls wore it in my absence.

At dinner, the family decided to go to the seashore on the weekend rather than wait until the following week. They enjoyed the tranquility of the summer home and showed me a photo album where they spent their summer holidays. The album was a thick three ring binder with plastic covers on each page to hold photographs in place. There were old black and white photos of girls as young children as well as color photos from their teenage years.

After dinner, the girls and I went upstairs to pack our suitcases. "You can remove the winter clothes from your bag and store them in the bureau next to your bed," Mineke suggested, "You won't be returning to the city with us before our vacation."

Bette added, "You will spend the summer in Ostende and return here before school starts in mid-August." I returned to that home for one last night before school started.

As I prepared for my next journey, Kathleen promised "It would take about ninety-minutes to drive to the cottage."

As much as I was aware of the plans from the letter I received before I left home, the time progressed quickly. It felt like I had no time to breathe. Bette came into the room to borrow a handbag and assured me, "Don't worry, you will have plenty of time to relax when we arrive at the cottage."

Ostende

I settled into the daily life of my new family at their summer home in Ostende, a village on the North Sea. The girls shared a large bedroom for the summer and opened a sofa bed under the window for my bed. I shoved my big red suitcase next to the couch as there was no space in the closet for an extra set of clothes and I was moving to their friend's home in a week.

Kathleen asked, "Do you mind sleeping under the window?"

"I prefer it for the fresh air after three days in cold air-conditioned buses and airplanes," I laughed. She climbed on the couch to open the window so the breeze could enter the hot stuffy room. They had not been to the cottage as they removed items from the closet to place them on open shelves for daily use.

The family mood suddenly changed when they reached the summer home, very cheerful and patient compared to their rigid demeanor in the city.

After lunch, the girls showed me the village, and we visited the Zwaan family to introduce me to my vacation hosts. It was exhilarating to romp along the sandy beach and wet my feet in the North Sea. The waves were calm; we splashed each other knowing our clothes would dry quickly in the hot sun. I spent a week with the girls at the seashore before they returned to Antwerp to depart on their vacation. We enjoyed the sandy beach each day.

Excited, but also bewildered, I wondered why the family would leave me soon after my arrival? Why host a student when their vacation plans would not include their guest? A holiday on the continent such as a road trip through Belgium and its neighboring countries to discover the history of the region made more sense to me, an immersive experience. Lost in thought as we roamed the beach, a tranquil place that I had not experienced since the Pacific coast of California last summer. Their abandonment disturbed me regardless of the special arrangements made to accommodate me.

Their itinerary began in Montreal where they would rent a car and take a road trip through New England, Philadelphia, and Washington D.C. They were excited to tour the White House and the Capitol. Then, they would return to Montreal with a detour to Rochester. I was not aware of the visit to my family home in New York.

My mother called Mama one day in June when I was at school to invite them for two nights. With the six-hour time difference she called in the morning to reach Mama before three o'clock in the afternoon so they could have a private conversation while the children attended school. She forgot to tell me that she met Mama on the phone. Mama invited Mom to Belgium for the Christmas holiday during that call.

There was tension at home during my high school years due to joining the Way Ministry, meeting Greg, getting sick, and fast tracking my high school plans. Did my parents agree to a year abroad so that I would forget about him? Was I supposed to aspire to the ambitious standards set by my older sister, Jan, who attended the University of Rochester and planned to go to law school? My mom was excited that I would be living in another doctor's home overseas.

I preferred creative pursuits and foreign languages; a small friendly arts college was more desirable to me than a large research institution. My acceptance to Elmira College arrived the day after the YFU assignment, so my future was set after the exchange program. I often dreamt of becoming a teacher, a translator at the United Nations, or a foreign service worker in another country, although those dreams never manifested. I was not interested in nursing; I hated the sight of blood working at the office. Eventually, I worked at a hospital, insurance companies, and schools in administrative and support services roles, not in executive decision-making positions.

Belgium had a unique culture and history nestled in between France and The Netherlands with a mix of French and Dutch culture. It was a battleground during the war when the Germans occupied Europe, and the Allied forces entered the continent through the beaches of Belgium, France and The Netherlands on the North Sea crossing the English Channel from Great Britain.

The language spoken in the northern region of Flanders, is Flemish, a dialect of Dutch as it bordered The Netherlands, but everybody was fluent in English as a second language. It was easy to include me in their conversations, but I needed to learn Dutch before school started. "*In Flanders Fields*," (c.1915) penned by a Canadian soldier, John McCrae, during World War I, refers to this region along the North Sea with the town of Ypres as its center.

On the tenth of July, eleven days after arriving in Antwerp, I moved into the Zwaan family home with my big red suitcase packed with all my summer clothes while the Van Leet family returned to Antwerp to leave on their vacation. I liked this family with four children ranging from age twelve to twenty-one years old. There were three girls and one boy, all their names started with "An...." The family hosted Janet, an American girl from Iowa for the summer. They enjoyed adding another American girl to their family for three weeks.

Introduced on that Sunday afternoon, with three kisses on each cheek, Mevrouw Zwaan repeated what Mevrouw Van Leet said upon my arrival, "Please call me Mama and this is your Papa" facing her husband. When he hugged me with three kisses on each cheek, he smiled, "Welcome to my humble home, Margot. One more princess in my castle, the more the merrier." Everyone chuckled. Immediately, I sensed it was going to be a fantastic vacation. He then excused himself to get ready for his drive back to the city for a busy work week.

Their cottage had two bedrooms in the attic, one for boys and one for girls. There was an extra roll-away bed for me and my big red suitcase fit underneath it. It was great to have another American girl to chat about our European experiences. I loved skipping along the beach with Anneliese, her sisters, and their friends. We bought ice cream cones at the beach house every day. We wore our bathing suits under sun dresses and carried towels in a large beach bag, so we could enter the water throughout the day. The nice leisurely pace during the summer reminded me of lazy days by the pool back home.

We checked in for dinner at five o'clock for barbeques or pizza. That was the easiest way to feed their large family as there were few pots and pans at the cottage. They did not have air conditioning in the cottages by the seashore. Microwave ovens were not present in homes at that time.

Papa Z worked at his office in Ghent and visited the cottage on weekends. He always brought groceries with him on Friday afternoons for the following week. He was an amicable gentleman who loved hanging out with his teenaged children. He reminded me of my dad and fun-loving uncles at our family reunions.

After dinner, we helped clean up the kitchen, then all the girls went to the local pub where I drank my first beer, never allowed back home where the drinking age was eighteen years old. I liked the taste of Heineken and Amstel beer, Dutch brands, stronger than Genesee beer in Rochester. Everyone was friendly and welcomed me and Janet into their social circle. One weekend, when all the teenagers in the village gathered at the park, Joost poured me a shot of whiskey, my first taste of hard liquor in my life. I felt sick and ran behind a bush to vomit. The girls sat me down on a blanket on the grass and handed me a thermos of water to drink, but I felt nauseated for the rest of the day. We moved to the shade of the trees to stay out of the hot sun. I never drank whiskey ever again.

At the end of July, my host family returned to Ostende for two weeks before school began. The Zwaan family departed on a vacation to show Janet the country as she had never been to Europe before the program. I thanked them for their hospitality.

Annelies and I exchanged addresses at the end of my stay at her house. We exchanged letters and cards for decades afterward, sharing future weddings, birth announcements and Christmas cards. I always received a separate note with photographs from Mama Z. We lost contact when Annelies moved to Italy with her future husband and young family in the nineties, twenty years after we met. I regret never contacting them when I returned to Europe on my future visits.

I reunited with the Van Leet family when they returned to their cottage for two more weeks in August. We roamed the village and lounged at the beach. We were not allowed to go to the pub. It was an awkward reunion. I could not spend time with the friends that I met while they were away. We returned to Antwerp in the middle of the week before school started. I went to my first YFU weekend retreat that weekend.

Tensions rose after their holiday in North America. Did they learn about Greg, the boyfriend I left behind? Did they see the letter he sent to their home? I secretly cried when I saw the letter from him after we returned to Antwerp, stating "I'm married!" written on the unopened blue airmail sheet that I sent him when I visited the school the day after my arrival, with **"Return to Sender"** stamped on it. While my smile disappeared, my heart broke into a million pieces. Did he purposely wait until I was overseas to break the news? My first love crumbled and there was nothing I could do to fix it. I was heartbroken although I put on a brave face to hide my sorrow.

What happened in Rochester? No one talked about it. I adapted to new situations easily, the move to Belgium was a perfect example. Working at the office while in high school taught me empathy and tolerance not just for health issues, but also cultural and social situations like my family vacations when we stayed in London for a month. Dad's office catered to patients of all ages, races, and stages of life. Adjusting my high school schedule from four to three years required flexibility to adapt to a full course schedule which I juggled with ease along with an illness, extra-curricular activities, and part time employment. I genuinely anticipated excitement living in Belgium and learning a new language. The three sisters appeared robotic rather than friendly the way they stuck together and took turns talking, so no one dominated a conversation. Their parents always pursued an agenda; there was no spontaneity. I remembered the brochure with the orange border that Franz discussed on the bus and spoke to a counsellor at the retreat on the weekend.

YFU Monthly Retreats

The weekend before school started in the middle of August, the YFU organization invited all exchange students in the Benelux (Belgium, The Netherlands, Luxembourg) Region to a retreat at Arnhem, The Netherlands. I took my big red suitcase with my summer clothes that I wore in Ostende and washed everything the day before we left the cottage. There was no time to unpack it as the retreat was the day after we returned to Antwerp and the following week school would begin. My winter clothes, new shoes, and school uniform remained in the bureau and closet in Mineke's bedroom in Antwerp.

As I traveled via train to these retreats, I fell in love with the beautiful landscapes of tulip fields, windmills and canals that defined the country. The Benelux region, connected to the Eurail system that expanded across Europe, made train travel fast and convenient between countries. The region was rebuilt from the destruction of World War II. Developed centuries earlier, the canals protected the land below sea level with a system of dikes to prevent flooding, that became major transportation and shipping corridors. Windmills throughout the country provided sustainable energy. Colorful rainbows of tulip fields added to the beauty.

When I arrived in Arnhem in the Netherlands, I saw a young man with blonde hair waving a YFU sign. He gathered all the students together to board a bus to take us from the train station to the camp. The students were separated into bunk rooms for sleeping and bathing, one for boys and one for girls, and ate meals together. Everyone was served the same meal, no substitutions allowed in a cafeteria style dining hall. Group sessions were spoken in English to discuss our experiences and we learned about our new home along with outdoor activities. One session was a film documentary about the German occupation of western Europe during World War II, and the Holocaust. It was interesting to learn history from a unique perspective, survivors directly affected by the destruction of the war. I never learned twentieth century world history at IHS, a grade twelve social studies course, graduating a year early. A field trip to the point of interest on the other side of the world was the perfect classroom.

I spoke to a counselor privately about the family in Belgium, "I barely stepped foot in the country and was suddenly pushed onto another family so they could take a holiday without me. I never felt welcomed after two months due to their hectic schedule."

He listened attentively while I talked, "I sensed competition and jealousy with three girls close in age instead of comradery and friendship. Conversations felt controlled, cold, and distant, no attempt to become friendly. After eight weeks, I never felt like a member of the family."

Meneer Hendrick did not comment about my concerns. He explained the process to transfer to another family, "Don't worry, it would be arranged quickly," he assured me. "I will take you to my home while we search for another family and arrange for you luggage to be shipped to Amsterdam. You don't have to return to that family after this weekend." I was not prepared for an abrupt relocation.

He sipped his beer and continued, "Do not contact the Van Leet family, the YFU regional office will communicate your request for a transfer and relay instructions to ship your luggage to your new location."

Unbeknownst to me, it took six weeks to locate another host family, attending another retreat a month later, filing another complaint against him, and staying with another counselor to find a host family. Thankfully, I had my big red suitcase with my summer clothes with me during this transition. I was so confused; I wanted to return home to America.

He drove me to his home in Amsterdam at the end of the weekend. His home was a private apartment in a hotel in central Amsterdam where he was the manager, as well as the director of the Benelux region of the YFU organization.

Instead of registering me in a separate hotel room, he had me stay in his apartment. There was no second bedroom, I had to share his bed, and he took advantage of me every night. No sex, but I did not like his advances and he would not leave me alone. Gray hair along the edges of his hairline, he looked like he was the same age or slightly older than my father. I felt helpless in the care of the leader of this organization.

As soon as he left for his office each day, I showered and dressed before entering the hotel café for breakfast where the clerk was informed to charge his daughter's meals to his room." After I ate a continental breakfast of bread and cheese with hot tea, I left the hotel to explore the city, walked along the canals, and returned to the hotel for dinner. He avoided greeting me in the lobby and restaurant, it was an awkward, private, one-sided affair also known as sexual assault. I never consented to his advances and felt powerless to retaliate. There were no vacancies for a separate hotel room when I inquired at the reservation desk every single day.

As I walked through the central square, the lines for the museums were long. I had no patience to mingle with the crowd or wait in lines on hot days. I noted the hotel's location for my return that evening. It was an ideal opportunity for sightseeing, free to wander in an international tourist area. However, I was not in the mood to visit any museums or go shopping. I wanted to move out of that hotel! At seventeen in a foreign country, I felt helpless, confused, and lost!

After a week with no updates, I asked him, "What is the status to transfer me to another host family?"

"I have been too busy with my work, no time to make inquiries," he replied, angry that I would question his motives.

The next day I took that YFU brochure with the orange border out of my big red suitcase and slipped it into my purse along with the stationery I brought from America to write letters. I purchased lemonade and vla (vanilla custard) from an outdoor vendor and sat at a table in the central square near the canal. I wrote a note about my situation and found a post office on a side street near the hotel to mail it.

A week later, I received a telegram at the hotel reception with the message,

"Meet Mevrouw Ebels at the next retreat in Leeuwarden in two weeks, in the middle of September. Bring all your luggage with you." The next day, I received the retreat announcement in the mail at the hotel. I was glad that the organization updated my address for communication purposes, so I was not totally lost in the system.

I had no choice but to tolerate this monster's advances for two more weeks. I never pursued therapy, but that sexual abuse bothered me for years.

The box of clothes from Antwerp arrived at the hotel the following week. I unpacked it and stuffed all my winter clothes back into my big red suitcase along with my summer clothes. I was relieved that everything I had brought to Belgium eleven weeks earlier was back in my possession. The hotel receptionist, Carrie, noticed my big red suitcase for a weekend retreat and gave me a wink and a wave. She knew I would not be returning to the hotel. I walked to the train station and bought a ticket to board a train to Leeuwarden.

Holding a YFU sign, Meneer Ebels hired a bus to pick up students at the train station in Leeuwarden to drive to the camp on Friday. Like the last one, it was a weekend of activities to discuss our experiences and learn more about The Netherlands history and culture. A film about canals and dikes explained how Dutch engineers reclaimed the land that sank under the sea. On Saturday morning, Mevrouw Ebels met with me privately to discuss my situation. We poured a cup of tea and grabbed a stroopwafel (a thin waffle stuffed with syrup) to sit outside in the beautiful flower garden while the other students went on a hike with her husband.

She began the conversation, "Margot, I am so sorry. When the head office received your letter, they called me immediately because I was hosting this retreat and had a vast network of host families to work with." She sighed, and asked, "How are you feeling?"

As tears welled up in my eyes, "Mevrouw Ebels," sobbing, "It was awful, I never experienced this in my life. He refused to stop when I asked him to. Every day when I inquired at reception about a hotel room, I was told they were fully booked for the rest of the summer."

I stopped to sip my tea and continued, "He made sure I could not book another room. I was prepared to pay for it; I could ask my parents to wire the money to cover the cost."

She grabbed a tissue from her purse and handed it to me, and asked, "Are your parents aware of the situation?"

"No, I have not communicated with them," I replied, "they don't even know that I left Belgium,"

Shocked, she grabbed my arm, "Why haven't you told them?"

"They would not understand why I did not want to stay with that family, I cried. "I am sure my mother contacted the Belgian family as they met in July and spoke on the phone before I left in June."

After a bite of the stroopwafel and sip of tea, I continued, "This new situation was too embarrassing to write home about and worry them. The last time I wrote to my parents was from the summer home after they returned from America, over a month ago. I described the village and the fun I had with the Zwaan family. I did not mention the tension that erupted after their return."

She took a sip of tea and said, "I read your file about that family. When they were asked to host, they reluctantly agreed, they could not cancel the vacation."

"There is more to it," I replied, "They met my American parents in person; my mother invited them to visit for two days. There were problems this past year before I left home."

I cleared my throat and continued," I loved the family in Ostende who hosted another American girl for the summer. It would have been nice just to stay with them after the other girl left. They also had four teenaged children, three girls and one boy about eight years apart in age and everyone got along well."

"Yes, they only wanted a summer student." She admitted. "My husband and I will take you to our home and I will make calls immediately to find another host as school started a month ago. I began the search for a new host when I received your complaint but needed to speak to you first." She turned towards me, smiling, and placed her hand on my shoulder, "In the meantime, we will take you to a library and assist you with the language and get you acquainted with our lovely little country."

I smiled, "That would be wonderful. I am homesick but at the same time, I don't want to give up hope."

She nodded no, "We would not send you home unless you were gravely ill, required hospitalization, or there was a family emergency such as a death in your family." She leaned in for a hug, "Don't worry, good things are coming. You will fall in love with The Netherlands, I guarantee it!" She sipped her tea and continued, "If you want, I can arrange for you to call home to America next week after we return to my home."

"Your home?" I asked.

She replied, "Yes, my husband and I will take you to our home while I make inquiries. Have patience, that is my job, a top priority unlike Meneer Hendrick."

I then asked, "Did this ever happen before? Why is he the Director if he takes advantage of teenagers?"

"This is the first time we heard of this problem," she said, "I have already filed a request with the head office for his removal from the board." She patted my back and smiled, "You were brave to speak up. Thank you for bringing his behavior to our attention."

She showed me the note in the file that my parents were worried about me. "Why is my daughter in a hotel?" read a telegram.

She suggested, "I want you to call home to America from my home next week. Let your parents know that you are ok." We stood up, exchanged hugs and smiles, and joined the group as they returned from the hike.

On Sunday, I accompanied Meneer and Mevrouw Ebels to their home near Leeuwarden in the northwestern province of Friesland. They were aware of my report in Arnhem a month earlier that brought me from Belgium to Amsterdam and prepared to make a successful transition for me this time. They assured me that they managed students within the vast network of the YFU organization and had an extensive list of host families to contact in The Netherlands. They urged me to have patience, suggesting it would take a week or two. They relied on families who sent their children on the program to return the favor of hosting foreign students. A requirement of the "exchange" same as when my parents hosted Louisa when Jan went to France for the summer.

The next day, we walked to the library to get a book about the country (written in English) and dual language cassette tapes in English and Dutch. She invited me to go shopping with her in the village to see the food they ate in The Netherlands. She introduced me to townsfolk who spoke both Dutch and English to me. They knew she was the crisis counselor who hosted students temporarily and assured me I was safe.

On Monday evening, Mevrouw Ebels contacted the overseas operator to ring a call to Rochester, New York. She had my home phone number in her file and asked me what time to arrange the call. I suggested anytime, knowing mom was not working. The call went through at ten o'clock at night, four o'clock in the afternoon back home after David and Paul arrived home from school.

Mom answered the phone, "Hi Margot, how are you? We have been worried about you. We had no idea how to reach you directly. We contacted the organization who informed us that you stayed in a hotel in Amsterdam?"

I replied, "Mom, I was under the impression it would only be a week, but it became a month. When I went to the next retreat this past weekend, I spoke with Mevrouw Ebels who is currently looking after me and she will find me a host family here in The Netherlands."

"Why did you leave Belgium? What happened?" Mom asked. "They were such a nice family when I met them."

"I don't want to discuss that now, it's hard to explain," I said. "I knew I would not be happy there for an entire year."

"Where are you now?" Mom asked. "Let me know when you have a new family."

"Mevrouw Ebels is a nice lady who takes care of students in transition situations in Leeuwarden," I smiled at her. "She will make contacts in her network to find me a family within a week or two."

Mom sighed with relief, "OK. You take care of yourself and keep me informed by letter or telegram when you move to a new family. I love you."

Relieved, "I will Mom. Say hello to Dad. I will be in touch as soon as I know where I am going. I love you and miss you." We exchanged goodbyes and disconnected the call.

Mevrouw Ebels suggested it was time for bed. She had a busy day planned for us tomorrow.

The next morning, I woke up early, showered and dressed. I asked Mevrouw Ebels if I could do my laundry. I had not washed my clothes since leaving Ostende a month earlier and was tired of rinsing and hanging garments in a bathtub. She showed me how to operate the washing machine. I sorted my dirty clothes and proceeded to wash and dry two loads over the next few hours.

She asked, "Do you have all your luggage with you? If not, I must arrange delivery of any belongings left behind when students come to the retreats with just a weekend bag."

I assured her, "That was the one thing his office arranged. A box of winter clothes arrived last week from Antwerp so I could pack everything together. I had my big red suitcase with me at the retreat in Arnhem because I only had one day in Antwerp after returning from the cottage before leaving for that retreat, no time to pack a weekend bag."

Meneer Ebels chuckled, "That is one large weekend bag!"

"I made sure I did not leave anything behind at the house of horrors," I retorted.

"You have lived out of your big red suitcase all summer, it is time to get you settled." He laughed, "My wife will make sure you move to a new home in record time. She gets results quickly."

They winked at each other and gave me a tape recorder to listen to the Dutch tapes we borrowed from the library. I sat on the couch and repeated the phrases to Zoite, (Sweetie) their cat. Meneer Ebels watched in amusement as she cuddled with me and purred in response. Dutch was a mix of German and English with slight pronunciation and spelling differences, very easy to learn but the sentence structure placing the verb at the end of a sentence was confusing.

After the laundry finished, I went for a walk in the neighborhood. I enjoyed the fresh air and scenery of the small town near the North Sea, four hundred kilometers north of Ostende. In mid-September, it was a bit cooler with the change of seasons. I loved the tranquil environment two hundred kilometers away from the hustle and bustle of Amsterdam.

Meneer Ebels grilled fresh fish and potatoes on the BBQ while his wife engaged in communications, contacting the regional representatives. She informed them, "I need a host family for a seventeen-year-old doctor's daughter from New York State who already missed the first month of school. Please respond promptly."

She received prospects from across the country and interviewed them on the phone for the rest of the week. I taught myself the language and history of the country from the library materials and explored the neighborhood each day until it was time to meet my new family in Veendam!

I enjoyed my stay in Leeuwarden; the Ebels felt like family and really cared about my wellbeing. They were genuinely concerned about my situation and eager to correct it quickly.

Chapter 5

Move to The Netherlands

Happy Days in Veendam

After ten days in Leeuwarden, on Tuesday morning during the last week of September, Meneer and Mevrouw Ebels drove me to Veendam in the province of Groningen, to meet the Van Der Veen family. We left after breakfast around 9:00 a.m. and arrived at Stationstraat 2 at 10:15, just in time for the morning coffee break. Mevrouw Van Der Veen welcomed us at the door along with their dog, a cocker spaniel named Flipje. Meneer Van Der Veen was sitting in the parlor anticipating my arrival. It finally felt like I had a home away from home!

Inside their home, Mevrouw approached me with three kisses on each cheek as Meneer Van Der Veen came to the foyer who also hugged and kissed me three times. He smiled and said, "Welcome to our home, Margot. We hope you will like it here. Please call me Papa and my wife is your Mama."

Mama said, "I hope you like dogs, this is Flipje. Our daughter, Jeannet is coming home for lunch to meet you."

"Mama and Papa, I am pleased to meet you and looking forward to meeting Jeannet." I smiled, "It will be nice to have a younger sister."

She asked Meneer and Mevrouw Ebels to sit down for coffee and cake. Meneer Ebels said, "You don't mind having a bank attached to your home?

Papa laughed, "It is a safe neighborhood. No robberies since we moved here."

Mevrouw Ebels changed the subject, "Margot has already missed a month at school. She would like to start right away."

Mama replied, "I notified Winkler Prins that she arrived today, and they made an appointment for tomorrow morning to register and arrange a schedule. Jeannet will walk to school with her and bring her to the office."

"I can hardly wait to get started." I smiled.

Mevrouw Ebels smiled, "That will be wonderful to introduce her to school immediately instead of waiting until next week."

Meneer Ebels intervened, "We have a long drive back home. Margot, you have our phone number and address if you need to reach us. I think you will be happy here now that you will be busy with school." He and his wife stood up and shook hands with Mama and Papa and gave me a hug and three kisses goodbye. I waved from the veranda holding Flipje as they drove away.

Papa excused himself to return to the bank. Mama led me upstairs to show me my bedroom and the bathroom. I brought my big red suitcase and placed it on the floor next to the bureau. "I will leave you to settle in your room, she sighed. "We will have lunch at 12:15 p.m. when Jeannet comes home. This afternoon you may stroll through the village to get acquainted with your new neighborhood."

Jeannet was so excited, she ran home at lunchtime. We greeted each other with a hug and three kisses on the cheek. She spoke good English for a twelve-year-old girl. We set the table and Mama served sandwiches. She brought out a plate with fresh sliced bread and Jeannet grabbed the cold cuts and cheese from the refrigerator.

Papa emerged from the bank whispering, "I don't join my family for lunch on school days but today is special to welcome our newest member of the family."

"Thank you for allowing me to move into your home," I replied smiling, "I am excited to learn what life is like in The Netherlands." It was the first time I smiled since leaving the Zwaan family in Ostende, two months earlier. My life was finally becoming the fairytale I dreamt about before I left home.

The food passed around, napkins dropped into our laps, and everyone made their own sandwich with the condiments and choices on the table. I waited until Mama and Papa started eating, noticed that they cut their sandwiches into bite size pieces, so I did the same. They served water with the meal, tea and coffee were served in the morning, afternoon, and evening with cake or cookies.

Jeannet talked about her morning at school, that she told her classmates I arrived at her home, and she could not wait to meet me. Mama looked at the clock and reminded her to finish eating so she could return to class on time. After we cleared the table, Jeannet and Papa excused themselves and I helped Mama tidy up the kitchen. She told me to take my time, unpack, and walk around town. She reminded me that Jeannet arrived home at half past three for tea and cookies and talked about her school day.

I went back upstairs to arrange my stuff. I opened the windows for fresh air in Eva's bedroom that had not been used in two months since she left for California. Eva enjoyed her host family and was happy that Jeannet had a new sister while she was away. It felt good to have a room for myself as I hung up my clothes in the closet and stuffed the bureau drawers. I also set up the wash basin with my toiletries.

Mama brought me towels and showed me the linen closet next to the bathroom. She explained she washed the linens on Mondays when her housekeeper came, and to put them in the hamper on Sunday evenings. She did all the family laundry on Fridays so she could hang it outside and after school Jeannet and I would sort and fold the clothes and bring them to each bedroom. She kept her weekends free from housework and laundry to enjoy visits with her son and friends. She then excused herself to lay down for her daily afternoon nap. She reminded me to leave the back door unlocked if I went outside; the front door was bolted facing the street. She would give me a spare key later.

At that time during the fall of 1973, The Netherlands along with other countries worldwide faced an oil embargo by OPEC (Organization of the Petroleum Exporting Countries) due to their support for Israel in the Yom Kippur War. Higher fuel prices led to drastic measures to reduce gasoline usage. I limited my use of hot water in showers and laundry. We also turned off the lights in rooms that were not in use. I adapted this habit to my daily routine for the rest of my life.

The government introduced "Car free Sundays," to encourage residents to walk and ride bicycles. People of all ages rode them everywhere. On future visits to the country, I noticed piles of bicycles parked at train stations and people carried their bikes in bags on buses and trains. It improved the air quality and cut pollution around the country.

After three months away from home, I happily felt like part of a family, not a guest. Jeannet welcomed me into her world, and we clicked instantly. Her bedroom was on the third floor, where we did homework, played games, and read books together. We walked the dog after school and before bedtime. We rode bikes along the canal in the center of town to go to the bakery and butcher for Mama. She bought a fresh loaf of bread every day.

Papa managed a bank attached to the house. I set up a savings account in Dutch Guilder. He also showed me how to send a telegram to my parents with their address and phone number. Upon receipt of that telegram, my parents wired $200 to deposit into my bank account.

My school day started at 7a.m., when I woke up to dress for school. I could wear jeans and peasant blouses; there was no uniform! A typical breakfast consisted of tea and crackers or stroopwafels (waffles stuffed with honey) topped with hagelslag (chocolate sprinkles). A short walk into town, school opened at 8 a.m. Classes stopped for recess at 10 a.m. for thirty minutes, to go home for coffee and cake. Lunch at noon for one hour, to go home to eat with the family. School finished at 3 p.m.

After school, at teatime with Mama, we talked about our day and helped prepare dinner. Every day, she boiled a pot of potatoes that we peeled in a special machine. We ate healthy meals with meat, potatoes, and vegetables for the main course and vla (custard) for dessert. At 8 p.m., coffee with cake was served when the news broadcast on television followed by British and Dutch sitcoms for the rest of the evening.

There were no commercials once the news began like (PBS) Public Broadcasting Service in America. It was nice to watch shows on television with no advertisements. We ate our meals at the dining room table away from the kitchen and the television in the living room. We walked the dog at 9 p.m. before bedtime. The evening walk was a habit I adapted when I returned home, a wonderful way to relax after a long day. Jeannet and I retired upstairs at 10 p.m. for the night.

Stationstraat 2, on the street corner, was a large home with three stories, a parlor, dining room and kitchen on the main floor, with a laundry mud room by the back door and powder room near the front foyer. The second floor had four bedrooms facing the street and a large attic facing the back. The main bathroom was on the second floor at the end of the hall with a bathtub / shower and separate WC or toilet next to it across from the parent's bedroom. Each bedroom had a wash basin to brush teeth and comb hair away from the bathroom. There were two small bedrooms on the third floor for Jeannet with a washbasin in one of the rooms, but she had to descend to the second floor and trot the full length of the hallway to use the toilet and the shower. Mama hired a housekeeper to help with cleaning and laundry on Mondays and Fridays.

Everybody, from preschoolers to senior citizens, rode a bicycle in The Netherlands. Cars and bicycles shared the roads without accidents. Main roads between towns had roundabouts to direct traffic encouraging slower speeds. There were no traffic lights in the villages, just stop signs and traffic ran smoothly. The land was flat, the towns were small and everything was close by. Canals ran through the towns with roads beside them.

The air was clean, with no pollution. Windmills, farms, and flower-adorned homes decorated the landscape. It was safe to walk or cycle throughout the countryside. Did I step into a fairytale? Veendam reminded me of something I read in my Brother's Grimm books.

I registered at Winkler Prins school, a century old educational institution, the next day after I arrived in Veendam. School began in the middle of August, six weeks earlier. The education system had three streams, a six-year GYMNASIUM program for university-bound students, a five-year HAVO program for college-bound students, and a four-year MAVO program for everyone else.

Placed in the HAVO five-year stream, I chose Dutch, English, German, Math, and History all taught in Dutch. I enjoyed learning German as it was like Dutch and not taught in my school in America.

Meneer Schnell, the English teacher, made fun of my American accent and pronunciation in his class. He taught British English to his students so I was going to learn the "proper" way to speak! Math, a universal language of formulas and numbers, was easy and History was a challenge, learning World History of the twentieth century was a course I never took back home. I was exempt from tests and grades although I wrote them anyway. Everyone spoke Dutch to me and before Christmas, I read, spoke, and understood the language comfortably. Immersion was the best way to learn a foreign language, not twenty or thirty minutes a day in a classroom where you never practiced it outside school. It was a friendly school environment where I felt welcomed from the first day when I arrived until the last day when I left.

I made friends at school. Girls invited me to their homes for tea after school to meet their families. We spoke both Dutch and English as people practiced their English skills with me. Through these friendships, I joined a volleyball team that met on Thursday afternoons and a swimming team that met on Mondays. I did not participate in the swim meets but I got exercise and improved my strokes at the practices. I enjoyed having that structure and activity. Two friends from school, Elly and Ankie, remained friends forever as we exchanged birthday, Christmas gifts and cards annually and visited each other later in our lives.

Another American girl on the YFU Exchange Program, Barbara from California, also attended the school. In early October, soon after my arrival, the local newspaper interviewed us in the school courtyard. As my Dutch was rusty, the reporter spoke English. It was nice to have a fellow American nearby and be welcomed by the Dutch community. We did not develop a close friendship because we lived at opposite ends of the town and had already forged a close group of friends separately. The journalist from **The Veendamer**, authored a fascinating article in Dutch and inserted a nice photograph of the two of us sitting together that graced the front page two weeks after the interview.

Jeannet's older brother, Hans often came home on weekends from university to visit his family. He had a close relationship with his parents as they sat in the parlor and drank beer and liqueurs before dinner. He had dark hair and glasses and was always dressed handsomely in a long-sleeved shirt and sweater or vest with dress pants. I never saw him in jeans and a tee shirt.

Papa invited me to sit with them and try a shot of liqueur. I sampled different drinks throughout the year, refusing whiskey after the incident in Belgium. They watched European football (soccer) on television which was exciting as the Dutch team reached the finals against Germany later that year. Papa teased me, "Margot, your move to our home brought the team good luck!"

"Thank you for the compliment, Papa." It felt great to be acknowledged with positivity and to be invited into that weekend afternoon familial bond. I was mesmerized by the friendliness of this family, the school, and the community right from the start. I applied stickers of the Dutch soccer players on my big red suitcase and orange became my favorite color. The national color, orange, traced back to William of Orange, who led the Dutch War of Independence against Spain in the sixteenth century.

I met Oom Lou and Tante Anja, dear friends of the family who lived in Winschoten, a town close to the border with Germany. An older couple with no children (their son died in a car accident), they were invited for dinner once a month on Saturdays and invited me to visit their home on a weekend as they had friends with teenagers.

I took the bus to Winschoten, and they arranged for Grietje to meet me. We walked to a pub and met her friends to enjoy a fun evening. I had a house key to let myself back into their home as it was past midnight when I returned. In the morning over breakfast, they asked about the evening and invited me to come back again. They enjoyed my visits as they reminded them of their son. I returned for a weekend visit every month, and became good friends with Grietje, her cousin, Derek, and their friends. The pub did not ask for identification; it was a fun evening of drinking and dancing. They walked me back to Tante's house by midnight.

The next morning, Tante Anja drove me to Veendam and joined Mama for coffee. She was pleased that I had a good relationship with everyone and had an enjoyable time. I stayed in contact with Tante Anja via letters and Christmas cards for about five years afterwards until she moved to an Old Age Home in Switzerland.

Living in a small town away from the big cities of Amsterdam and Rotterdam was tranquil without traffic, crowds, and noise. The family life was relaxed and there was no sibling rivalry with the four-year age difference with Jeannet. We were both happy to form a sisterly bond. Just like at home in America, I helped with daily chores setting the table and cleared it after meals, washed dishes, walked the dog, picked up groceries, tidied my bedroom and folded laundry on wash days.

In the evenings while watching television, Mama relaxed with embroidery (cross stitch or needlepoint). She knew that I liked to sew. She gave me a kit that included the cloth, threads, hoops, and needles along with a floral pattern sketched on paper. I enjoyed creating handsewn scenes in a couple of weeks. Cross stitch was delicate and tedious as one sewed a small row of "xxxxx" to recreate the pattern on the canvas. We bought more complicated patterns of Dutch skaters and dancers that I embroidered that year and gave to my mother in America. Those pieces were framed and hung on her wall for decades. The handmade creations were passed back to me to grace my walls; a reminder of that European charm I experienced in my youth. I continued embroidery when I returned home to America and dabbled in other handicrafts like macrame, sewing, and weaving.

Family Ties

It was important for me as a student to treat my host families with the utmost respect as they became my parents and siblings while I lived with them. There were rules to be followed regardless of how I felt about them. Throughout my story, I refer to my American birth parents as Mom and Dad or Mother and Father. My host family's parents were called Mama and Papa, that is a requirement of the Student Exchange Organization to help ease transitions for students to feel welcome in their host family's homes. As a courtesy, I refer to the Dutch adults as Meneer and Mevrouw out of respect for their culture while American adults are known as Mr. and Mrs. I also refer to Tante and Oom also known as Aunt and Uncle for those adult friendships that I developed a close relationship with. My European hosts and friends insisted that I address them as such to nurture the close relationships that we shared.

I wrote letters to my parents in New York on blue airmail sheets where I wrote on one side, folded them into an envelope to write the address, and put the stamp on the outside, a flat 3D postcard. The mail took about a week. It became increasingly more difficult to write in English as I immersed myself in the Dutch language and culture. They were happy that I adjusted to life overseas and enjoyed myself. I was happy that I had the strength to overcome the difficulties I encountered during the summer and found a new family that became forever friends as we stayed in touch for the rest of our lives, visiting each other on both sides of the ocean.

My American family wanted to come for a visit. My brother Mark spent the fall semester of his college year in Greece while I was in Europe. He sent me a postcard that he wanted to visit on a weekend in October. My Dutch family was eager to meet him, especially Hans, who was the same age. Mark flew to Zurich, Switzerland, and boarded a train for The Netherlands. We worried as he did not arrive on time. The next day, when he returned to Greece, he sent a telegram:

"Sorry Margot, I could not visit. I flew to Switzerland and switched to the train for Groningen. The conductor thought my passport was fake and asked me to leave the train. I changed my flight and returned to Athens. Love, Mark."

My sister, Jan, spent the spring semester at her university in Paris in January. She flew to Amsterdam with my mother and six-year-old brother, to spend the holidays with me before her school began. The train station connected to Schiphol, so I instructed them to take it to Assen where Papa and I met them to drive to Veendam. They brought a small red suitcase packed with my winter coat, boots, scarf, and hat to wear during the winter months that I had placed on my bed before I left last summer.

The Van der Veens had two spare bedrooms, so they welcomed my American family for the holiday. They arrived before Christmas and spent five days in Veendam. We took long walks to show my American family the village where I lived. It was not cold with a light blanket of snow. Homes and businesses were beautifully decorated with Christmas lights. Mama cooked the traditional holiday meals of kroketten (stuffed hash-like sausages) and Bahmi (rice) and Nasi (noodles) Goreng (Indonesian flavored stir fries). She also prepared delicious fondues to dip chunks of fresh baguette into a variety of cheese and chocolate sauces. Tante Anja and Oom Lou joined us on Christmas Day so my mom could meet them as I wrote to her about my weekend visits to their home in Winschoten. Jeannet and I enjoyed having the extra company and playing with my little brother David. He liked walking the dog with us.

We traveled via train to Antwerp for New Years to visit the Van Leet family. We spent three days with them and attended a New Years Eve party together. It felt awkward returning to their home after I left abruptly at the end of the summer holiday, however, this invitation was arranged during that trip to America between my two mothers. I had no choice but to accept their plans. I was glad that my American sister, Jan, was present, to act as a shield between me and the Belgian family.

My mom slipped and broke her wrist while dancing at the party, so Dokter Van Leet asked for a large serviette or a dishtowel from the banquet hall to wrap a sling around her wrist to elevate her arm for the night. He took her to Emergency the next morning on New Years Day to get it set in a cast. Jan and I managed the luggage while my mom looked after David for the rest of that vacation.

From Belgium, we traveled via train to Paris to help Jan get settled into her apartment. We stayed at a hotel near the university so we could walk to her apartment, and the central location was ideal for sightseeing. It was fun to visit museums and cafes and speak French.

It was nice to see my American family to reassure my mother that I was happy with my Dutch family and enjoyed the slower pace of village life in The Netherlands that was different from the fast pace of city life in America. She was impressed with my new family and formed a lifelong friendship with them as Mama, Jeannet, and Eva corresponded and visited her in Rochester in future years.

In Paris, mom asked me again, "Margot, why did you leave Belgium?"

"I did not have a good relationship with the girls. I felt like a stranger, not like a family member." I replied. "There was no time during the summer to get acquainted with them before the school year started."

"You didn't give it a chance," Mom suggested.

I was annoyed that my mother followed through with the visit after I left that family. She could have written a letter to cancel their invitation as a show of support for my decision to leave them. We could have spent the three days over New Years in Brussels on the way to Paris.

My sister, Jan, noticed the sibling rivalry between the three sisters aged three years apart during that weekend visit, understood my frustration, and explained it to her. There were other reasons, but I decided not to discuss those details. She was satisfied with Jan's explanation. I never had any further contact with the Van Leet family after that holiday visit.

To change the subject, I asked, "How was Dad? It was too bad that he did not accompany you on this trip."

"He did not want to leave the boys home alone during the holidays, so they took a road trip to ski in Vermont," Mom replied. "Paul got his driver's license last summer as soon as he turned sixteen, so they had three drivers, and it was good practice for him to drive in winter conditions." My dad and brothers loved snow skiing in the winter as they pursued it for the rest of their lives.

I kept the breakup with Greg a secret. Mom did not ask about him, so I did not volunteer any information. That unopened returned letter affected my mood when I returned to Antwerp after their visit to America that also affected my relationship with them. I wondered if the Van Leet family received that letter when they returned to Antwerp before or after their trip to America prior to returning to their summer home when they picked me up from the Zwaan household. Was it possible they mentioned or showed it to my mother privately which added to the tension between us after their vacation to America?

My mother and brother took a taxi to Paris Charles de Gaulle Airport to fly home, and I took the train to Assen the weekend before school resumed. I phoned Papa to pick me up when I arrived at the station. Jeannet and Hans accompanied him in the car so that Hans could take the train back to university. I enjoyed seeing my American mother, brother, and sister halfway through my year abroad. It was nice to have a reunion over the holidays in a magical setting like Europe, far away from America. I was glad my mom met my new host family that I fell in love with and developed her own relationship with them to cherish for the rest of her life. It made my year abroad more genuine sharing that bond with her.

The weather in The Netherlands was like the weather in New York. A mild winter with a blanket of snow where temperatures hovered above freezing at zero Centigrade or thirty-two Fahrenheit. I unpacked the small red suitcase and added those items to the closet in my bedroom so I could wear the winter jacket to school.

Happy New Year, 1974

I resumed the Dutch routine after the holidays, adapting to the customs, culture and village life in Veendam. At school everyone shared stories about their holiday traditions and family visits. In The Netherlands, St. Piets arrived on horseback from Spain three weeks before Christmas on December 5th, where families exchanged small gifts. Christmas and Boxing Day (the day after Christmas) were reserved for festive dinners with extended family. They celebrated the holidays with chocolate letters representing your name. I adopted this chocolate letter tradition years later with my future children.

The YFU spring retreat took place in Schiermonnikoog, an island north of the country, in the North Sea, in the middle of March, the weekend after my eighteenth birthday. All the American students shared stories of their adventures in Europe. This time Mevrouw Ebels advised me, "The Van der Veen family requested a transfer due to illness and Mama needed her rest without an extra person in her home."

I was aware of her migraine headaches, that she rested in the afternoons before Jeannet and I came home from school. Without hesitation, Mevrouw Ebels arranged a transfer for me to Stadskanaal, the next town, so that I did not have to change schools. She asked me to join her and her husband for breakfast, away from the other students and she and her husband drove me to Stadskanaal on Sunday with the small red suitcase given to me at Christmas for my winter jacket.

Meneer Ebels joked, "Where is the big red suitcase you clutched last fall?"

I laughed, "I did not need it, I was going back to my Dutch home."

Mevrouw Ebels added sincerely, "Margot, I felt bad that you were being moved again. Please understand it's not your fault." We sipped our tea and she continued, "I convinced Mevrouw Dirkse that we did not want to disrupt your school routine. I also reminded her of the 'exchange' obligation that her son would travel to America next summer, so she agreed without hesitation."

The Dirkse family welcomed me at the end of the weekend. It was a smooth transition because they drove me to Veendam to collect my luggage on Tuesday evening after school to bring it to their home. I slept in their daughter Rena's bedroom who moved out to attend university. They conversed with Van Der Veens in the parlor for a few minutes while I went upstairs to pack my clothes. They had a seventeen-year-old son, Peter, who attended Winkler Prins School and registered for the YFU summer exchange program. We rode bikes to school together in the morning and afternoon until I learned the route myself. They spent their weekends on a houseboat cruising the rivers and canals of the country, a fun weekend experience.

I continued my after-school activities of swimming and volleyball. I saw Jeannet at school who invited me back to Stationstraat for tea with Mama on Wednesdays. Mama explained that her migraine headaches were getting worse, and the doctor recommended the change to ease her anxiety. They wanted to ensure a smooth transition for me in the middle of the school year. I was pleased that they stayed in touch with me, as Jeannet and I developed a close kinship over the past six months. I was disappointed but also empathetic, having been aware of the illness and their consideration to keep things as normal for me and Jeannet as possible. The time was flying by; I would be returning home in four months in July. I endured the anxiety of living with a third family knowing it was temporary, maintained my routine at school, and kept my friendships intact. It was a huge relief that I did not have to start over again from scratch in another province!

After two months apart, I noticed that Mama had rosy cheeks and felt better. When I visited after school for tea, Mama asked about my day.

"My day was good." After a sip of tea, I cheerfully remarked, "Mama, you are looking much better, how are you feeling?"

She smiled back, "It must be the warm weather, I am feeling great."

Jeannet sat down with us after walking the dog, "Mama, I miss not having a sister to hang out with in the house," she sighed. "Can Margot come back for the rest of her stay? She would be leaving before Eva returned home."

Mama looked at her youngest child and noticed the sparkle in her eyes, "I hear you on the phone with Margot every day."

"I like her as a sister, we are good friends," Jeannet exclaimed.

Mama was pleased to see her daughter happy, "I will arrange it." She called Mevrouw Ebels the next morning.

I hugged and kissed her on three cheeks when it was time to return to Stadskanaal. I wanted to ride the bike while it was still daylight and arrived on time for dinner. Mevrouw Dirkse cooked erwtensoep (pea soup) often with sausages, not my favorite food but a Dutch custom that I endured.

The next day (Thursday, the first week of May) when I came home from school and volleyball, Mevrouw Dirkse served tea and boeter koek (butter cookies) to me and Peter and explained her communications with Mevrouw Ebels and the Van der Veens during the day. She preferred that I waited until the end of the program when Peter traveled to America for the summer. However, she realized that the request came from the younger sister and her parents wanted to honor their daughter's wish.

Meneer Dirkse had a conference that weekend where they would not be on the boat. After dinner, I excused myself to wash a load of laundry and packed my big red suitcase. Mevrouw Dirkse drove me to Veendam on Saturday. I was relieved and thanked her for her understanding and appreciation to be my host.

I telephoned Mevrouw Ebels, "Thank you for making the arrangements."

"This was the easiest transfer I ever made," she laughed. "I was glad that your year became a positive experience."

It was Mother's Day weekend when I returned to Veendam. I was so happy that I walked to the village centrum and bought a bouquet for Mama. She loved the colors and variety of flowers and found a vase to display them on a table near the front door. When Tante Anja visited for dinner that weekend, she thanked me for that kind gesture and invited me back to her home for another weekend stay. It was the last time I would see them that year as they had a cruise vacation planned in the summer.

Two weeks later I took the bus to Winschoten on Friday after school. I was thrilled to see Grietje one last time before returning to America. We met her friends at the pub for a "farewell" party and exchanged addresses. Her cousin Derek was not present this time, but Grietje handed me a note from him,

"Lieve Margot, I am sorry I missed you this weekend, I had to attend an interview in London. I hope you are well and enjoying the time you have left in The Netherlands. I have applied to a hospitality management program that might bring me to America. I hope we can meet again. Viel Liefs, Derek."

Everyone was quiet as I opened the envelope and read it silently under the table. The girls were curious as I smiled and frowned at the same time, "Good news!" I perked up, "Grietje, here is my Rochester address and phone number so he can contact me." I put the letter in my purse and wrote my American address on the envelope and gave it back to her. We ordered another round of drinks.

On Saturday morning, both Tante Anja and Oom Lou drove me to Veendam and stayed for coffee and boterkoek. They came together to say goodbye to Mama and Papa; it would be months before they would meet again. I thanked them for their hospitality on my monthly visits and making new friends. Tante Anja winked at me; she was friends with Grietje's mother, knew that a romance was blossoming, and was pleased to help make it happen.

The school year ended the second week of June and a ceremony for all graduating students took place in the school courtyard on the following Sunday. I attended the ceremony with Jeannet. At school, the principal told the teacher who collected the tickets at the entrance to flag me and Barbara to go to the office. He handed both of us gowns and caps so we could line up with the other graduating students. We were pleased to be included in the ceremony.

A week later, Ankie's family invited me for a vacation at their summer home, "Arcadia" in Ameland, an island off the northern coast of Friesland by the North Sea. I visited her family often for tea after school. The only daughter in the family with four brothers, her parents allowed her to bring a girlfriend to their summer home after school finished. I was honored to have this opportunity.

We explored the island on bikes, swam in the sea, and gathered around the campfire in the evenings. Oom Bernard and Tante Trees asked me to leave a greeting in their cottage guest book. During the summer break, everyone took turns cooking dinner every night. When it was my turn, I cooked spaghetti and meatballs which everyone loved. I never cooked a meal at home in Rochester or during this year abroad, but I figured it was a universal entrée that everyone would enjoy. The vacation on the island with the Schmidt family was a memorable conclusion to my year abroad.

PART III

CONFUSION

Back Home In the USA

(1974 – 1979)

Chapter 6

Return Home to America
Thursday July 18, 1974

A Warm Welcome Home

After graduation day, a letter from YFU explained the departure details to return home to America. The letter stated,

"All students are expected to meet at Schiphol Airport in Amsterdam, The Netherlands on Wednesday, seventeen July 1974 at 12 noon for a 5 p.m. flight to Washington D.C. Students in the Benelux region (Belgium, The Netherlands and Luxembourg) are responsible for their own transportation to the airport and look for the YFU representative to receive your airline ticket. All other students will be contacted by their European regional representatives with the itinerary from their host country to Amsterdam."

"Upon arrival in Washington, all students will be bused to a reception at YFU headquarters and spend the night at the Holiday Inn. At this reception, locate your American regional representative to receive your instructions on returning to your home the following day.

There are no exceptions, all students must attend this reception and stay at this hotel."

I was excited to depart from Amsterdam, a two-hour drive from Veendam. My visit to Ankie's summer home in Ameland ended on the weekend before my departure. I washed my clothes and packed my big red suitcase for the last time, on Monday, July 15. On Wednesday morning, I hugged Mama goodbye with three kisses on each cheek and thanked her for everything.

She said, "Stay in touch! You are welcome to visit anytime!" She was not traveling to the airport as it would be a full day of driving for her, and she did not want a headache while she was recovering from her illness.

Papa, Jeannet, and I left the house at 8 a.m. for the two-hour drive. We picked up Hans at his apartment in Amsterdam to help with my luggage. He drove back to Veendam with his father and sister afterward to visit Mama. When we arrived at the departure lane, counselors held YFU signs around the terminal. We hugged goodbye with kisses on three cheeks.

With tears in our eyes, I promised Jeannet, "We will meet again!"

Everyone received their tickets on their bus rides to Schiphol. I asked a lady with a YFU sign where to pick up my ticket coming from The Netherlands. She pointed towards a tall blonde gentleman holding a sign for "**Benelux students**." I walked over and recognized Franz from the bus ride last year. He remembered me but forgot my name. He found my ticket near the bottom of his pile and handed it to me. He told me to stay close by until his group of students arrived so he could brief us on the flight and reception details.

As we waited for other students, he mentioned, "I am boarding this flight to escort everyone back to America and spend a month visiting my cousins in Canada. I will return to Europe in the middle of August with all the European students on the program in the USA and Canada." Eva would be returning home to Europe at that time.

When all the students from various points in The Netherlands and Belgium arrived in Amsterdam and found Franz, he handed out the remaining tickets and a copy of our flight instructions. He did a quick head count and explained what was printed on the flyer:

- "Please line up to check your luggage and receive your boarding pass then proceed to Gate B18 for the direct flight to Washington, D.C.
- When we arrive in Washington, you will collect your luggage and go through customs.
- In the Washington airport, follow the YFU signs to board the buses to attend the reception.
- Remember the bus number where your luggage is stored and return to it for your trip to the hotel once the party ends.
- At the reception, locate your regional representative to receive instructions for transportation to your home tomorrow morning.
- **There are no exceptions. Everyone must attend the reception to get your tickets for your trip home tomorrow."

At 4 p.m. we lined up to board the plane. It was a clear sunny day as I walked on the tarmac and up the stairs to find my assigned seat, 28 F, a window seat near the back of the aircraft. Knowing I would be gaining hours traveling west through six time zones, I pulled down the shade, rested my head, and closed my eyes. It was going to be a long day attending the three-hour reception once we landed on American soil.

The plane landed on time at 5 p.m. in the evening in Washington. We collected our luggage, went through customs, and boarded buses to attend the reception. All the buses had cardboard signs in the front window with the number assignment. My bus was **YFU # 12**. I wrote it on the back page of my diary as a reminder when it was time to go to the hotel.

We were welcomed home by special guests, First and Second Ladies, Mrs. Pat Nixon and Mrs. Betty Ford, who addressed the crowd with a short speech, "Welcome home. We, Mrs. Ford and I, trust you had a wonderful time on your world adventures this past year. Memories you will cherish for the rest of your lives. A unique field trip to share with your family and friends. You are now global citizens, the next generation of leaders to move the world forward into the future."

Mrs. Ford noted, "Please enjoy this beautiful sunny evening coming together with friends and tasting the refreshments. It is a pleasure to meet you and hear your stories. We wish you the best in your future endeavors and trust your year abroad inspired you to make the world a better place." After their greeting, they were escorted to a waiting car by their security team.

It was truly special to attend an event with the first ladies of our country. Their appearance was short but sweet and I could barely see them standing far away from the podium. It was an honor that they accepted the invitation to attend this reception to welcome the weary teenaged travelers back home in a nonpolitical, bipartisan gathering.

I was not aware of the Watergate scandal that unfolded over the past year in my absence where President Nixon resigned from office in August and the Fords moved into the White House three weeks after I returned home.

Delicious refreshments were placed on tables for students' consumption while mingling with the crowd before heading to our hotel for the night. It was a casual affair to feed hundreds of hungry teenagers as the flight attendants did not serve a meal; they handed out cracker snacks and beverages during the flight.

At the reception, signs were posted for the various destinations across the USA where students lived. There were two tables for New York State, "Western NY" and "Hudson Valley." I walked over to the "Western NY." John, the escort on the bus to Detroit and flight last year, would guide us back home. He asked me my last name, found my ticket near the bottom of the pile, and handed it to me. As the group gathered in front of the table with their tickets in hand, John announced, "Please don't lose these tickets. You will collect your boarding pass tomorrow morning when you check your luggage at the ticket counter. Meet me at the bus outside the hotel entrance tomorrow morning at nine o'clock sharp. Your parents have the flight information and will meet you at the airport upon arrival."

What a relief to have a much shorter commute with a ninety-minute flight to Rochester! A bus trip would have taken all day to travel north from D.C. through the mountains of Pennsylvania and New York to Irondequoit. After the reception, we were bused to the hotel, and the concierge at the reception desk handed out our room assignments. Exhausted, I found my room, met my roommate, soaked in a tub full of bubble bath and went to bed. The alarm clock was set for 7 a.m., breakfast was served at 8 a.m., and the buses to Washington National Airport departed at 9 a.m. It was a tight schedule to move hundreds of students that morning, but the YFU organization deployed an army of volunteers (former exchange students) for assistance.

At the departure desk, I checked my big red suitcase, received my boarding pass, and proceeded through the terminal to my gate. We did not need to pass through customs, but we were required to go through the security checkpoint. I stopped at the bathroom and found Mary waiting in line. We were thrilled to bump into each other, hugged, and checked our boarding passes. We were on the same flight. I switched seats with Bill once we were on the plane. Mary and I chatted nonstop the whole way home. We agreed to phone and meet for lunch the following week after reuniting with our families in Rochester.

On Thursday afternoon when I arrived in Rochester, Dad greeted me at the airport. It was his day off for meetings, appointments, and family stuff. I was glad to see him after a year since he did not make the trip at Christmas with Mom but stayed home with Mark and Paul to go skiing. We drove home to unload my red suitcases, dressed up and then the whole family piled into the maroon Mercedes to eat dinner at the URMC (University of Rochester Medical Center) Faculty Club. I loved those dinners, the food was delicious, and it was fun to meet children of other physicians at the club.

When the family entered the building there was a huge display with tulips and balloons and a sign that read, "**Welcome Home Margot**." During the evening, when Dr. Williams, the President of the Club (they were elected for 3-year terms) approached the podium to start the festivities, he announced "There is a special guest with us tonight." He smiled towards our table and said, "Margot, please stand and tell us about your European adventure, it was no ordinary vacation." I was surprised and embarrassed that my dad arranged this. Everyone clicked their glasses as I approached the podium. I did not have a speech prepared as I expected an ordinary buffet dinner.

I excitedly grabbed the microphone, "Thank you for the lovely surprise, I had no idea that I would be welcomed home in such a manner. I am truly honored to be here tonight."

Everyone started clapping and Dr. Jones shouted from the back of the room, "Tell us about it, the club has sponsored trips everywhere but not to The Netherlands."

Focused on the positive aspects, I explained, "I wanted to go on the exchange program for a year, a summer was too short. I fast tracked my high school credits to graduate a year early. The Netherlands was not in my original plan, but I was transferred there. When I requested French on my application, the initial assignment was Dutch Belgium. Three months later, I was placed with a family in The Netherlands that I loved. Moving to a small village in Europe, it felt like I stepped into a fairytale. The YFU staff and host families provided support throughout the year."

A round of applause erupted while I walked back to my table and Dad stood up and hugged me whispering, "Good job!" Dr. Williams then murmured, "We will consider adding The Netherlands and Belgium to our itineraries in the future; a lot of history and culture to experience in both countries." Already seated next to my dad, I raised my voice, "By the way, the people were friendly, polite, and spoke English fluently." More chatter across the room as everyone considered the possibilities.

Summer in Irondequoit

I spent the weekend sleeping, swimming, unpacking, doing laundry, and reorganizing my bedroom. I opened the windows for fresh air. At 10 a.m. on Monday morning, I called Mary.

The phone rang three times before someone picked up, "Hello, who is calling?"

I answered, "Hi, this is Margot. Is Mary there."

A deep male voice replied, "She's outside, I will go get her." I heard a door screech open, and he yelled, "Mary, the phone is for you." A minute later, Mary was on the line.

She said, "Hi Margot. I lost your number last year and we forgot to exchange numbers on the plane coming home."

I remarked, "I found the napkin crumpled in the bottom of my purse when I unpacked this weekend and I could barely read it. I checked the phone book to verify your number before I called you."

"You are kidding. How are you?" she laughed. "It is so hard to get back into the Rochester groove after being away for so long."

I agreed and asked, "Would you like to come over to my house one day for a swim and lunch?"

"Sure. I drive my dad to work and pick him up every day so my brother and I can use the car," she sighed. "You are in Irondequoit? I pass by it on Ridge Road all the time."

We arranged to meet on Friday because the following week I would be working at the office and taking Driver's Ed, and she would start her summer job at Kodak in her father's department. I gave her directions to reach my home. She was familiar with Northside General Hospital at Ridge Road and Portland Avenue.

I said, "When you reach the hospital, head north on Portland to Titus. Go through the light and down the hill to Oakview Elementary School and I will meet you in the parking lot."

She said, "That is great. I can be there around 10 a.m. and stay until 3 p.m. when I must head back to Kodak."

On Friday morning I walked over to the school at 9:30 a.m. and sat on the swings until I saw her approach the school. I hopped into the passenger seat and directed her to Old North Hill.

She remarked, "Thanks for doing this, I would not have found your house on my own."

"I will take you back to the school this afternoon," I said. "It is confusing to find your way around here."

It was a beautiful sunny day to lounge by the pool, and we enjoyed a picnic lunch of tuna fish sandwiches on the back porch with my mom and siblings.

At lunch, Mom said, "Mary, I heard you spent the year in Switzerland, how did you like it?"

"It was great, I improved my French that was taught in school." she said. "It is so much better to live and learn a language in a country that speaks it."

I agreed, "It is the best way to learn a foreign language."

Mom continued, "Have you been to Europe before? Did you travel while you were there?"

"No, it was my first time, but not my last," she grinned. "At Christmas, I traveled to Glasgow, Scotland to visit my mother's cousin's family, who I met in America when I was a young child. We had a wonderful time together. "

When lunch was finished, we cleared the table and brought the dishes to the kitchen and then returned to the pool. We spent the afternoon reminiscing about our experiences with our families and countries and jumped in the water to cool off as the sun beat down on our bodies sitting on the green lounge chairs.

She stayed with the same family all year and her advanced French language skills from fifth to twelfth grade eased her transition. Her host family took her on a road trip through the country and into Austria for two weeks before school started. She took the train to Paris with her host sister at Easter. She loved the trip to Scotland during the Christmas holidays to reconnect with her relatives. She was surprised about my situation in Belgium but happy that the organization resolved the problem with a successful transfer to The Netherlands. We were both pleased with our year abroad, memories created forever in our hearts.

At 3 p.m., she thanked my mother for lunch and swimming, and we left to pick up her father. I accompanied her to the school so she could find her way back to Ridge Road and then walked back home. She moved to Texas to attend university in the fall; we never met again. When I arrived home, I collected the towels on the lounge chairs and hung them on the clothesline to dry outside the porch.

It was a warm summer with the sun shining daily without rain. I used the pool every day. I worked at dad's office, arriving at 1 p.m. in the afternoon, and closed at 5:30 in the afternoon for Irene and Lucille so they could go home to their families. Patients welcomed me back on the job and inquired about my year abroad. Dad proudly told all his patients about his daughter's European adventure. They looked forward to more stories when they returned for future appointments.

One patient, Jane Smith, an older heavy-set woman, remarked, "You always loved adventure. I remember your accident in the driveway years ago."

Stunned at the mention of that vague memory, I remarked, "Oh, you were there?"

"Yes, I was outside as the car rolled into the street and ran inside the office to tell your dad what happened," she replied, "I hope you have your license now."

"I'm taking Driver's Ed this summer." I answered,

As she moved towards the door, she winked, "Be careful. Good luck."

Happy to be back home, I missed my Dutch family in that idyllic fairyland. I thought and spoke in Dutch, correcting myself to speak English often. On the weekend when I unpacked, I took my film to the camera store to be developed. The clerk said, "It would be ready for pick up by Wednesday." I rode my bike back to the store on Thursday, picked up the envelope of four by six-inch color photographs, and bought picture frames and a photo album to display those images on my bedside table and organized a scrap book of those memories.

I practiced European cultural habits at home. I took my shoes off as soon as I walked into the house although mom said, "You don't have to do that."

I told her "It is a good habit that I like." It was common around the world to remove shoes in people's homes to prevent germs and bacteria from spreading.

Eating all my food including sandwiches with a knife and fork, my brother with his usual sarcasm said, "Everyone eats with their hands in America."

I laughed, "It is good table manners." I poured milk into my mug before the coffee to let it blend and always placed a napkin in my lap. I followed these habits for the rest of my life. My emotional maturity developed as I adapted to some of the formalities in Europe different from the casual habits in America.

I was so busy with school before I graduated that I never learned how to drive when I turned sixteen years old. At eighteen, it was time to get my license. I took a Driver's Education course at Irondequoit High School in the mornings before I worked at the office in the afternoons. It was a three-week course where I passed the road test on the first try. Learning in a group setting with an unknown instructor forced me to pay attention and learn the rules of the road correctly.

The first hour was spent in the classroom and the second hour on the road taking turns in the driver's seat. With ten students in the class split between two instructors (teachers from two schools in the district) and two station wagons, all students learned to drive in big cars. At that time, station wagons had two bench seats with three seatbelts in the front and back to accommodate six passengers. Front row bucket seats were not standard in cars.

The first week, we drove around the school parking lot to practice braking and parking. We had to practice forward and backward parking between the lines, using the rear and sideview mirrors. Back up cameras would not be introduced as standard equipment for several decades. The second week, the instructor guided us to St. Paul Boulevard towards the lake to practice accelerating. During the third week, we turned onto the Ontario Beach Parkway (I-18) that followed the lake from Greece to Hamlin Beach to practice highway driving. In the mornings, the roads were not busy as we drove west against the commuter traffic entering the city, which made learning to drive easier. I became familiar with that highway on my future trips to the border.

On the last day, the instructors drove the students to the local New York State (NYS) Department of Transportation Driver's License Bureau. We waited in the lobby while a test examiner took each student on the fifteen-minute road test separately in the instructors' vehicles. I was the last person evaluated in my group. It felt like an eternity waiting for my turn. I practiced at home driving my mom's station wagon with her, dad, or my older brother in the evenings. After my test, the examiner handed our results to our instructors who drove us back to school.

Chatter commenced in the car as we were all excited and relieved to have finished the course and passed the test. Upon arrival at the school, the instructor handed each student their test results, a temporary driver's license with our names printed on it. We all jumped for joy accomplishing that life goal.

The instructors, John and Kathy, said a final goodbye in the school parking lot. John addressed the group, "Before you go, I want to congratulate everyone for doing a fantastic job in driving and passing your test!" We all clapped for each other. "Present this certificate to your insurance company to qualify for a discounted automobile insurance rate."

Kathy added, "We enjoyed teaching you how to drive this summer."

John remarked, "Please follow the rules you learned to avoid tickets and accidents."

"Hang on to your paper. Put it in your wallet, you need to carry it with you every time you sit in the driver's seat," Kathy reminded us, "it's a temporary license until you receive your permanent card in the mail in the next few weeks." We shook hands and were dismissed to leave.

I was assigned to Kathy. I noticed that John was the same guy who was on my YFU flights and bus trips. When I shook his hand, we both stared like we knew each other. He was a teacher in the WISD (West Irondequoit School District), He taught driver's ed in the summer in between his trips for YFU at the beginning and end of the season to accompany students on their journeys to Europe and the return trip home. That way he worked with students in both programs, those who traveled overseas for the summer as well as those who chose the year program. He was certified through the New York State Department of Motor Vehicles to teach Drivers Education.

John knew that I wanted to go into teaching from our conversation at the reception in Washington, D.C. He also recognized my last name and acknowledged he knew the doctor. Everyone in the school and the town knew him.

John said, "I live at home with my parents and work in Irondequoit, so I asked permission from the district administration office pointing to the small building at the end of the lot next to Dake Middle School to use the IHS parking lot for the YFU pickups and the driver's ed course."

I nodded in agreement, "It was convenient for us but not for the students who traveled over one hundred miles in every direction from central and western regions of the state to meet here. A school or mall closer to the Thruway would be more convenient for them."

"Yes, but it is more private and less congested to congregate here," he answered, "this location also has easy access to the highways to leave the city in all directions and the extra-large parking lot serving two schools was perfect for the busloads of students and their families in the program."

"Hmm, good point, I never thought of that," I sighed.

He cleared his throat, sipped his thermos, and continued, "I recall at the reception that you plan to teach school. You will soon find out how difficult it is to get a job in this community. You can supplement your income with temporary summer jobs until you get settled in a permanent teaching position."

"Yes, two months in summer is a nice vacation but no steady income." I laughed.

He smiled, "You are still young, enjoy life and enjoy college, it is a lot of fun."

It was getting close to noon; we said goodbye. I walked home for lunch and changed my clothes to work at the office in the afternoon. I thought about his job with YFU, the desire to travel with expenses paid for. The responsibility of mentoring the students on their journeys would be something to consider during my college years. Spending each summer in various locations around the world was inspiring.

My mind was daydreaming all afternoon at the office. It was a slow day on a Friday in the middle of summer with very few patients in attendance. The phone rang constantly with cancellations as patients called to reschedule their appointments on another day. I pulled out my diary and pictures in my purse as I recalled my European adventure.

It felt good to borrow mom's car when I needed to go places without asking for a ride. I was told to be careful and come home on time in case she or my siblings needed the car. Jan and Mark moved back home that summer after living on campus at their schools. With four teenagers at home, the car was always in use by one of us. The driver's license was my first official ID (identification card), a sign of independence after turning eighteen! I could go to bars and vote in elections with this plastic identification card in my hand.

Living at home, I enjoyed swimming in the backyard pool. My siblings were happy that I resumed the weekly cleaning, a chore I loved before I left for Europe. Having joined the swim team in Veendam, I practiced the skills I learned to improve my strokes; a sport I enjoyed all my life that has benefited my health and wellbeing.

In August, Tim and Nan invited me to accompany their family on a vacation to Cape Cod as the designated caregiver for their daughters, Kristin, and Kelly, who were nine and seven years old. I accepted the invitation without hesitation. We traveled together as family; I was introduced as Tim's younger sister at social gatherings. The vacation in lieu of babysitting money was an offer I could not refuse. My family arrived at the end of the week for a second week of summer fun at my favorite ocean playground.

They stayed at a cottage in Dennisport, a resort town in the middle of the Cape. We relaxed on the beach, splashed in the ocean waves, climbed sand dunes and built sandcastles, visited Provincetown, and ate fresh seafood. Provincetown, a trendy little village at the furthest point of the Cape, was a haven for artists to explore their passions. During the summer season, vendors sold handmade items and paintings. I loved turquoise jewelry and bought myself a pair of dangling pierced earrings with a matching necklace and bracelet. The main street in the center of the town was closed to traffic all summer so artisans could set up tables to display and sell their creations every day.

On the drive home with my family at the end of the second week, we stopped at Plymouth Rock for a picnic lunch and watched a Red Sox baseball game at Fenway Park in Boston, my brother's favorite team. Dad let me drive between rest stops on the Massachusetts Turnpike and on the New York State Thruway so I could practice highway and night driving. He felt confident with me behind the wheel and slept for an hour before resuming the task. We arrived home at midnight after the game. A fantastic way to end the summer before going back to school. Cape Cod was always a favorite beach vacation with its proximity to home and cooler temperatures in the northeast.

Chapter 7

Off to College and Beyond

Campus Living

On Labor Day Weekend, September 1974, I packed my big red suitcase again to attend college in Elmira, New York. I received the acceptance letter last year before I left for Europe, and they deferred my admission for one year until January 1975. I did not have to pack everything for a year since it was a short drive on the Thruway to the campus and I came home on school breaks. I packed casual clothes for class and socializing, my toiletries, linens and towels, a lightweight jacket, sweatshirts, and sweater when the temperature cooled down in the evenings as brisk winds swept through the town from the Finger Lakes and Bristol Hills nearby.

I shared a room with Patty from Poughkeepsie. We got along well but she was very depressed and lonely after losing her mother to cancer during the summer. She dropped out of school after the first semester in mid-December. Reassigned to a single room in another dormitory, I moved my stuff across campus on the weekend before classes resumed in

January. The dormitory rooms were furnished with a single bed, bureau, and desk with a small closet for each resident. I switched my lightweight jacket with my red winter jacket, hat, gloves, and boots at home over the holiday. The hall supervisor gave me a cart to transport my stuff to the new building. My cart rental was assigned for 10 a.m. Saturday for two hours. I returned it by noon for other students to borrow. Moving between residences became second nature to me along with making new friends.

Elmira College was a small liberal arts school for approximately eight hundred students near the Pennsylvania border nestled between Corning and Binghampton, New York, founded in the middle of the nineteenth century. Originally a school for women, it opened its doors to men five years earlier. The College was home to the **Center for Mark Twain Studies** attracting scholars from around the world. Mark Twain was one of my favorite American authors that I studied in high school, but I did not pursue literature courses in college.

The mandatory Freshman Core Program was a combination of Language, Math, and Science, like a high school review course. I took French and German as my two electives, I wanted to improve my foreign language skills. At the college level, the professors spoke the language during class and the textbooks were written in the language, an immersive learning experience unlike the high school language classes I took previously. I considered a future career as a teacher, enrollment in teaching courses happened during the third year of study.

At home during the Christmas holiday, a letter from Derek was sitting on my desk in my bedroom, postmarked "**Chicago, Illinois November 30, 1974.**"

The letter arrived in Irondequoit the week after the Thanksgiving holiday when I returned to school. He moved to America to join a hospitality management program in Chicago and wanted to visit me sometime during the school year. I wrote him a note to apologize for the delayed response, listed my college address and phone number, and suggested we meet in Elmira sometime during the winter semester.

Living on the third floor of a dormitory, each floor had a pay phone in the center of the corridor that girls answered as they passed by and yelled a name who the call was for and left the handle dangling until it was answered. When no one answered the call and that annoying buzz started, I hung the phone on the hook as my room was across from the booth. No one knew who was calling until the phone was answered and no one received messages; the caller was told to call again later if a girl did not respond when her name was yelled down the corridor. Caller ID was not available on landlines and pay phones. To call home there was a long-distance charge, so you put the coins in the slots when the operator told you the cost or requested a collect call. I called collect, and whoever picked up the phone at home "said yes" when asked by the operator, "Margot is calling, do you accept the charge?"

I usually had my record player blasting my favorite albums of Elton John and the Beatles to block out the noise in the hallway. I did not own a pair of headphones, and all the girls played their favorite music in their rooms with their doors closed when they did not want to be disturbed.

Derek called me at the dorm one evening in the middle of January after receiving my letter. Instinctively, I heard the ring and answered the hall phone, so no one had to call or look for me. We arranged to meet a month later during the President's Day long weekend in February. He took a bus to Elmira, and I walked to the station to meet him.

When we reached my room and removed our coats and boots, he crawled into my green beanbag chair, and I pulled the wooden chair out from my desk to sit down. He began the conversation,

"Margot, I liked you from the moment we met. I was happy every time my cousin, Grietje, told me you were visiting for the weekend. It must have been ten times that Tante Anja invited you to her home?"

Thoughts were swirling through my head of small-town gossip where everyone knew each other's business. He continued, "She is a jolly old lady who everyone called, Tante. I don't know her last name.

"A lovely lady who graciously welcomed me into her home and a dear friend of the Van Der Veen family," I remarked.

"Grietje's mother is my mother's sister, why our surnames are different, and there are few familiar features," he replied, "and Tante's son, Jan, (Yon) was a sweet young lad, taken to the Lord way too soon."

"I liked Grietje. She was a nice girl to include me in her inner circle. I felt welcomed and it was a nice break from Veendam to get away on a weekend," I said. "It was the only time I went to a bar, not allowed or should I say not encouraged in Veendam." Whenever I was offered a drink in my friend's homes, I politely accepted.

Changing the subject, Derek continued, "My hotel management program will take me around the world to learn the ropes. I know you love to travel. Why don't you come along for the ride?"

I was thinking, very tempting, he knows me like an open book. "Derek, I like you too, why I invited you here. I apologize that you are sleeping on the floor and endured a long bus ride," I took a sip from my diet coke, "I don't have a car, and the closest airport would be Rochester, and well, you know, I am not involving my family in our rendezvous."

He nodded in agreement drinking his root beer. I continued, "I was transferred to a single room over the holidays when my roommate dropped out of school at the end of last term, so there is no extra bed. Girls invite their boyfriends here when their roommates go home for a weekend. Being an American holiday, the dorm is half empty."

He interrupted, "You are not answering my question."

I intervened, "I'm getting there, let me finish."

He winked. I continued, "Your program is a wonderful way to see the world." After another sip, "The exchange program was a wonderful experience for me and I fell in love with your country. It took years of planning and convincing my parents to agree to it. It was the best way to visit a foreign country and immerse myself into the culture."

I took a deep breath, not sure if I should keep going with my line of thought.

He yawned and said, "Pardon me, continue, you have a lot on your mind."

"My first three months were miserable before I landed in Veendam." I sighed. "As you have noticed, living in Chicago, America is nothing like the small towns you are used to back home."

He smiled, "It's been quite an adjustment for this country boy," rubbing his grumbling stomach. "You never talked about the first three months, what happened?"

I almost cried and he got up to hug me. "I was placed with a family of three teenage daughters, four years apart in age, and the father was a dentist. A perfect match to my American family."

Derek got up to stretch, "And, so, what happened?"

"Then, they took off on an American holiday ten days after my arrival where I stayed with their friends at their summer home on the coast," I explained with a frown. His expression changed from excitement to concern. "The three weeks they were gone were fabulous. But when they returned the mood changed, they met my American family and who knows..."

He sighed, "I hate people like that. So, what happened?"

"When I went to the first YFU retreat, I spoke with a counsellor, and their immediate response was to remove students from the situation and arrange a transfer within their network of host families." I coughed and cleared my throat, "I was taken to Amsterdam and stayed in a hotel for a month until the next retreat where I complained to another counsellor who lived in Leeuwarden and placed me in Veendam."

He noticed the tears, "What happened in Amsterdam?"

I cried, "Molested by that counsellor." He gasped. "I sent a note to the organization, but they could not intervene until the next monthly retreat. The worst four weeks of my life!"

Holding me closer, "Wow, does anyone else know? Frightening!"

"No, you are the only one outside of the organization that I have told. Trying to forget about it."

He nodded in agreement and asked, "What are your plans now?"

After another sip, "I need to spend at least four years earning my college degree." I said, "I can't put it on hold."

I broke that commitment halfway through the program and it would be three more decades before I fulfilled that promise to myself and my parents.

"Think about it. You know how valuable travel is and it is a work holiday, paid for by the companies that hire me. You can work in the hotel too." He sounded very convincing, "There are all kinds of administrative jobs for you to experience, not just housekeeping and cooking."

Was that a premonition? I worked as a motel chambermaid six months later near the college that I had transferred to, that only lasted three weekends!

"Whenever we have a holiday or school break, we can meet for a vacation," I suggested. "It would be a great way to develop our friendship while we pursue our education separately." I was getting used to long distance romances.

He didn't agree and felt defeated having traveled 700 miles to see me. He got up from the beanbag and announced, "I'm hungry, let's get some dinner."

We put on our boots and coats and ran down the stairs to the foyer that opened to the campus. It was cloudy and snowing, but not cold. We trudged through the fluffy white powder that formed around our boots and gleefully threw snowballs at each other as we walked to the dining hall.

He found a table at the back of the room while I lined up at the cafeteria counter. I loaded two trays of food to show my school ID to the cashier. She commented, "You must be hungry," and I smiled, "The other tray is for my sick roommate."

When I approached the table, Derek was surrounded by a group of girls who thought he was a new guy on campus. I overheard the conversation from Stacy, "I love your British accent, where are you from."

Bonnie added, "What are you studying?"

Leslie boldly asked, "Where is your room?"

Carla replied, "No, he is visiting Margot for the weekend." They saw the trays of food in my hands and backed away so I could place them on the table.

Derek, the ever-polite, charming European gentleman, said, "Ladies, nice to meet you. Please allow me and my girl to eat our dinner in peace." They went back to their table and collected their jackets to leave, defeated in their quest to lure him away from me.

Thinking as I sat down, "Hmmm, my girl???" I liked that comment and hoped he meant it.

We went to the pub on campus for the evening and returned to my room after midnight. We bought snacks at the pub to eat for breakfast the next day and checked the bus schedule for his return trip to Chicago. I snuck him into the bathroom when it was empty and no one was roaming the hallway; it was not a co-ed dormitory, adding a bit of mystery to our visit.

The next morning, we walked to the bus station together and hugged and kissed goodbye for the last time before he boarded the Trailways coach bus. He had a long day ahead with two connections, arriving in Chicago after midnight, why I suggested the long weekend to travel; he could rest on Monday before class on Tuesday.

He knew my birthday was a month later and sent me a sweet birthday card with a thank you note in Dutch,

"Lieve Margot, Hartelijk bedankt en gefeliciteerd. Veel liefs, Derek."

"Dear Margot, A heartfelt thank you and happy birthday. Much Love, Derek."

That was the last time I heard from him. I liked Derek but also knew I had to stay grounded to finish school. A sweet memory of a Dutch boyfriend. Disappointed but not heartbroken that I could not fulfill his dream.

The spring term was shortened to eight weeks with one core program instead of classes. Kitchen Chemistry was fun learning cooking and gardening with field trips to gourmet restaurants, farms, and wineries in the Finger Lakes region. During this program, Annie, a sweet young lady with short red curly hair who lived in Elmira with her parents, and I formed a friendship that lasted beyond college for about a decade. Once we married and moved to other places, we lost touch with each other. Invited to her wedding in Elmira a few years later, Annie and Tom moved to Hartford, Connecticut after graduation.

I transferred to Nazareth College in Rochester to pursue a Fine Arts Degree for my second year of college that also had a teaching credential built into the third year of the program. After transferring to a single room in the second semester of Elmira, I loved the independence, freedom, and privacy of living alone. Dad agreed to pay the extra cost of a private room so I could concentrate on my studies.

It was fun learning art and design, opera, voice, and classical piano, as well as theatre production, designing and creating sets for stage plays. I met Laurie from Penfield who also lived on campus and our friendship lasted forever. This program, paired with an Elementary

Teaching Certificate, would allow us to teach art, music, and drama in addition to elementary grade levels.

In January of that year, my brother, Mark, married Sue in Connecticut, a fellow student he met in Greece when I was in the Netherlands. She was a lovely lady who became a wonderful addition to our family for more than half a century. It was a very cold, snowy weekend when Dad drove the family to the wedding in a snowstorm.

The three bridesmaids, her cousin, a college roommate, and I wore beautiful long sleeve velvet red gowns with white lace trim and Jan wore a red dress and played her guitar during the ceremony. It was a beautiful reception with dinner and dancing. The wedding was attended by her relatives and their friends from college. We met those relatives and friends again decades later when their children married. My cousins did not attend this wedding due to the unpredictable winter weather when travelling across the country.

I dropped out of Nazareth College at the end of that year because I had doubts about teaching. I feared standing in front of a classroom leading twenty children with diverse backgrounds and learning disabilities. My friend, Laurie, embraced the program, working with Special Education students her entire career. The education system transformed in the late twentieth century incorporating Special Education, Mental Health, and English as a Second Language (ESL) programming into the curriculum.

After two years of college, my heart was still in Europe. I missed the village life far away from the large cities. I had a tough time adjusting to campus living. I was confused about my future. I loved learning foreign languages but anticipated that I would never use them without working in a foreign service job. It was a dilemma about how to proceed. I missed Derek and his proposal to travel roamed through my brain as I gave up my dream of teaching.

While I was at Nazareth, I worked at a grocery store, with manual cash registers where one must tap the number buttons carefully like a calculator when checking out groceries. It would be another decade before scanners were invented.

I was scheduled to work Thursday and Friday afternoons until the store closed at 10 p.m. The supervisor always offered me a ride back to campus so that I did not walk alone in the darkness. On weekends, I was scheduled alternating morning and evening shifts. The grocery store, located in Pittsford Plaza, was a twenty-minute walk or a five-minute drive from the campus.

I worked at the store for about two years. I bought my first car, a used purple AMC Rambler (American Motor Company) in the summer after I quit Nazareth and moved back home, to commute to work by myself. During that summer, I also worked afternoons at the office when I was not scheduled at the store and enjoyed the pool. In September 1976, I was twenty years old and a college dropout, it was time to make tough decisions about my future.

My First Full Time Job

Most office jobs required secretarial training, including typing, dictation and shorthand along with basic business skills. It would be more than a decade before computers became standard in every home and office. In the fall, I pursued a four-month secretarial program. Shorthand was like learning a foreign language, but I could not grasp the symbols nor increase my transcription speed; I never used it in my future office careers.

The job board at the secretarial school posted an ad for an Admitting Assistant at Highland Hospital. At the interview, I would work the evening, night, and weekend shifts. I liked working alone and most evenings were not busy compared to the day shift. I had a good rapport with all staff in the department and throughout the hospital. This position carried a huge responsibility assigning beds to patients from the emergency and maternity wards in consultation with the nursing staff.

Dad saw the ad at one of his meetings, but I had already applied through the secretarial school when he brought it to my attention. He stopped by Human Resources and introduced himself to Howard, the Director of Admissions, to promote my application. I started the position right after Thanksgiving on the first of December 1976, a huge responsibility for a young twenty-year-old woman.

I dealt with patient's family members, secured their health insurance information, and assigned appropriate room accommodation for their illness. Upon assurance of the great care their loved one would receive at the hospital, I requested signed consent forms for treatment. The hospital forms consisted of seven duplicate copies to distribute to various departments and a blue card with the patient's information stamped on all documents circulated for lab work, x-rays, and billing within the facility. That was the paper trail I created for a patient's hospital admission long before computer technology developed.

I was in daily contact with nurses, billing clerks, information and switchboard operators, as well as housekeeping and security staff. I spoke with parents of car accident victims near death, new parents who lost their baby in childbirth, as well as family members of terminally ill patients. Truly heartbreaking moments showing empathy that toughened me up emotionally to deal with trauma later in my life.

One weekend in the New Year after I joined the hospital, Dad asked me, "What time do you finish your shift?

I replied, "My shift was three o'clock in the afternoon until 11:30 p.m."

He asked, "Can you get it changed to come home an hour earlier?"

"I doubt it." I explained, "The morning shift ends at 3:30 p.m., and I work alone, so I must be on time. At quitting time, I roll a cart with forms and blue cards to the switchboard office." I sneezed and continued, "The operator does double duty answering calls and admitting patients overnight. She works from 11 p.m. to 7 a.m. when the day shift starts."

I covered that shift on her vacations. At that time, I was not familiar with the guidelines that hospital workers followed about shift work outlined in the union contract.

Dad remarked, "Oh, so it is a precise schedule change for each shift that can't be altered." He realized I worked in a unionized environment.

I sighed, "Is there a problem?"

Mom chimed in, "We are awakened every night when you come home, and it is tough to go back to sleep."

"I try to be quiet, but your bedroom is over the garage, and you may hear me lifting and closing the heavy door" (no electronic garage door opener). I suggested, "I will start using the front door if that is better. You leave that light on and I always turn it off before I go to bed."

Dad interjected, "Can you rent an apartment? I saw the want ads board last week when I was at a meeting and there are rentals posted in the cafeteria."

I stared, "Dad, I never go to the cafeteria, I always make a lunch here before I leave and go to a staff lounge near my office. I didn't know a want ads board existed."

He said, "Go have a look at it on one of your breaks."

They were serious. Were they kicking me out because I dropped out of school? Education was a big deal in my family, a status symbol, and I was carving another path to follow.

I watched the ads in the lunchroom where employees advertised car sales, home and apartment rentals, babysitting, and sales of household items for the next few weeks. I called a nurse looking for a housemate on Park Avenue where I stayed for four months and then moved back home for the summer. It was a trendy neighborhood with shops and restaurants close to the Memorial Art Gallery and George Eastman Museum. The Frog Pond was one of my favorite restaurants. That shared house on Beverley Street was a ten-minute drive to the hospital.

I lived with three other girls in their twenties in a large older home where we each had our own bedroom but shared the kitchen, living room and bathroom. Kathy, who posted the ad, was a night nurse on the orthopedic floor. Debbie and Jane held office jobs in downtown Rochester. They were friends from high school in Buffalo and needed a fourth roommate when Brenda moved out to get married. As we worked different shifts and occasional weekends, we shared the main floor without conflict. The girls used the washer and dryer in the basement, but I brought my laundry home on weekends when I visited my parents.

The homes on this street did not have driveways, all cars parallel parked on both sides of the street. It was a cold snowy winter that year. The snowplow buried our cars in snow drifts, a challenging task to clear it off to drive to work on time. The neighbors helped each other clear the snow off their cars when we all gathered outside. When the lease expired in June, everyone moved out and I lost contact with them.

After living at home for the summer, I searched for another apartment near the hospital. This time, a nurse in the Intensive Care Unit (ICU), Barbara, wanted a roommate in a building above a restaurant, three blocks away from the hospital on South Avenue. This was perfect for walking to work and a short drive to Monroe Community College where I enrolled in an Associate of Science Business degree on a part-time basis in the mornings.

It was a one-bedroom suite, but she made room in her den for a roommate to supplement her income to pay the rent. I had to walk through her bedroom to get to my room, which was difficult when her boyfriend visited. It was an old building with three flights of stairs. No elevator made grocery shopping and moving furniture challenging.

When Barbara moved out, I stayed in that apartment for two more years, working at the hospital and attending school. Living above a restaurant was noisy on weekends and in the summer, but I tolerated that inconvenience due to the proximity to work and the affordable rent on my clerical salary. I enjoyed independent living. The building had four other tenants who were quiet, so it was perfect for studying during my free time. A twenty-minute drive home to Irondequoit, I visited every weekend to do laundry and enjoyed a meal with mom and dad. They were pleased with this arrangement. It was also nice to be close by in the summer to use and clean the pool.

After I returned home from my year abroad, it was difficult to reconnect with former high school friends. Most students had their own circle of friendships formed during their senior year while I was away and moved on to college and other pursuits in and around Rochester and beyond. We reconnected at the class reunions that I attended every five years and later social media platforms like Facebook and Instagram. IHS staged class reunions where former students gathered for a weekend at a local pub on Friday evenings, a tour of the high school on Saturday mornings, and a formal dinner at a local banquet hall on Saturday evenings. These reunions, organized by groups of classmates in every graduating class, brought former students together to reminisce about old times and to catch up on the present.

I attended the Saturday evening banquet at each reunion. I met new people at the banquets as classmates I used to know as a teenager often declined invitations. My graduating class celebrated its fiftieth anniversary at the time of writing. As former students relocated to other cities across the continent to pursue their careers, coming home to celebrate these weekend events generated business for the local economy.

Eager to make new friends, I called Marisa, the oldest daughter of my father's receptionist, Lucille. My family had established a friendship with her family years earlier when my cousins moved out of state. We enjoyed holiday meals together. Her parents and grandmother always prepared savory Italian and Portuguese dishes with enough food to feed an army, there were usually twenty people or more at these festivities.

Marisa and I went to the movies, bowling, shopping, and bar hopping to scout the music scene in Rochester on weekends. During that time in the mid to late seventies, discos were popularized by the movies, "*Saturday Night Fever*" and "*Grease,*" starring John Travolta, Karen Lynn Gorney and Olivia Newton John, dance films with musical hits by the BeeGees. We dressed up in our fancy bell bottom pants and peasant blouses enjoying Saturday nights on the town. I did not drink alcoholic beverages at the dance halls because I was the "designated driver." We always had a fun time listening to the music and dancing with other girls in groups while the guys drank, smoked, and watched from the bar.

In the spring when the weather warmed up, Marisa asked me, "Margot do you want to go away for a weekend?"

I loved travelling so a suggestion from a close friend sparked my interest. I said, "Where to?"

She replied, "I don't know, I want to get away and check out Macy's in New York City. It is a big department store that we don't have in Rochester."

Every year, I watched the Macy's parade televised on Thanksgiving Day to kick off the Christmas season and caught a glimpse of the city along the parade route. I thought for a moment knowing it was more than three hundred miles away at the opposite end of the state, and replied, "How will we get there? It is too far for me to drive, at least seven hours on the Thruway. Hotels would be expensive."

"But there is so much to do in New York City," she said, "like walking through Manhattan, Greenwich Village, Central Park, and Times Square. It would be fun to explore it."

"It would be a fun place to visit on a weekend; I love Broadway plays!" I agreed, "We should investigate the cost of the train or airfare, as well as hotels in a central location."

Marisa visited a travel agent in her neighborhood after work and picked up brochures. The next time we met, we went bowling and ate white hot dogs at the bowling alley. White Hots, a Rochester delicacy, was a hotdog composed of unsmoked pork or veal that allowed the meat to retain its naturally white color. It tasted like the bratwurst sandwich I ate on the bus in Germany and occasionally in The Netherlands.

She pulled brochures out of her red cloth bag with an airplane on the front to show me the tourist spots and hotels in the "Big Apple" a popular nickname for New York City. She had an Amtrac schedule, United Airlines brochure, Holiday Inn, and other hotel brochures. I looked at them and quickly calculated in my head an approximate cost for a weekend getaway. She said, "What do you think, should we do it?"

"Marisa, it would cost us more than $500 each for transportation, hotels, and restaurants." I explained. "It may be glamorous, but the news reports about crime in the city, I would not feel safe walking or taking the subway, especially at night." We were both making minimum wage at our jobs, so that was a lot of money to put aside for a weekend trip.

She agreed and said, "You may be right. Any other suggestions? My family had never travelled to New York City."

"Have you been to Canada? Toronto was fun when I went with my family," I sighed. "It is a three-hour drive, a direct route on the highway."

She replied, "Yeah, we went camping in Canada when I was younger, but not Toronto."

"I will ask my mother where we stayed the last time," I smiled, "Not a luxury hotel, but nice rooms and a short walk to the Eaton Center where there was shopping and restaurants." The City Hall and CN Tower were nearby with a large fountain and parkette.

She sighed, "Do we need Canadian money?"

"I am not sure; I will ask at the bank." I remarked. "We also need valid ID, like a passport or driver's license."

She smiled, "Ok, let's plan on it in a month or so on a long weekend this summer."

I reminded her, "We better check with our parents too."

Although Toronto was nearby, it required entry into a foreign country, something she had never done alone, and I had not done without supervision. The YFU program was a carefully controlled experience.

She said, "My mom mentioned it to your dad when she worked at the office."

The next time I went to the bank to deposit my paycheck, I asked the teller, "What is the currency exchange for the Canadian dollar?"

"It is not necessary to exchange currency in advance of your trip," she confirmed and explained. "When you pay for items with your American dollar, you will receive change in Canadian dollars, a different colored bill for each denomination. Canadian and American coins are interchangeable in both countries." The Canadian coins had a picture of

Queen Elizabeth on one side while the American coins had a different president on each denomination.

Mom called me at work on Friday to invite me home for dinner that weekend. I brought my laundry, and my parents broached the subject of a weekend trip with Marisa at the dinner table. Dad relayed the conversation he had with Lucille at the office and mom gave me a map and brochures of places to visit in Toronto. There was a wicker basket attached to the desk next to the phone in the family room full of maps from all the road trips we traveled as a family.

That summer we went to Toronto on three long weekends together. I switched shifts on Friday evenings with Cassie who worked part time on weekends. When she worked on a Friday for me, I worked the following Saturday or Sunday for her. There was no sick or overtime involved as my time sheet totaled eighty hours and hers showed four shifts with the switch. Our supervisor supported the switch, if it stayed confidential within the department, and it did not happen often. She did not want any problems with the Union.

Marisa and I left Rochester on Friday morning for the three-hour drive to Toronto. When we reached the border, I showed the Canadian agent my driver's license and her birth certificate. When we approached the city, driving seemed chaotic, bumper to bumper and terribly slow. We were not used to the crowds we encountered, and we never ventured outside the downtown core from the waterfront to Bloor Street alongside Yonge Street. We found our hotel, checked in, and parked the car in their parking lot for the weekend. We did not use it until it was time to drive home.

My first time traveling with a girlfriend, the responsibility was enormous at twenty-one years old. It was the first time I drove my car on a vacation outside of Rochester. I was nervous about a breakdown, but I was covered by the AAA family membership if I needed a tow or other assistance. We felt safe in our choices and enjoyed each other's company.

We hiked up Yonge to Bloor St and crossed the street to walk all the way down to the Lake Ontario waterfront, shopped, ate at various restaurants, and discovered the night life. We loved Eaton's and Simpsons, huge department stores that anchored the Eaton Center at Dundas and Queen Streets. We did not buy anything but admired the fashions and browsed for hours with big smiles on our faces.

We found a disco in Chinatown in the basement of a hotel, near City Hall, called *Floating World* and joined the queue for admission on Friday evening. There were young people all dressed up who paid the $5 cover charge. We chatted with the people behind us who lived in Toronto. They realized we were Americans by our accents and that we paid for our admission with greenbacks (American dollars).

We stayed two nights at the Chelsea Inn north of the Eaton Centre for a reasonable price and drove home on Sunday morning. At that time, gas was fifty cents a gallon in both countries; our travel cost was under fifty dollars for the round trip compared to the cost of a train or flight to New York City. That savings paid for our hotel, shopping, and entertainment. We returned to Toronto for two more long weekends that summer. Renting an apartment and maintaining a vehicle, I was self-conscious of my spending habits when I was living independently; solely responsible for all my living expenses coming out of my salary.

Marisa and I remained friends for life, reconnecting decades later with her mother and sister, where we enjoyed Friday game nights playing Scrabble, eating pizza, remembering old times, and sharing stories of our future families.

Chapter 8

Romance in the Air

Another Long-Distance Boyfriend ... Toronto, Canada

At the Floating World, Alberto and Nick introduced themselves while we were waiting in the line outside to enter the disco. They were well dressed in a suit and tie and sported chin length curly hair and asked for cigarettes. We politely declined; we did not smoke. They invited us to sit with them and bought the first round of drinks. At the end of the evening, they walked us to our hotel. We met at the disco again on Saturday evening and enjoyed another night of dancing. Alberto and I exchanged addresses and phone numbers at the end of the second evening.

At that time, smoking and drinking was allowed in public places, but I never enjoyed the smell of tobacco or alcohol as it lingered in my clothes and my hair. I was self-conscious of secondhand smoke, deliberately avoiding it whenever I was in a public place and I never allowed smoking in my future homes. Decades later public health concerns resulted in government legislation banning the practice in public places.

On Sunday morning, we packed our bags, checked out of the hotel, and loaded the car. We walked across Yonge Street for breakfast at Fran's Restaurant before leaving the city. It was a family restaurant with reasonable prices. I ordered poached eggs on toast with coffee. Marisa ordered strawberry pancakes with tea. I was a little nervous as we started the drive home with a lot of traffic in the city on the first long weekend of summer filled with tourists. We noticed license plates from different states and provinces. Following the map, she guided me down Yonge Street to the Gardiner Expressway westbound. When we crossed the city limits, the highway became known as the Queen Elizabeth Way (QEW).

The drive along the highway was long and boring with most exits surrounded by green space, no residential or commercial development near the highway. At that time, it was one hundred miles of two lanes in each direction with a speed limit of sixty miles per hour. There were no tolls like the New York State Thruway. It was the middle of the long weekend, the highway traffic was light, and the sky was clear. The QEW followed Lake Ontario, heading west to Hamilton, a city that cradled the western curve of Lake Ontario, and then east to Niagara, ending at the international border. A fork in the road as we approached Hamilton, veered left for Niagara and right for downtown Hamilton. On the Niagara bound highway, "Ontario Street" was the name of an exit in each town that we passed, a bit confusing. I was relieved when I saw the exit for the bridge to the USA, the halfway point of our journey.

At the border, there was a twenty-minute wait as each car was inspected. I handed my driver's license and Marisa's birth certificate to the agent through my opened window when I stopped at the booth.

"Hello ladies, please remove your sunglasses so we can match your face to your ID," barked the agent. "Where did you go? Do you have any goods to declare?"

I replied, "We spent the weekend in Toronto. We did not buy anything."

In disbelief, the guard hesitated and asked me to open the trunk. He did not see any shopping bags and opened our suitcases, satisfied that I told the truth. I watched him through the rearview mirror. As he searched through the trunk, he looked behind our car and noticed the line was getting longer, it was going to be a busy day for him. He closed the trunk and pulled a card out of his pocket.

When he returned to my open window, he gave me a "What to Declare" card along with the passport and birth certificate. "Please review this information before your next trip to understand your spending limits." He waved to us to leave the booth. I was relieved that the inspection was finished, nervous during those two-minute inspections, an annoyance that became part of my future travels for the rest of my life.

I handed the card to Marisa, and she asked, "What's that?"

"Read it to me while I'm driving." I replied. She put on her glasses to read the small print and pictures with slashes through them. She flipped the card over and noticed it was the same information printed in French.

She explained, "It is a list of items we are not allowed to bring across the border like animals, plants, and food. There is also a price list of the value of goods to declare, $0 for twenty-four hours, $200 for forty-eight hours. What does that mean?"

"I must concentrate on the road to follow the signs to the parkway. We passed an ice cream stand on Friday," I replied. "We can stop there for a cone to review the card."

She agreed, "It is so hot and humid, let's take a break when we get there."

My car did not have air conditioning. A nice breeze swirled through the car with the windows open; driving at a high speed was refreshing. Twenty minutes later I saw cars parked around a small brown building with a swing set next to it. A sign on the shoulder of the road read, "**Brown's Custard OPEN**," I pulled into the last parking spot and bought two vanilla and chocolate swirls while Marisa sat at one of the picnic tables by the playground. There were four children playing while their parents watched with glee, slurping their cones. The ice cream was dripping so we licked our treat quickly before it melted. This became a popular rest stop on future family visits with my children.

When I sat down, she placed the card on the table. I scanned it, "I did not know there were restrictions of what you can bring home. My parents never mentioned it when we discussed the trip."

"Oh, so we could have spent two hundred dollars since we were there for two nights?" she said.

I nodded, "Yeah, it means we pay tax if the stuff we buy costs more than that."

She sighed, "We will always be safe, we can't afford to spend that much money." I smiled in agreement.

Marisa continued navigating with the map in her lap until I reached the Ontario Beach Parkway where I was familiar with the rest of the route home.

She started the conversation, "It appears you and Alberto hit it off."

"Yes, he seems like a nice guy," I said.

She continued, "Do you want to see him again?"

I smiled, "Let's wait and see what happens."

Changing the subject, I continued, "Did you like the Eaton Centre? It may not be Macy's, but it was certainly glamourous."

She replied, "Yes, I would like to go again on another long weekend. I will bring more money next time to buy something."

"Me too," I nodded in agreement.

We had no regrets dodging New York City. It did not bother us that we were in a foreign country. The foreign exchange rate was on par, no need to calculate the actual cost in American dollars. Everything appeared normal except for the crowds and traffic congestion which we would experience in any large metropolitan area. Toronto was much closer to home and the Canadian department stores had more to offer than our local Sibley's and McCurdy's. Eaton's and Simpsons became a desirable alternative to shopping at Macys. It would be another twenty years before Macy's opened in Rochester and Eaton's and Simpsons were bought out by Sears (American) and Hudson's Bay Company (Canadian).

Alberto called the following weekend. He did not want to disturb me at work in the evenings, and he woke early to start his job, so weekends were the best time to talk. He also wanted to call when his parents were out shopping so they would not ask questions. He told me not to call or write to him for that reason. He promised to call every weekend around the same time.

The ladies at work were curious about my weekend adventure. I described the stores along Yonge Street and inside the mall. They noticed the glow in my eyes and asked if anything else happened. I described the discotheque. I assured them we had an exciting time and planned to go back again.

The first trip happened on Memorial Day weekend of May 1977, when I was twenty-one years old. Marisa and I made two more weekend trips that summer on July 4th and Labor Day weekends. Traveling home on Sunday, we avoided the long waits at the border on Monday, the last day of the long weekends. In the fall, Marisa met her future husband in Rochester, so I drove to Toronto alone, and stayed at the Chelsea Inn.

Diane continued to allow the weekend shift changes with Cassie as long as we kept quiet about it.

After the third weekend trip, I invited Alberto to come to Rochester to stay at my apartment. He traveled by Greyhound bus on a Friday evening and I met him at the station at midnight after my work shift ended. He told his parents he was camping with friends that weekend. I cooked a lasagna casserole for a late dinner that I prepared earlier that day and we watched late night talk shows before going to bed. On Saturday, we drove to a mall and took a walk through Highland Park during the day and went to a movie in the evening. It was a tight squeeze in my twin bed; he refused to sleep on the floor. On Sunday morning, I dropped him off at the bus station to return home. It was a five-hour trip and he wanted to be home for dinner with his parents and go to bed early for his job on Monday morning.

In the fall, I missed my period; the pregnancy test was positive at Dr. Williams clinic. The doctor showed concern because he and my dad were colleagues. I remembered meeting him and his daughter at the Faculty Club when I was welcomed back from Europe. He came back into the examining room after I dressed to discuss the results.

He started the conversation, "Margot, you are only twenty-one years old, and these accidents happen to young women. Did you use protection? I don't see a prescription for the pill on your file."

"No, I don't have a prescription, and I only see this guy one weekend each month," I replied. "He used condoms but forgot them last time."

"Do you want to have the baby? It is a huge responsibility that will change your life," the doctor continued. "Does he and your parents know about this?"

Staring at him, I raised my voice and sternly shouted, "NO …. NO" to both questions.

He pulled out brochures from the display case on the wall above the writing desk and wrote notes on my file while I moved from the examination table into the chair.

"Are you familiar with abortion? Are you aware it is now legal?" he continued in a measured tone, "It is a simple procedure I can perform at the out-patient clinic on a weekend when you are not working and with rest you can return to work the following Monday."

"I heard about it but not familiar with the procedure or the law." I asked, "What will it cost and when can you do it?"

He handed me a brochure, "It would have to be immediately, I can schedule you on Friday evening at seven o'clock." he assured me. "Bring a trustworthy friend to drive you home and plan on bed rest the entire weekend so you can work on Monday. No one needs to know what happened."

"At Highland? Everyone will find out with my name associated with my dad." I was getting worried.

Anticipating my fear, he took my hand and calmly explained, "I thought about that. I will charge you $200 cash; no insurance claim will be filed. You will be registered as Melanie Stein. Wear an outfit and a hat or sweatshirt with a hood to cover your face that your colleagues won't recognize." I was aware that all hospital records were confidential.

He pushed a form in front of me and said, "This is a consent for treatment that all patients must sign to be filed in the Melanie Stein record." I read and signed it "*Melanie Stein*" and passed it back to him. I wondered if he changed names and charged cash amounts without filing insurance claims for other patients to protect their privacy.

As he closed the file, he noticed my apartment address, "You live near the hospital?" I nodded affirmatively and he said, "Please arrange a ride to and from the clinic. You won't feel like walking home. Any other questions?" We shook hands and he left the room to see the next patient.

As I left the office that familiar "Don't you worry, you will be fine, it will be taken care of" rang through my head. I stuffed the brochure in my purse to read at work later that afternoon when it was not busy.

The abortion, a dilation and curettage procedure, also known as D&C, happened in the outpatient clinic three days later. I phoned a girlfriend I knew from school who agreed to accompany me to the appointment. The procedure was performed in less than thirty minutes, and Melanie was monitored for an hour afterward with the blood pressure cuff on one arm and IV hooked up to her other arm and then discharged to go home. That Friday evening was the only time I called in sick at work. The nurse who supervised my recovery and the clerk who collected the payment did not recognize me. I never had any contact with the Outpatient Department while working on the evening, night, and weekend shifts; my secret was safe.

My friend walked with me up the three flights of stairs in my building and asked if I needed anything at the store. I nodded no and she left so I could rest. I took aspirin before I went to bed and slept twelve hours, awakened by my phone ringing on Saturday morning.

"Hello" I said in a groggy tone.

"Hi Margot, Did I wake you? Are you coming home this weekend for dinner?" Mom asked.

"No Mom, I had to work the night shift last night and tonight, so I am going to stay here to rest. It is difficult to adjust to the shift change." I replied.

"Ok," she sighed. "Sorry I woke you up. Go back to sleep. Good luck tonight."

"Thanks, I'll see you next weekend." I hung up the phone and crawled back into bed with my business textbook for an hour. When I got up to make breakfast, it was uncomfortable to sit at the table, so I spent the weekend lying down on the couch watching television and reading the brochure along with my course assignments. After two days of rest, I felt better mentally and physically on Monday at school in the morning and work in the afternoon. Nobody questioned my Friday evening absence.

Abortion was legal in the United States following the Roe v. Wade (1973) case by the Supreme Court. At age twenty-one at conception, I would be twenty-two by the due date. I had no desire to carry a baby for nine months, give birth, raise a child alone, or pursue adoption. I had no regrets terminating that pregnancy in the first trimester while it was a tiny fetus and the sex was unknown. I threw out the brochure in the restaurant garbage bin when I went to school Monday morning.... Fait accompli!

I kept it a secret for a long time. The girlfriend who accompanied me to the clinic went through a similar experience six months later. I returned the favor, driving her to the clinic. The whole ordeal was dealt with in two weeks from the time I missed my period to the procedure. I was anxious during that time but also knew in my heart that I could not proceed with pregnancy and childbirth. Thankfully, I lived alone in my own apartment to deal with it on my own, without involving a roommate or my parents. As abortion was a controversial issue, some considered it murder of a fetus or human; I never thought of it in such terms. I was satisfied that it was a simple procedure without complications that was resolved with a quick recovery.

The following weekend on the phone, Alberto denied paternity. When I assured him, he was the only one, he agreed to help cover the cost. I made the decision alone, without consulting him. Occurring early in our friendship / relationship, it was a long-distance romance without a commitment. At that time, we lived separate lives. Then, he stopped calling, was it over?

Christmas in The Netherlands

Enrolled in the HAVO program at Winkler Prins, Jeannet rehearsed for a part in the Christmas play. I received a blue airmail letter from my little sister one week after my operation.

It read in Dutch, "Lieve Margot, I hope you are well. It has been a long time since you left Europe. Do you plan to return? I am performing in a school play during the Christmas holiday. I would like you to come to my performance. Viel liefs, Jeannet."

The next paragraph in Mama's handwriting, read "Lieve, Margot, do you have plans for Christmas? We would love to see you again. Please come for a visit in December. Viel Liefs, Mama."

It would be Jeannet's seventeenth birthday the day after Christmas, so it would be nice to celebrate with her. The holidays in Europe would be magical. I needed a vacation. My two-week vacation allotment had to be used before the end of the year. I never touched my vacation days with the weekend trips to Toronto. I checked the calendar posted in my supervisor's office for availability around the holidays. There were no vacations slotted for the last two weeks of December. There were no restrictions to book off during the holidays. Cassie and Dottie, part time colleagues who covered my shift would be delighted, they needed the extra money and the Christmas bonus.

The day after I received the letter, I went to the post office to send a telegram, "Lieve Jeannet, I accept your invitation. I will mail my itinerary as soon as I make the reservations. Veel liefs, Margot."

A Christmas holiday, to my favorite place … Veendam! I was super excited to be invited back for a visit! After making the reservations, I realized I needed three weeks off to cover the return trip home after New Years Day. Diane suggested allocating that extra week to next year's vacation time, and I could book a second week off later in the year. I had no intention of booking another week of vacation, so I took five single days off as needed for appointments or long weekends.

My parents added me to their American Automobile Association (AAA) family membership plan as soon as I got my driver's license. The emergency road service was dependable when I skidded into a snowbank on the I-490 overpass last year, the first snowfall of the season in November and my first year of driving my own vehicle. It was a frightening accident losing control of the car on an icy snow-covered patch skidding into the guardrail that overlooked the highway below.

A pickup truck pulled up and stopped behind me. A middle-aged man got out of his truck and walked over to the driver's side door. knocked and looked inside. "Hey lady, are you ok?" he shouted.

I was startled but relieved someone stopped as it was after midnight. I opened the window, and cried, "I need a phone to call the AAA."

He opened the door and helped me get out of the car and noted, "You are lucky, it appears just your front fender is damaged." He drove me to a bar at the next exit so I could make a phone call and waited with me until the tow truck driver arrived to bring me back to my car. He bought a beer and offered it to me to help me relax, but I declined, so he asked the bar tender for a glass of water for me and drank the beer while we waited for my ride.

As Jim waved and pivoted to leave the bar when the tow truck arrived, I shouted, "Thanks for your help, Jim."

He winked and shouted, "I have a daughter your age."

The tow truck driver towed my vehicle to a garage and then drove me to my apartment. The next day, I reported it to my insurance company who arranged a rental car while the front fender was being replaced. My parents were relieved that I survived as that overpass on the I-490 was known to be dangerous, causing fatal accidents and was eventually restructured years later. The seat belt saved my life and I was not injured, just a headache and a few aches and pains for a few days.

Requiring their services again, I visited the AAA travel agency to make my reservations. I was pleased with their services, as I never would have figured out this itinerary on my own. It was more than just booking a flight across the pond and coordinating the timing and connections at each location. It was much more complicated than the flights I booked to California when I was in high school.

A flight to Toronto and London, a train to Harversum, a ferry crossing the English Channel to Hoek van Holland, and a train to Assen, became a forty-eight-hour journey. A similar journey was arranged for the return flight home two weeks later.

The following account was from my diary of this memorable vacation.

Tuesday December 20, 1977, Day One

"Laurie, my friend from Nazareth, drove me to the airport and offered to pick me up when I returned home two weeks later. She wrote the return flight info in her calendar. The American Airlines flight from Rochester to Toronto was diverted to Buffalo due to a snowstorm and the shuttle to take us to the airport was delayed. Three British businessmen who had a meeting at Kodak sat beside me on that flight. They rented a car and invited me to join them since we were booked on the same overnight flight to London. I accepted their offer to travel together as it was my first time navigating through the Toronto and London airports alone. They were teased by airport personnel for being my chauffeur and bodyguards. Professionally dressed in business suits and overcoats following their meeting, I felt safe and trusted them."

"A lot of chaos and confusion at the airline ticket counter as connecting flights diverted due to the weather. The flight departed Toronto ninety minutes behind schedule at ten o'clock in the evening. We flew British Airways from Toronto to London. The aircraft, a deluxe DC10 accommodated hundreds of people. Dinner was a tough steak, but I was hungry and ate it. Drinks were served before dinner and wine with dinner, a first for this weary traveler. The weather in London was foggy, causing more confusion and delays, changing airports, and sitting on the tarmac, it finally landed at Gatwick Airport."

Wednesday, December 21, 1977, Day Two

"As the crowd of weary travelers waited at the baggage claim, I thanked Ben, George, and Leon for their assistance traveling across the pond. Leon, the older gentleman commented, "You are the same age as my daughter, it was the natural thing to do." Ben saw my bag and lifted it off the carousel for me, stating, "Have a safe journey and enjoy your visit with your Dutch family." George, the quiet one who drove the rental car through the storm, smiled and gave me a hug, "Bon Voyage." I wished them a "Merry Christmas" and went to the bathroom before joining the line at Customs."

"Checking my AAA itinerary, I had hours to kill before boarding the ferry at eight o'clock in the evening for another overnight voyage. I also had to figure out how to get there. I took the British Airways shuttle to King's Cross in London and sat next to Dave. He and I shared a locker to store our bags for a couple of hours, and we went to a pub for a drink."

"When we fetched our bags from the locker, he walked with me to the underground subway at Liverpool Street where I took the train to Harversum to hop on the ferry to cross the channel to The Netherlands. This ferry was an old yacht, and everyone sat on the outdoor deck on a wintry night. I chatted with Marija and Jan, a Dutch couple hiking in Europe. We found blankets to wrap around us and fell asleep on the benches on the deck."

Thursday December 22, 1977, Day Three

"When the ferry docked in Hoek van Holland, I boarded a train to Amsterdam Central Station. I bought a ticket to Assen and arrived at twelve noon."

"Papa and Jeannet greeted me with three kisses on each cheek, we loaded my big red suitcase in the trunk of the car and drove home to Veendam for lunch. Mama looked tired and greeted me with three kisses and a hug. She spoke Dutch to see if I understood and I picked up the language like I never left the country. After lunch, I moved my big red suitcase to Jeannet's attic bedroom, showered and changed my clothes after forty-eight hours of travelling."

As promised, I met Jeannet again! We were elated to reunite in Veendam three and a half years later. So excited, there was no mention of the play that day. Upstairs in her bedroom, I asked, "Jeannet when is your school play?"

She laughed, "I used that excuse to fool you. I wanted to see you again."

"I smiled, "Always a joker, it worked. I am here!"

Smiling, "Don't worry. We will be busy," she laughed.

"Why I came back! I knew it would be fun," yawning from lack of sleep.

At seventeen years old, the same age as I lived with her, she matured into a beautiful, kind, and friendly young lady.

"We walked through the Promenade and Kerk Straat to shop and admired the Christmas decor. Mama made Macaroni Salad, a delicious meal after all the weird eating and drinking from the last two days. Eva and I finally met in person for the first time. She met my mother at the end of her year abroad in 1974, she flew to Rochester after her school year finished for

a week vacation before she returned to Europe. After dinner, Evelien went to work and Jeannet went to a party. Still recovering from jet lag and the six-hour time change, I chatted with Mama and Papa, watched television, and walked the dog before I went to bed exhausted at 10 p.m."

Friday, December 23, 1977, Day Four

"I slept for twelve hours and woke up in time for coffee at half past ten in the morning. Eva and I walked the dog to the post office and bought groceries. After lunch, we drove to the train station in Assen to pick up Oma. It was the first time I met Oma; she visited the family on the weekends I was away at the retreat and Winschoten and during the holiday break when I traveled with my mother, brother, and sister. Dinner was meatballs, salad, potatoes, and vla. After dinner, I walked through the village and checked in on old friends. Babs lived in Groningen and Ankie was in England for a year, but their parents invited me into their homes for tea. It felt great to be welcomed and learn about their daughter's adventures. When I returned home, Eva and I watched television and walked the dog before bedtime."

Saturday, December 24, 1977, Day Five

"On Christmas Eve, I visited Christa who moved to Borgerspark. It was a street with new homes that was hard to find. Riding the bicycle, I found Eva on the Promenade to give me directions. Christa attended teaching school in Hilversum. I went home to call Elly who was moving to Borgerspark next week. We arranged to meet on Friday after the move."

"Hans arrived in the afternoon; we chatted and drank before sitting down to eat *Boeren Kool* also known as *Stamppot* (green kale with mashed potatoes and sausage) for dinner. After watching television, we went to Church for a midnight service."

Sunday, December 25, 1977, Day Five

"On Christmas morning, Jeannet and I went to an open house at Veen Leist. All day long there were interactive craft booths, children's plays, films, and a choir. It was fun to join in the activities. After lunch, Eva took me and Oma on a drive through the countryside. When we returned, Bert arrived to visit Hans."

"Mama served meat fondue with all kinds of sauces and ice cream cake for dinner. After dinner, we opened gifts. Everyone liked what I gave them, and I received a feather pen, pineapple candle, jade bracelet and an embroidery book with patterns that would keep me busy creating designs for a long time."

Monday, December 26, 1977, Day Six

"The day after Christmas, also known as Boxing Day, was Jeannet's seventeenth birthday. Tante Anja and Oom Lou came for a visit. It was nice to see them again. They liked the pillow and Christmas cloth with tulips that I gave them."

"In the afternoon, Eva, Oma, and I took the dog for a walk in the woods at Gieten, a small village near Assen. We ate beef with sauces and *vegetables for dinner and played cards until midnight, a very enjoyable evening to celebrate my sister's birthday.*

Tuesday, December 27, 1977, Day Seven

"Jeannet played in a volleyball tournament. It was great to reunite with people I knew from the school. We ate Zuurkool (Sauerkraut) for dinner and watched the movie "High Society" (1956) a musical version of "The Philadelphia Story" starring Bing Crosby, Grace Kelly and Frank Sinatra set in Newport, Rhode Island, a millionaire's playground.

I phoned Meneer and Mevrouw Ebels in Leeuwarden who were pleased that I returned to The Netherlands for a visit.

Wednesday, December 28, 1977, Day Eight

On Wednesday, Papa drove the girls to Oldenburg, Germany a small town near the border of The Netherlands. Despite the rain, we shopped at the Kerstmarkt, had coffee and cake at a bakery, enjoyed a great meal at a hotel, then drove home.

"In the evening, I met Babs and her boyfriend in Groningen. When I visited her mother the first day, she promised to take me to Groningen to visit her daughter during the holidays. I was pleased that her mother arranged it. As Babs was employed as a dental hygienist, and I worked at a hospital, we had a lot in common".

Thursday, December 29, 1977, Day Nine

On Thursday, Hans drove me to Tante Anja's home in Winschoten. We went shopping on the Grote Markt where I bought embroidered stationery and a Japanese lantern. We ate a delicious chicken dinner with coffee and cake. Grietje came by with Annet, Claire, Ernst and Anton inviting me to join them for the evening at Café Chanton. We stopped at Derek's parents' shoe store to say hello. They were pleased to see me and told me that he was working in England but spending the holidays down under with his Aussie girlfriend. They promised to send my greetings to him."

"At the café, Grietje remarked, "Derek told me about his visit at your college."

"I was surprised to hear from him six months after leaving the Netherlands," I replied.

"She continued, "He was very fond of you and disappointed you turned him down."

"I never turned him down," a bit shocked at that accusation. "I suggested we both pursue our education and meet for vacations."

"Then, he misunderstood you," She remarked, "I agree that was a good compromise." They were close cousins, born months apart and grew up together in Winschoten. "He admitted to me last year when he came home from Chicago before he transferred to London, that he missed you."

"Really!" I laughed. "A thank you / birthday card a month after his visit was the last time I heard from him, over two and a half years ago!" She sensed my disappointment and we ordered another beer.

Getting depressed thinking about him, I changed the subject, "I currently work an administrative job in a hospital in Rochester and attend a business program at a local college."

"Oh, you are not in the teacher's college?" She replied. "Is that where Derek visited you?"

"After two years of teacher's college, I quit and moved back home," I sighed. "I had a tough time figuring out what I wanted to do. My heart missed Europe." Taking a sip of beer, "I love that job for now. Who knows what the future holds!"

"She agreed, "Yes, I love teaching little children, but someday, I would like to teach teenagers."

"At midnight, she walked me back to Tante Anja's home. We hugged and kissed on three cheeks and wished each other good luck."

Friday, December 30, 1977, Day Ten

"The next morning, Annet and Claire came to Tante Anja's home to take me to Pleintje for a coffee before I returned to Veendam."

I never exchanged addresses to stay in touch with these ladies, but it was nice to see them again. It was the last time I would see Tante Anja and Oom Lou. I sent them a thank you note when I returned home to

Rochester and never heard from them again. They moved to a senior's residence in Switzerland.

"After returning from Winschoten, Jeannet and I took the bus to Groningen for an afternoon of shopping, pizza, and beer, and watched the James Bond film, "The Spy Who Loved Me." I loved James Bond. We hustled back to the bus station, flagged down the driver as he pulled out of his parking spot. He let us board the bus, noting it was his last trip for the day. We thanked him for stopping and arrived home in Veendam around midnight."

Saturday, December 31, 1977, Day Eleven

"On New Years Eve during the day, Jeannet and I strolled through the village looking for gifts to bring home to Rochester. I wanted to buy a Dutch t-shirt for David but could not find one. The village did not have any souvenir shops like you find in airports. I bought silver teaspoons with everyone's initials for my family instead. We ate Bahmi Goreng (Fried Rice with Indonesian spices) for dinner, and I finished macrame hangings for Mama while we watched television. At midnight, we toasted each other with drinks, then Jeannet and I went to see the fireworks on the Promenade. We stayed out until five o'clock in the morning visiting friends' homes for drinks and snacks. It was a long fun night." I never celebrated New Years Eve like that, ever!

Sunday, January 1, 1978, Day Twelve

"New Years Day was a lazy day. We slept in and watched the Austrian Orchestra and ballet on television with Papa. I felt lousy with all the drinking and snacking the night before. Olie bollen are a traditional New Years treat of breaded deep-fried donuts. I went out for a walk in the middle of the afternoon and packed my big red suitcase for my departure. We had a light early dinner of ragout (meat, vegetable, and potato stew) and then Mama, Papa, Hans, and I drove to Winschoten to wish Tante Anja and Oom Lou a Happy New Year. They served nice hors d'oeuvres and we came home at midnight."

Monday, January 2, 1978, Day Thirteen

The day after New Years, I bought traditional Dutch treats of cheese, chocolate and hagelslag at the grocer, Albert Hein, to bring home to Rochester. I purchased a bouquet of flowers as a thank you for Mama. In the afternoon, Jeannet and I cycled to Borgerspaark to visit Elly and her family in their new home. Then back to Ankie's home to say goodbye to her parents. When they called her on Christmas, they told her I visited, and she was disappointed that she missed me. Next time? ... twenty-two years later when she visited me in Canada.

Tuesday, January 3, 1978, Day Fourteen

On the fourteenth day my magical vacation ended. Mama and the girls drove me to Groningen at five o'clock in the afternoon to take the train to the overnight ferry. We ate soup at the station before my departure.

We hugged and kissed goodbye on three cheeks. I invited them to come to Rochester."

"I changed trains in Amersfoort where I met a British couple taking the ferry. This time, it was a luxury cruise ship with an assigned seat. I was elated to travel in such luxury and sleep."

Wednesday, January 4, 1978, Day Fifteen

The ferry docked in England at half past seven in the morning and I walked through customs to board the train to Liverpool Street. I walked to the Underground and found the train that took me to Gatwick Airport, arriving at eleven o'clock in the morning. This train had a cabin to seat four people, like the Canadian train I took to Alberta ten years earlier with my family. I sat with an American girl who was studying architectural restoration in Germany. At the airport, I had no choice but to buy lunch of steak, vegetables and potato in an expensive restaurant that tasted awful."

"I boarded the British Airways flight to Toronto at half past three in the afternoon, but it was delayed until five o'clock. I was assigned a seat next to Yvonne and Maureen, and we had a nice chat. The plane landed in Toronto at eight o'clock in the evening and it took ninety minutes to collect my bag and go through Customs. There was no hotel reservation made in advance in Toronto, and I was too exhausted to arrange it. I walked to the American Airlines counter and slept on a chair in their lounge for the night."

Thursday, January 5, 1978, Day Sixteen

My connecting flight to Rochester was at eight o'clock in the morning. At seven o'clock I checked my bag and received my boarding pass. I walked through the security check point and proceeded to the gate. The plane was on time, boarding at quarter to eight. The Christmas rush was finished, with parents back to work and children in school, the plane was half full, so I was able to stretch my legs and placed my extra bag of gifts on the seat next to me."

"Laurie waited for me at the baggage claim in the Rochester airport. We greeted each other with a hug, and I told her all about my adventure as she drove. We stopped for breakfast at the restaurant below my apartment and she helped me drag my luggage up the three flights of stairs. This weary adventurer was finally back home by twelve noon. I had three days to rest and prepare for the new year before school and work began on Monday."

When I booked this trip in October, I had two choices, a direct flight from Toronto to Amsterdam that would be double the cost during the Christmas holidays or the money saving flight / ferry / train that totaled five hundred dollars. Living on a very tight budget renting an apartment and maintaining a car, I chose the latter. I had to factor in the journey from Rochester to Toronto and Amsterdam to Veendam both ways. I could not ask anyone to drive those distances in unpredictable winter weather conditions, recalling my car accident last winter.

The itinerary was incredibly detailed with all my connections; the travel agency coordinated with their overseas partners allowing extra time for delays. The most difficult and unpredictable issue was the

Toronto airport closure on my first day. I was grateful that the three British gentlemen offered me a ride with them in their rental car and drove safely to make that flight. They wanted to go home, and I wanted to cross the pond, advantageous for the four of us.

It was nice that Mama invited me to come back, I did not have to ask. It was also nice to have a place to stay and eat for two weeks, which saved me money. I enjoyed sleeping until ten o'clock every morning, especially fighting jet lag, but I was not prepared for the busy schedule and late nights every day. Progressing from elementary to high school, Jeannet exhibited more freedom, independence, and maturity.

I was not used to all the alcohol consumption, but I adapted, drinking slowly. I was welcomed by everyone I called and visited, even when their adult child / my friend was not home. That hospitality was heartwarming. These friendships lasted a lifetime with annual birthday and holiday cards as well as future wedding, birth, and death announcements. It would be more than three decades before I crossed the pond again, so I hosted my Dutch family and friends in North America while we pursued careers and raised families.

An International Move Inquiry

Alberto and I reconnected after my vacation, three months after my operation. He called me the weekend after I returned home from Europe to wish me a belated holiday greeting. I was confused but happy at the same time. We resumed our monthly weekend visits alternating between Rochester and Toronto for another year before our engagement to marry. In Toronto, I stayed at the Chelsea Inn, and we met downtown during the day. In Rochester, he traveled on the Greyhound bus and stayed at my apartment. I arranged my weekend trips to Toronto on my days off, Saturday and Sunday nights, returning home Monday morning to work my regular afternoon shift. There was gossip in the office about my long-distance romance; shifting my visits to Saturday from Friday to avoid requesting coverage for my shift, curtailed further gossip and speculation. Alternatively, he arrived at midnight on Friday midnight and left Sunday morning by bus so there was no disruption in our work schedules.

On one of the summer visits, I confronted him, "What are your intentions with me?"

He looked surprised, "Can't we just be friends?"

I countered, "I am making sacrifices, paying for a hotel, meals, and gas when I visit Toronto and entertaining you in my home in Rochester."

He argued, "I am also making sacrifices, making excuses to see you behind my parent's back."

I contained my anger, "We have been sneaking around for over a year, I want a commitment if these visits continue. I am not taking any more chances after my operation last fall."

He was surprised that I mentioned that after months of silence, "I don't know what I want right now. Give me time to think about it. I would not see you if I did not care for you!"

I met his parents and cousins at his uncle's fiftieth birthday party in the fall. Once that introduction occurred, I stayed at his parent's home on our monthly weekend visits. I was relieved that I no longer had to pay for a hotel in Toronto.

He came to Rochester for my twenty-third birthday, twenty-two months after we first met at the disco. I picked him up at the bus station on Friday at midnight after my shift ended and cooked his favorite dinner, a lasagna casserole. He popped the question and I said "**YES!**" I was pleased to finally have that commitment of marriage. The next day we met my parents for dinner and announced our engagement. I had attended several weddings of my friends who were already starting families. At that time, couples married in their early twenties upon graduation from college. I did not want to lag too far behind that trend.

My parents were concerned; it meant one of us would move across the border. Dad started the discussion, "Alberto, I have contacts through my medical practice to arrange job opportunities for you here in Rochester. There are good career choices here like Kodak."

Alberto insisted, "Margot should come to Canada. I work for the City of Toronto and want to stay close to my parents." They were not aware that he was an only child. He reminded them, "Margot lived in Europe and Toronto is only a three-hour drive for weekend visits."

Noticing my excitement, my parents agreed. We looked at a calendar and set the wedding date on Memorial Day weekend the following year. It would allow relatives and friends to plan a visit and give us a year to make the arrangements. The wedding took place exactly three years from the weekend we first met.

I continued the discussion, "I checked into the Canadian Immigration Office in Toronto on my last visit and received the application with instructions and documents to submit for approval. It will take several months to process."

My parents looked surprised that I did this without telling them. An independent working woman, I did not have to seek parental approval for decisions affecting my life. It was best to inform them that I made the necessary inquiries for a life changing move; I did not walk into it blindly by showing up at the border without the required documentation.

One month later I received notice to report for an interview at the Canadian Consulate in Buffalo. I used Irondequoit as my "permanent address" and saw the letter on the counter when I came home for my weekend visit. Mom drove and I booked a vacation day. She asked me to stay for dinner to discuss the interview with Dad.

When we arrived at the Consulate, we were directed to the Immigration Office where I signed in and waited my turn for the meeting. There were a dozen people with family members in the waiting room. A little nervous, Mom needed to be home when David arrived home from school. She had a book to read while she waited. Interviews were conducted in six cubicles. My name was called about ten minutes after my scheduled time.

Ian introduced himself and started the interview. "Margot, you want to move to Canada alone at twenty-three years old?"

I answered calmly, "Ian, I am engaged to marry a Canadian who lives and works in Toronto."

He glanced at my file, "There is no indication on your application that your fiancé is your sponsor."

"That is correct. I applied independently and will search for a job upon my arrival," I responded proudly. "I made inquiries at employment placement firms who assured me there were many administrative opportunities." I purchased a *Toronto Star* newspaper on my last visit to scan the want ads and made phone calls.

He looked over my application and spoke in French, the second language in Canada. I could not follow him. He said, "Your application says you speak French which is required for all government positions."

I corrected him, "I took French in school, but I don't speak it fluently. I read and understand the language when spoken slowly." He made a note on the file. French Immersion was one of the streams in their school system for students who wished to become bilingual.

He continued, "All applicants are expected to take English skills testing. It will take about an hour. Can you do that today or would you like to make an appointment for another day?"

They schedule an hour to accommodate non-English speaking applicants. "I traveled here from Rochester with my mother," I said. "I would prefer to stay and do it now if possible."

"Take a ten-minute break and let your mother know what is happening," he said. Handing me a bracelet, "Show this green bracelet to the guard who will let you back into the room when you are ready and I will set up the examination."

I nodded, "Thank you, I will be back shortly."

I went to the lobby and talked to mom and we both went to the restroom. She whispered, "You are a smart girl, you'll be finished in less than an hour." I nodded in agreement and promised it would be quick.

When I approached the office door, the guard saw the bracelet and opened it. I returned to Ian's cubicle in five minutes, and he gave me the booklet and set a timer for one hour. I sat at a small table in the corner while he continued working quietly at this desk. It was an easy test that I finished in thirty minutes.

He took the completed test and said, "You will receive a letter in the mail in a couple of months when a decision is made on your application. Please confirm your mailing address with the receptionist."

As he shook my hand, I said, "Thank you, have a nice day." I asked the receptionist to update the mailing address on my file to my apartment, so I could check for its arrival every day.

Mom was pleased that I was finished before noon, and we left the building. As she drove to the Thruway, she said, "We will stop at the Service Area for a quick bite and gas up the car. I don't want to waste time at a sit-down restaurant." I agreed and we were home before 2 p.m., an hour before David came home from school.

After lunch while she was driving, she began, "Margot, you are taking on too much responsibility with work, marriage, and another move to a foreign country."

"Mom, I am twenty-three years old, a typical age to marry, the same age when you married Dad," I answered, a bit annoyed. "Many of my friends are already married and having babies." I took a sip from my thermos, "Alberto and I dated for two years, a normal courtship."

I sensed she was concerned that I did not have a university degree to get a decent job. She thought the hospital job could lead to a future promotion and career; it was a permanent job that would keep me close to home in Rochester. I wondered if she hoped that I would meet and marry a doctor someday.

I took a sip of water and continued, "People move around when they finish school and look for jobs. Mark, Jan, and Paul live in different states, and my distance would be the closest for coming home." She nodded in agreement. "To me, it felt like moving to a neighboring state, not a foreign country."

The immigration documents arrived in the mail three months later at the end of June with an expiration date of December 31, 1980. I had an eighteen-month window to move to Canada. The wedding was scheduled for next May. I wanted to relocate before the wedding. I gave up my apartment at the end of July and moved back home while I prepared for the move. I resigned from my job two weeks later in August, a job that I loved for three years. As this move was close to home, I left things behind until I needed them.

PART IV

PATIENCE IS GOLDEN

Living in Canada

(1979 – 2010)

Chapter 9

Canada, here I come Tuesday, August 28, 1979

Moving Day

I packed the trunk of my new car, a silver Datsun 310 hatchback, and left my parents' home in Irondequoit on Tuesday morning, August 28, 1979. A peaceful drive along the scenic Lake Ontario Parkway, listening to my recorded cassette tapes of my favorite rock bands. The custard stand was open, so I stopped for a cone and sat at a picnic table to stretch my legs and thought about this new adventure. I arrived at Canada Customs in Niagara Falls at noon.

When I showed the guard my document and passport, he placed a pink sticker on the windshield, pointed to the building on the right, and said, "Park your car over there to get your paper approved and car inspected." I nodded and drove into the parking lot and opened the trunk for another guard standing in the parking lot directing traffic.

I waited an hour, and then the guard behind the counter shook my hand, "Welcome to Canada, Margot." He informed me, "You must show this stamped immigration document with your passport every time you cross the border into Canada. Don't lose it, keep it in a safe place."

"Thank you, Sir," I said with a big grin across my face. Another dream came true.

The yellow document was a mimeographed copy of a multi-layered form, like the admission forms I created; copies for the applicant (me) and various government departments to keep on file. Wrinkled and crumpled around the edges, it was barely legible folded up in my passport case for the rest of my life. It became required evidence for permanent resident renewals and my citizenship application decades later.

I followed the QEW Toronto eighty miles around Lake Ontario and arrived at Strathmore Blvd at 3 p.m. when Alberto arrived home from work. Alberto's father signaled for me to drive around the block to the alley behind the houses and he opened the garage door to park next to his car. The garage doors were not numbered and close together. I had to memorize the spot, counting the structures from each corner so I could find it when driving alone. It was a heavy double door without an electronic opener, so I parked on the street if I planned to go out again.

Waiting for me outside, Nello gave me a hug with two kisses on each cheek, smiling, "Welcome to Canada, Margot."

"Thank you for allowing me to stay at your home," I smiled.

Emilia stood inside the back door and said, "Hallo Margot, glad you are here."

"It feels great to finally move here," I beamed excitedly.

They opened the trunk and grabbed things to bring into the house. Once the car was empty, I locked it and Nello shut the garage door. We placed all my belongings under the stairs so I could move them upstairs to the spare bedroom later.

Alberto appeared and looked surprised at my collection under the stairs. He gave me a hug and said, "How was your trip?"

I sighed, "Ok, but I'm tired."

He picked up my big red suitcase and brought it upstairs and I followed him with smaller items. We made more trips up and down the stairs until everything was in my room. He showed me the empty closet and bureau to use. He excused himself to shower and nap while I spent the rest of the afternoon organizing the spare bedroom until we were called downstairs for dinner.

More culture shock as I immersed myself in Canadian culture. Although Canada and the USA were neighbors and the distance from my parent's home was less than two hundred miles, I adapted to the new lifestyle.

My previous visits to Toronto centered around the downtown core near Bloor and Yonge Streets where there were commercial and retail businesses, hospitals, and hotels for tourists. The subway network traveled north / south below Yonge Street and east / west below Bloor

Street. I had only stayed at his parent's home four times in the past year. Alberto's parents lived near Woodbine Station on the Bloor / Danforth line, a fifteen-minute commute downtown. It was the best way to navigate through the city as driving was congested, and parking was expensive. It was a short walk to the subway and to Danforth for shopping, restaurants, banking, grocery, and drug stores from his home.

The city had semi-detached homes with mutual driveways between houses shared by neighbors. The front and back yards were small for a garden and close to the sidewalks near the street. Garages were in alleys behind the homes rather than attached to the front or sides of houses facing the street. High density housing to squeeze more people into a city block was the standard in Toronto, compared to the large homes on large lots in Irondequoit and the villages of Europe. At that time, the population of Toronto of six hundred thousand people was three times the size of my hometown. Strathmore Blvd was one block north of Danforth where the subway ran underground. I heard the rumble of the trains inside the house.

In this neighborhood, the homes were two-story, three-bedroom houses with a living room, dining room and kitchen on the main floor and the narrow hallway running down the side of the home was attached to the neighbor's home. The attached home mirrored an opposite layout. One heard voices and televisions on the other side of the wall. These homes, built in the early part of the 20th century, had two kitchens, one in the basement and one on the main floor, where two families or two generations of a family lived together under one roof. Alberto's mother did all the cooking in the basement where meals were served daily. The main floor kitchen and dining room were reserved for holidays and entertaining guests. The finished basement was designed like a separate apartment with a kitchen, family room with a sofa bed, and three-piece bathroom which was used for daily living. The laundry room had a washing machine, no dryer. There were clothes lines hooked up to the house by the back door strung across the yard to the garage and in the basement hallway near the furnace and water heater. The paneling on the wall resembled the paneling in my parent's home.

His parents immigrated to Canada from Italy in the 1950s when he was a baby accompanied by cousins on both sides of the family. His mother's sister's family settled in Montreal, Quebec while his father's sister's family settled in Willowdale, a suburb north of Toronto. The neighborhood, populated by Italian immigrants, was dubbed "Little Italy." The residents spoke Italian at home and learned English on the job and the children learned English at school. His mother and aunts learned English watching television as they stayed home. Like my father's childhood in Rochester forty years earlier.

Toronto was home to various ethnic groups residing in different areas, with local businesses reflecting the backgrounds of the neighborhood residents. As one traveled along Bloor Street there were Greek, Polish, Indian, Arab, Ukrainian, and Italian neighborhoods side by side, all spoke their native languages. It was multi-cultural, unlike the "melting pot" in the USA where immigrants learned English to blend into the American culture.

I wasted no time exploring job prospects and apartments. The next day, I took the subway downtown to register my car at Service

Ontario, changing my license plates and driver's license to the Province of Ontario. I applied for a Canadian social insurance number required for banking and employment at Service Canada. The brochure from Service Canada explained how to apply for citizenship after five years.

I found the secretarial employment agency I contacted months earlier and completed application forms, clerical tests, and interviewed for job opportunities. They put me on a temporary call list to accept job assignments immediately. By the end of the week, I received my first assignment to work the following week. On the weekend, Alberto and I took the subway downtown to that location so that I knew exactly where to report at 9 a.m. Monday morning.

Blending into Canadian Culture (early 1980s)

A few weeks later, I attended a job interview at St Clair and Yonge, north of Bloor Street to work for a lawyer in an insurance adjustors office, F.C. Maltman & Co. It was amazing that I found full-time permanent employment within a month of moving there; this position was nothing like the jobs I had in Rochester. This company represented lawyers and other professionals sued for malpractice; an interesting introduction to employment during my first year in my adopted homeland.

The office spanned an entire floor, with ten adjustors' offices by the windows and ten secretaries' desks lined up across from them. Each adjustor and secretary partnered as a team and adapted their own professional work relationships, whether it was dictating letters and reports, transcribing handwritten pieces, or explaining and creating documents. Jason informed me to look through the file to familiarize myself with each case as I worked on it, to create documents from his handwritten instructions for his signature. He made corrections but was genuinely satisfied with my submissions, making his job easier and praised me for my work ethic.

I found a three-storey rooming house near the office where there were five bedrooms rented to young single women, and we shared the kitchen and bathroom, on the second and third floor of the home. There was no living room, we socialized in our studios and in the kitchen. Laundry had to be taken to a laundromat. The first floor was the landlord's business. There was no garage or driveway to park my car, so it stayed at Alberto's parents' home in their garage and I gave him a key. This rooming house was a five-minute walk to the St. Clair subway station on the Yonge Street line north of Bloor Street, conveniently located to travel anywhere in the transit network. Alberto picked me up on weekends to bring my laundry to his home and grocery shopping.

The landlord made three hundred dollars per week or twelve hundred a month in rental income, charging tenants sixty dollars per week. There was no lease, the renters gave him a minimum of two weeks' notice upon moving. I lived in this home for six months before the wedding and made friends with the housemates. I informed the landlord that it would be a six-month commitment when I moved in. The rent included utilities but we had to order our own telephone service. Julianna and I shared occasional meals together and walked to the Eaton Centre and Mirvish Village on weekends to shop. We lost contact when I moved out.

I was familiar with the Eaton Centre from previous shopping trips. Mirvish Village was a unique discount department store owned by the family that staged live plays in the city near Bloor and Bathurst Streets. It reminded me of Park Avenue in Rochester, a "trendy" neighborhood with boutiques, restaurants and crowds of people shopping for groceries, household items, and clothing. It was fun to watch people and eat ethnic food at the snack bars.

In April, eight weeks before the wedding, I moved to an apartment building near Islington Subway station, the last stop on the west side of the city that was close to Alberto's workplace. We rented a two-bedroom apartment on the seventh floor in a new thirty-storey building for a year before purchasing our first matrimonial home. There was an underground parking garage, a fitness center with a dozen cardio and weight machines, and a laundry room with coin operating machines in the basement so I could park my car, workout, and do my own laundry at home. The building was a ten-minute walk to the subway station, a large grocery store and other amenities. I bought a 4-wheel cart to haul my groceries.

It became a forty-minute commute to work each way, adding ninety-minutes on to my seven-hour workday. On my first commute downtown by train, I recognized Louise and Laura when we exited the station at St. Clair. We walked into the office together a bit frazzled at 10:30 a.m., during the morning coffee break.

The head secretary, Margaret noticed us with our jackets draped on our arms, "Ladies, welcome to the office," with a bit of sarcasm, "Did you sleep in? Its already break time."

Laura spoke, "Margaret, as you can see there are three of us, we came from different directions on the subway."

"It is on the news, I heard it on my transistor radio," Louise added. "A power failure shut down the system this morning."

"My first trip that was supposed to take forty minutes, lasted two and a half hours," I sighed. It was refreshing that there were two senior secretaries with me, so I did not face her wrath alone.

Margaret stared at me, "Don't you walk to work, Margot?"

"I moved into a new apartment this past weekend at the end of the subway line near my fiancé's workplace. An extremely exhausting weekend," I remarked. "I will give you my new address and phone number by the end of the day."

She glared, "Oh, welcome to the commuting world of chaos. I wondered why no one picked up the phone at your house this morning."

Everyone giggled, as Doug, an older balding stocky gentleman, one of the partners, walked in to get a cup of coffee. He grinned, "I took a head count earlier when I heard the news, is everyone accounted for? I did not notice our new addition, the Americano."

I smiled, "Yes, Doug, I'm here." We found our coffee mugs in the cupboard above the sink, filled them up, and returned to our desks to start work.

When I stepped out for lunch, Doug waved me into his office and shut the door. There were windows on the wall, so everything was visible when holding meetings. "When I heard you and Louise, who is my secretary, come in this morning, I decided to interrupt the conversation." He sighed. "I hope you were not offended. It was meant to be a joke."

"It was a nice gesture to break the tension," I smiled. "Is there a problem?"

He continued, "Confidentially, Margaret always complains about you. I thought something happened on Friday, why you were late this morning."

"I would have called if I stayed home sick or had an appointment," I joked. "I'm well aware being the new kid on the block, and also being American, that people will talk about me."

"Don't worry, Jason is pleased with your work. He thinks you are the best assistant he has had in a long time," Doug remarked.

"That is reassuring," I replied. "I enjoy working with him."

"It is my job to ensure the vertical partnerships between adjustor and assistant work," Doug continued. "I don't care about the horizontal relationships between the secretaries."

"Thank you, that is good to know, it is my first experience in this type of office environment," I replied. "It's been a hectic time for me, adjusting to life in a new city and country along with my upcoming wedding back home that my mother is planning."

He got up to open the door and smiled, "Sorry, it took me six months to meet you, it is a busy workplace. I will be organizing a friendly staff softball season soon, I hope you will join us." It was a nice social gathering every week after work for a game and pub night in the spring.

I grinned a wide smile, "I'm looking forward to it."

It was a friendly office environment; everyone was on a first-name basis and dressed professionally every day. I told Alberto about the game nights and he met me after work to cheer me on the baseball diamond. Everyone participated, and teams changed weekly based on attendance. I enjoyed that social event with colleagues from all levels of the company.

There were two young junior secretaries getting married that summer. Margaret planned a surprise bridal shower for us on a Friday night after hours in the conference room. The ladies gave thoughtful wedding gifts, and everyone brought delicious treats for refreshments. Connie and I were both getting married in our hometowns far away from Toronto and she was also new to the company, so the office staff were not on our guest lists. It was not necessary to set up a gift registry in Toronto because the Italians on my list would not understand it. The bridal shower at the office was a pleasant surprise and friendly acknowledgement of our upcoming nuptials. I locked the gifts in a corner of Jason's office for the next week and I brought a few things home each day on the subway. Alberto picked me up at the station so I did not have to carry the gifts while walking home.

Chapter 10

The First Ten Years of Marriage (1980s)

The Wedding May 24, 1980

I drove home every month to assist with the wedding arrangements. One weekend in January, my sister, Jan, and Mark's wife, Sue, joined mom and I to shop for bridal and bridesmaid dresses. I chose a simple empire waist bridal gown off the sales rack that fit perfectly, having lost forty pounds since moving to Canada. The bridesmaids' gowns were cream color with purple flowers and a purple empire waist sash. Mom created a head band of dried flowers attached to her wedding veil for my headpiece and the garter belt had a blue ribbon. The traditional "something old, something new, something borrowed, something blue" was evident in my simple but elegant ensemble. I saved it for years but never wore it again. Decades later, I kept the veil and discarded the dress because I could not remove the stains from storage and it ripped stuffed in the back of a closet. Will the veil be worn again someday?

My school friend, Fiona, did not show up for the bridal fittings and did not answer my calls. I needed a third bridesmaid in the party.

I called the hospital information desk one evening, "Good evening, Information, Donna speaking."

"Hi Donna, how are you?" I replied.

She recognized my voice immediately, "Margot, I'm good. Surprised to hear from you."

"Donna, I need a favor and you have been a great friend the last few years," I said nervously.

"Ok," she replied, "What is on your mind? I miss our daily chats on our breaks."

"I need a third bridesmaid and thought of you," I was more relaxed. "Would you be interested?"

"Of course," she said without hesitation, "Your wedding is marked on the calendar and my mother, husband, and four-year-old son will be attending."

Smiling, I explained, "I plan to come back to Rochester in a few weeks if it is not snowing, can you meet me at the Bridal store for a fitting?"

"Sure, no problem," I could sense the excitement in her voice.

"Great, I will let you know when I am back in town so we can meet," I said excitedly.

She was getting nervous as visitors hovered over her desk, "I must go now so keep me posted and we will meet soon. Bye." And the phone clicked.

I knew I could count on her and was relieved she agreed to step in on short notice. She was the same age as Sue, so the four of us would get along well on my wedding day. Two weeks later we met at the bridal store for her fitting and everything was ordered. I addressed all the invitations that weekend and prepared them for the mail. Mom picked a green script that matched the spring garden theme I wanted for the décor.

A family friend, Hazel, and her daughters hosted a bridal shower at their home in Irondequoit one month later. It was a large party with twenty women that Mom invited who gave very thoughtful gifts from the gift registry at Sibley's that I had arranged when I came home for the dress shopping. The food was delicious; Aunt Hazel was always a gracious hostess. Her daughters used to babysit when we moved to Old North Hill.

Recalling the list that I prepared when I moved to Toronto last year, I presented the registry list at Canada Customs when I drove back home and the guard waved me through the gate without an inspection. The value of goods exceeded the allowable $200 limit for a weekend trip.

On Memorial Day weekend, Alberto and I got married at the University of Rochester Interfaith Chapel. Rochester weather reports claimed it was the hottest May 24th on record at one hundred degrees Fahrenheit for years. I was a bit nervous as Dad walked me down the aisle. I almost tripped in the long gown and high heels that I wasn't used to wearing. Everyone stood in the pews and smiled as we passed them. The bridal party pivoted when the music changed to announce my entrance. It felt weird being the center of attention and all eyes watching me. The priest was not feeling well after four ceremonies that day dressed in a heavy white robe and whispered if he could shorten our service, his last one for the day. Alberto nodded in agreement, he was not comfortable in his heavy suit and wanted to get the event over with.

It was a traditional non-religious ceremony. Although Alberto's family and relatives were Catholic, we did not opt for an hour-long mass, just the nuptials to appease everyone on both sides of the aisle. My brother Mark and one of Alberto's cousins stepped up to the altar for the two readings. Immediately following the service, our families and relatives proceeded outside for professional family pictures on a paved walkway with lush greenery and the Genesee River in the background. The other guests drove across town to the reception that was scheduled immediately following the ceremony, and doors opened at 6:30 p.m. in the evening.

Mom made all the arrangements for the Reception at the Hospitality House in Perinton, including the meal, the cake, the flowers, and the invitations. The meal was set up as a buffet with lasagna, chicken, and beef entrees along with hors d'oeures, antipastos, appetizers, and vegetables. I recalled her weekend buffets in the dining room when friends came over for dinner. It was easier than a sit-down meal so everyone could serve themselves and have a variety of choices. All the food was prepared and cooked to perfection. The cake was delicious. The flowers, table settings, and decorations were beautiful. Mom did an excellent job planning all the details. She only organized my wedding.

My sister had a small ceremony in her home state ten years later, and my brother's wives arranged their own weddings and receptions.

We did not have a seating plan except to reserve a few tables in front of the head table for our families and relatives. The guests chose their own seats and sat among friends and some made new friends with ten place settings at each round table. Everyone enjoyed the evening of dinner, open bar, and dancing to a local band.

The band played a mix of soft rock, some polkas and halfway through the evening asked us to line up and form a train while they played an instrumental number. I led the crowd around the venue and ventured outside for a breath of fresh air. Many guests stood up and joined the line; it got the crowd moving and dancing. Alberto and I had the first dance, my dad and I had the second one, and then our guests were invited onto the dance floor for the rest of the evening. At the end we had the traditional garter belt removal, caught by one of the ushers and the bouquet toss, caught by one of Alberto's cousin's girlfriends. We fed each other a piece of cake after the traditional cake cutting. The band did a wonderful job providing the music and mood for these traditions.

At the end of the evening, I changed into a blue empire waist cap sleeve dress and we were escorted out to my car to go to the hotel. We stayed at the same hotel as our out-of-town guests. One of the ushers had my keys for the day to drive to the chapel, the reception, and the hotel. We did not hire a chauffeured limousine for the bridal party; they followed in their own vehicles. An hour later, my brothers and sister and all our cousins knocked on our hotel door with bottles of champagne to continue the celebration. It was a nice surprise to conclude the festivities.

We were pleased that fifty of Alberto's parents' friends and relatives made the trip from Canada for the weekend. One aunt and six-year-old cousin, Serena, from Italy also attended the wedding. We booked rooms at the Marriott Hotel for our out-of-town guests. I invited colleagues from the hospital and close friends from school and Mom invited relatives and family friends that I had known all my life. I was happy that my aunts and uncles flew to Rochester for the weekend to celebrate with us. I enjoyed the friendly atmosphere because I knew everyone and stopped at every table to welcome them and introduce my husband. I was glad that my parents did not invite any doctors from the faculty club. Even though they paid for it, it was my party, not a time to impress his colleagues.

The next day we returned to our apartment in Toronto so Alberto could unload a trunk of clothing and personal items. We did not live together before the wedding. The following day, we flew to San Francisco for a ten-day honeymoon exploring the west coast of California. We rented a car and drove along the Pacific Coast Highway, from San Francisco to San Luis Obispo, visiting my cousins along the way. I was in the driver's seat when the rental car broke down as we traveled through hairpin turns on a cliff overlooking the Pacific Ocean. My life flashed before me as I braked and recalled the skid into a snowbank a few years earlier. Alberto took over the driving and we called the rental company to give us a replacement when we could exit the highway in the next town. We were offered a huge Cadillac to replace our Chevrolet sedan. Alberto was happy to drive in grand style. We stopped in Salinas for lunch at Nepenthe with my cousin, Sandy and her husband, Steve, and later in Los Angeles, we met my cousin, Randy, and his wife, Gail, at Yuk Yuk's.

At midnight, Steve Martin, a famous comedian, presented his new material to the audience. As newlyweds in the front row, we became his target. Everyone laughed at his monologue. At the start of his career in the 1970s, Steve was a writer for comedy shows, the *Smothers Brothers* and *Sonny and Cher*. The Smothers Brothers aired on Sunday evenings after the Ed Sullivan Show, a fantastic night of entertainment. Steve was transitioning to movie roles at the start of the new decade; his film debut was *The Jerk* (1979) and *Dead Men Don't Wear Plaid* (1982). One of my favorite comedians at that time, it was exciting to see him live; we were seated in the front row next to the stage.

As our drive down the Pacific Coast Highway #1 was scary and treacherous when the car broke down in the middle of nowhere, the comedy show transformed our honeymoon into a joyous occasion. We booked a hotel in Marina Del Rey, near Los Angeles Airport, to visit my aunt and uncle in Garden Grove. It was great to see the whole family again with my new husband, after that strange summer visit years earlier before Europe when I dated Greg in Upland. Once we returned to Toronto, Alberto settled into his new home, his first time living independently away from his parents.

My Employment as a Newly Married Woman

During my honeymoon, my employer reorganized due to resignations, including Jason's, the lawyer I worked for. I was aware that he was leaving at the end of the month while I was on my honeymoon. I was not satisfied with his replacement, Don, and requested a transfer, but nothing was available. Jason opened a private legal practice. We maintained a professional relationship for years where he managed my personal legal affairs, and I could rely on him for reference checks at job interviews. I had to start building Canadian connections in my professional network. With all the life-changing moments in my life, including marriage, a new home, and longer commute, I yearned for a new work environment.

I found another job downtown at North American Life Assurance Company (NALACO), where I worked for the next five years, until I went on a permanent maternity leave. I preferred to work downtown, an area I was familiar with, so I could travel a direct route by subway and occasionally shop or attend concerts, movies, and plays in the evenings without returning home and going out again. Alberto met me downtown on those occasions.

During the first two years in a branch office as the Manager's secretary, I coordinated sales training and agent recruiting. However, when two branch offices merged, I was demoted to receptionist due to my low seniority as the last one hired. All the ladies in this merger were single and good friends from years of working and socializing together. As an American and obvious outsider, I felt their ice-cold attitudes towards me. A post on the job board for a Manager's Secretary in the

Facilities Department at the Corporate Headquarters in downtown Toronto appealed to me. I transferred there for the next three years.

When that department expanded due to a corporate merger, Janet, the department manager, offered me a promotion. I was flattered but also nervous with this job offer, because I wasn't used to this type of recognition. A fellow American who also married a Canadian, we shared similar concerns about life in Canada and the USA, both happy to reside north of the border. She was five years older and had been living in Toronto for a decade at that time. She did not have any children. I was four months pregnant but it was not noticeable yet.

Janet called me into her office on a rainy September day, "Margot, as you know the office is expanding and will be moving to a larger building in north Toronto next year."

"Yes, it is very intriguing to be a part of this relocation and involved in the planning process in this department," I said nervously.

"I would like you to move up to Jerome's position as a Facilities Assistant and he will step into a new position as a Project Manager to help plan the relocation." she explained.

"That would be wonderful," smiling, hiding my disappointment knowing I was not planning on returning to work at the new location after the baby was born.

I visited my parents in Rochester the following weekend to go shopping for maternity clothes. I shared my pregnancy news in person since they were aware of my health issues, when my mom visited after my surgery last winter. They were happy that the baby news happened soon after the surgery.

Two weeks later, I wore maternity dresses as my belly started to show. Janet always asked how I was feeling, making sure I could handle the increased responsibility. I played along with her plans to keep my job safe until I was ready to leave it. At the end of October when we had a Halloween dress up day, the Director came down to the department to greet everyone and take pictures. He stared at me and marched into Janet's office, slamming the door. I sensed the tension. A few minutes later, she buzzed me to join the meeting.

In a condescending tone, "What are your plans?" asked Ray. "You never announced your pregnancy."

"At this time, I am not sure," I replied confidently. I inquired about unemployment benefits during the summer and was told I didn't have to say anything until I was ready to give them my two weeks' notice.

Janet looked at me and said, "When is your due date, you are entitled to seventeen weeks off and I will have to hire a replacement in your absence?"

I recalled the bumping in the branch office before I came to this position and replied, "I will let you know when I give notice about my leave." She could figure it out when a baby bump occurred at the midpoint of a nine-month pregnancy.

I sensed another demotion forthcoming. I stopped by Human Resources the next day and they assured me my job was secure until I gave them notice. They put a freeze on job transfers until after the merger took place next summer. I was relieved and continued working for the next five months pretending that nothing was going to change. I left the job on the first day of March 1986 five years after I was hired and submitted my resignation in the middle of June. My maternity benefits ran out at the end of that month.

At that time, my pregnancy and landed immigrant status worked against me. Although employment laws were changing to reflect diversity and challenged human rights abuse in the workplace to protect all employees from discriminatory practices, the private sector didn't enforce the new legal regulations unless the victim challenged their misrepresentation. I kept quiet and played their game until it was time to leave; I had a new career called motherhood to look forward to.

The company relocated to an office tower at Finch, the northernmost stop on the Yonge Street line that summer. As much as I enjoyed these jobs learning new skills, it was a long commute each way by train from Etobicoke in the west to downtown Toronto, adding two hours to my workday. I was also self-conscious of my landed immigrant status, not being Canadian. The five-year anniversary to apply for Canadian citizenship passed and I chose not to, putting that decision off indefinitely. I wanted to leave the door open if I (we) ever decided to relocate back to the USA.

During the years before we started a family, we enjoyed many reunions attending nuptials on both sides of our families as well as a few surprise visits from my Dutch friends.

Family Weddings and Visits

While I was working at the insurance company, we celebrated family weddings in Canada and the USA and welcomed my Dutch friends and family in Canada. It was nice to greet the extended families on both sides each time nuptials occurred and see them again after our wedding. We scheduled our vacations for time off work around these events and traveled together to see the continent and introduced ourselves to our extended families.

In Montreal, the marriage of Alberto's cousin, Georgietta, was more culture shock as French is the first language in Quebec, not English. Although I took French in high school and college, I never used it in Toronto. Alberto's cousins spoke French and Italian fluently, little English. Subjected to Italian conversations between Alberto and his parents at home, I understood the context, following the conversations with ease. It was a beautiful wedding and reception, with food, drink, and dancing.

It was great to experience the Quebec culture in their home and community as my previous visit to Montreal with my high school French Club, toured museums, cathedrals, and historical battlefields. A decade later in the early nineties, her younger sister, Edi, transferred to Toronto for employment. Edi was fluent in all three languages, Italian,

French, and English and a few years younger than me. It was fun to connect with her on weekends to visit Toronto Islands, High Park, and shop at the Eaton Centre since I didn't go downtown very often after my children were born. I never asked her to babysit but she enjoyed hanging out with us and entertaining her younger cousins.

Giovanni and Pasquale, in Willowdale, his cousins who were groomsmen in our wedding, also got married. We traveled to Kanata near Ottawa for one wedding and to Thornhill north of Toronto for the other. These weddings mixed Italian with Eastern European traditions for one ceremony and Greek customs in the other with hundreds of guests. Alberto was asked to do a reading at both ceremonies. Eventually, we celebrated the baptisms of our future children together as Godparents. After annual holiday celebrations with their parents and families during my first decade in Canada, we drifted apart to raise our families and pursue our careers until funerals for the parents and my children's nuptials reunited us with Alberto's extended family.

We also attended weddings for his cousins Paulo and Stefano related through his father's sister's husband in North Bay and Burlington. North Bay was a five-hour drive north of Toronto heading towards Lake Superior. We drove together with Alberto's parents for the weekend and saw many of the same relatives that came to our wedding in Rochester. It was fun to attend these authentic Italian weddings and reconnect with his relatives that had moved to Canada.

In the spring, Dad broke his leg skiing. I drove to Rochester to visit him. It shocked me seeing my hero, in pain with his leg in a cast, helpless. "Hi Dad, how are you? What happened?"

"Your brother and I wanted to hit the slopes one last time and I fell at the bottom of the hill at the end of the day," he said calmly. "The Ski Patrol were alerted, quickly rescued me, called an ambulance, and another friend drove David home."

"You have been skiing for a long time without getting hurt before," I cried seeing my dad in so much pain. He put his arms out for me to lean into a hug.

"I enjoyed twenty years of skiing and happy you kids embraced the sport," Dad continued. "I'm glad we joined the ski club, they acted quickly to get help, something that might not happen at the larger ski resorts around here."

"I liked skiing but after introducing it to Alberto, he was not interested, he preferred ice skating and hockey," I sighed. "I went a few times with a girlfriend by bus from Toronto to Blue Mountain. When she married and moved away, I gave it up."

"You can always come home for a weekend and take David skiing, I will keep the membership going for him while he is in high school," Dad replied.

"I will keep that in mind, Dad," I said. "Maybe Alberto will reconsider too." The following winter I came home alone a few times to go skiing with David. I didn't like long distance driving in snow, but I made the effort to keep my promise to my father. David was sixteen, with a learner's permit, so I let him practice driving to the ski hill in winter driving conditions. David joined the school ski team and had lots of friends to enjoy the sport together.

"Look Margot," Dad sighed, "I don't know if I can make it to your brother, Paul's wedding in Denver this summer. Would you and Alberto take David, to the wedding?"

Without hesitation, I said, "Sure, of course, I will look after him. Alberto and I are planning a week's vacation to visit Yellowstone and the Grand Tetons in Wyoming before the ceremony."

"Thanks Margot. I knew I could count on you. What about Alberto?" Dad asked.

"Dad, I will let him know when I get home that we are bringing David. They get along well, like brothers," I said.

"Maybe I'll call him on the phone too," Dad said. "He may prefer to hear the request directly from me. Make your flight reservations from Rochester and I will reimburse you."

Six months later we embarked on a vacation with my little brother that reminded me of the family road trips in my youth before he was born.

I laughed each time people asked me, "Is that boy your son?" reacting, "No, he was my baby brother, and we attended a family wedding together." We had a twelve-year age difference between us. I could not imagine being a teenaged mother, that memory haunted me.

The following summer we traveled to my cousin Will's wedding at Cape Cod. An exciting road trip, driving east along Lake Ontario to Montreal and then south through New England to the Cape. A grand affair, with an outdoor wedding on his fiance's family property. A fun family reunion with all my cousins on my dad's side of the family. They ended the evening sailing into the sunset. Our road trip continued south along the Atlantic coast to New York City, Philadelphia, and Washington DC, visiting historic sites and attending major league baseball games. Will moved his family back to Japan where he grew up for several years, so we lost contact, but always stayed connected through Christmas cards and updates through his mother, my Aunt Toni, whenever she visited my parents in Rochester.

In June 1983, ten years after my first European adventure, Elly and Peter arrived in Canada. They flew to Toronto with friends who had relatives in Ottawa. I scheduled a week off work to welcome them to my home.

I sat on my veranda waiting for their arrival in the middle of the afternoon. When I went inside to answer the phone, I saw their RV pull into our driveway so I ended the call. I loved hosting them in my home. They removed their luggage and placed it on the sidewalk leading to the veranda.

They pivoted to wave goodbye to their friends who left to set up their campsite. We grabbed the luggage and entered my house. I showed them the basement family room where the sofa bed was ready for their use. I pointed to the bathroom at the other end of the basement and told them they could shower upstairs in the main bathroom.

Elly and I hugged each other with three kisses on each cheek. She pointed to her husband, "Do you remember Peter?" He attended Winkler Prins in classes a year ahead of us."

Peter leaned in for a hug and three kisses and said, "I was a friend of Pete's, the family you lived with in Stadskanaal."

"Sorry, I don't remember you or much about that family. It was not a good time for me," I replied. "His mother always cooked pea soup for supper, not my favorite food."

"You did not stay there very long, about two months." he recalled.

"Because it happened in the middle of the school year, the YFU representative wanted to make my transition as smooth as possible," I explained. "She convinced Mevrouw Dirkse to take me in for the remaining months since her son was scheduled to go to America that summer. It was fantastic that I could retain my connection to Jeannet's family, the school, my friends, and after school activities. When I noticed Mama was feeling better in May of that year, Jeannet and I begged for my return for the remainder of my stay."

Elly commented, "Yes it was nice that you did not have to start over and visit Jeannet often."

"She plans to visit here in Canada at the end of the summer. She will be working at a camp in Michigan," I smiled. "I am looking forward to seeing her again."

"Are you hungry for lunch?" I asked. I prepared a tray of bread, cheese and ham slices earlier. "Can I offer you a drink?"

Peter suggested, "Do you have tea and we can have a sandwich with it?"

"Yes, I forgot about the afternoon tea tradition." I admitted. "Have a seat at the table."

A few minutes later I served the tea with quartered ham and cheese sandwiches. Alberto arrived home from work, I introduced them, and he grabbed a cold beer from the fridge and sat down with us.

"Are you familiar with baseball? The Toronto Blue Jays are playing at home this weekend," Alberto asked. "We could go downtown for a game."

"We don't have it back home, but I've watched it on television," Peter said. "It would be nice to attend a game in person."

"There are a lot of things to do while you are here," I said. "Downtown Toronto has a lot of shopping, CN Tower, Royal Ontario Museum, Harbour Front, and a ferry to the islands. Another day we could go to the Toronto Zoo and take another day to visit Niagara Falls."

Elly smiled, "That sounds like a lot of fun. It will be a busy week as tourists."

It was nice that our spouses were comfortable around each other; sports were always a safe bet to bring guys together. We ate at various restaurants around the city, to experience the culture and vibe of big city international living, quite different from the small towns in The Netherlands. After a week, their friends returned with the RV, and they departed on a camping trip exploring the provinces of Ontario and Quebec as well as parts of New England for three weeks. They spent a month in North America, and it was a pleasure to host Elly and Peter in my home.

Elly was like a sister to me as we exchanged letters frequently describing our lives, our feelings, and our travels. She wrote in Dutch, and I wrote in English, so we both improved our language skills. I often read her letters to myself out loud to practice speaking the language. After the tragic death of her sister, our sisterly bond grew stronger.

Jeannet visited Toronto in August for two summers after her summer camp ended in Michigan while attending the University of Groningen. She loved combining work with travel and visiting North America for the first time in her life.

She had a full itinerary visiting friends in various cities around the country. She sent me postcards with dates, names, phone numbers and addresses where I could reach her, long before cell phones, email and texting allowed instant long-distance communication. She was not afraid to travel alone and visiting friends made it a safe journey to save money on food and lodging. I was thrilled that she enjoyed travelling outside the EU. Our sisterly bond was strengthened during her visits.

In the middle of August, I met Jeannet at the Bus Station in downtown Toronto. She looked radiant having enjoyed her summer abroad. She collected her luggage and ran down the platform when she saw me.

"Lieve Margot, good to see you!" she said excitedly.

"Jeannet, I am glad you came to Canada to visit my home," as I hugged her and we kissed on three cheeks. "Tell me about your adventure here in America."

Jeannet said, "I don't know where to start. It was so much fun working with the children, teaching them to draw and paint."

"It is a lot of fun teaching young children," I smiled, "They listen and want to learn. What have you done since leaving the camp three weeks ago?"

"I sent you my itinerary where I would be visiting my friends, other counselors that worked at the camp," She laughed.

"Yes, you had a busy vacation after the camp, traveling around the country. How did it go?" I asked.

Jeannet smiled, "I absolutely love it here. I have made a lot of friends, speaking English, visiting many historical places and shopping."

"We will do a lot of that here in Toronto for the next few days so you can experience both American and Canadian culture. On Friday, we will drive to Niagara Falls to meet my mother and brother and you will spend time with them in Rochester. I know June will take you to the museum and art gallery and of course you can swim in her backyard pool. David is growing up fast since you last saw him." I explained to her that my parents recently separated and no longer lived together, but Dad had access to the children and visited often, so that she was prepared for it.

Excited and smiling, "That will be wonderful. I am looking forward to it. It has been ten years since they visited us at Christmas in Veendam. That was a lot of fun."

"I don't like to drive downtown; my car is parked at the subway station close to my home," I sighed. "I hope you don't mind a train ride and I can take your handbag so you can drag your suitcase up and down the stairs?"

"You know me Margot, I don't mind traveling by bus and trains. I don't drive back home," she said.

An hour later, we arrived at my house and I showed her the basement where she would be sleeping. I was thrilled to have more guests from Europe that summer. She took a nap, showered and settled in while I unpacked groceries and prepared some food for dinner. Alberto would be late, attending a baseball game after work that day. When she came upstairs, she made the salad while I cooked the pizza. It was nice to have her company as we caught up on our lives. When we sat down to eat dinner, I handed her two letters addressed to her that arrived a few days earlier.

"When did you receive these letters?" she asked anxiously. The postmarks were smudged.

"One came last week and the other yesterday," I replied. "Good timing as the mail delivery in Canada is very slow,".

"I was getting worried because none of my friends received mail for me and I gave Mama their addresses and dates like I sent you," she remarked.

"I also got a separate letter from Mama and she wrote it a few weeks ago and sent to me so that it would arrive in time for your visit here," I showed it to her. "She told your boyfriend to do the same."

"I am happy that he spoke to her and took her advice. I missed him this summer and this is the only letter I received from him," she started crying. I hugged her and assured her that his letter meant he was thinking of her. She wiped her tears with her napkin and felt a little better.

After we cleaned up the dinner, we went for a walk and I showed her the neighborhood. She looked at the paper map I left on the table to show her where her Canadian adventure would lead.

She was getting excited and said, "This is easy to follow. I love Toronto and I saw your bus stop around the corner." The public transit network (TTC) was a grid that was easy to navigate and tokens cost a dollar at that time, very affordable.

I booked a week off work for her visit, so I could entertain her. Alberto did not take vacation days so that she and I could bond alone. It was a fun girl's week together. On Friday, we drove to Niagara Falls and crossed the border to the American side where we met my mother for lunch. We were flagged to stop at the Customs building to get her passport stamped. When we arrived at the Niagara Falls Parking Lot, we found my mother and David and Jeannet transferred her luggage to mom's station wagon.

Mom enjoyed entertaining her with David, as they were both young adults who were easy to please and interested in visiting historical and cultural places; they were happy to spend a few days together. My Dad and David treated her to a Rochester Red Wings baseball game, her first time in an outdoor baseball stadium that she thoroughly enjoyed as it was not a European sport. She was booked to fly home at the end of August from Rochester with her overseas connection in Boston, Massachusetts.

She sent thank you notes to all her hosts when she arrived home. Mom and I received separate letters of gratitude.

She wrote, "Lieve Margot, I really enjoyed visiting you and seeing where you lived. I am curious if you would allow me to move to Toronto and live with you after I graduate from university? I could stay in your basement and find my way around Toronto myself and apply for school employment. Please think about it and let me know. Veel liefs, zusje, Jeannet."

I wanted to help her but also knew Alberto would not appreciate a boarder in our home, especially in his man cave where he blasted his stereo and worked out. We only had one full bathroom on the main floor of our bungalow for three adults to share, not a good fit.

I wrote back a few days later,

"Lieve Jeannet, I enjoyed our visit immensely. We developed a beautiful familial relationship these past ten years. I hope you felt welcome to visit me again. You will always be my little sister. Moving to Canada was a very long and difficult process to apply for immigration when I moved here. The government does not recognize diplomas from foreign countries. School boards may expect you to attend a Canadian university to get a Canadian teaching credential."

"I am trying to get pregnant to have a baby so our family will be expanding. Alberto does not want anyone else living in our home. I believe Mama and Papa would prefer that you stay in Europe to teach, there are many countries for you to pursue opportunities much closer to your home. I am sorry that I can't honor your request but you are always welcome to come back for a visit. Veel Liefs, zusje, Margot."

When she returned home, her boyfriend ended their relationship. Sadly, this was the last time I saw Jeannet in person. She continued her university program in Groningen, but this breakup depressed her, affecting everything in her life. Her mother and sister wrote letters describing her anxiety, seeking medical and psychiatric assistance for her. Jeannet refused treatment and eventually gave up hope.

A year after our visit, at twenty-three years old, she ended her life on October 5, 1984. She hung herself in the shower of her dormitory, devastated over the breakup from her boyfriend. This was truly the saddest day of my life coping with the tragic death of my adopted little sister. Her favorite song was "I Just Called to Say I Love You," by Stevie Wonder. Each October, as Canada marked Thanksgiving, I cooked a turkey feast in her honor and quietly prayed for her peace. I often wondered if I should have sponsored Jeannet's immigration to Canada and welcomed her into my home. Were her visits and letters to me a cry for help? At that time, I could not offer a lending hand to my dearest friend.

Six months later, another tragedy struck a family friend. Kelly, who I babysat in high school and accompanied her family to Cape Cod after my year abroad, passed away. On her eighteenth birthday, walking home from a party, a hit and run accident by a drunk driver ended her life. My parents showed me the obituary in the Rochester newspaper when I came home for a weekend visit. Learning about another young friend's fatal accident was devastating. I stayed in touch with her parents via annual Christmas greetings and we met for lunch at their home in the Finger Lakes region of central New York state, decades later to reflect on family blessings.

Mama and Eva exchanged letters describing their grief. Papa retired from the bank to enjoy time traveling with Mama in their golden years. Five years after losing her youngest child, Mama visited me in Toronto and my mother in Rochester. I was pleased that she maintained our familial bond after Jeannet's untimely death. You could sense her sadness; death of your child was heartbreaking. Mama and Papa would remain my adopted parents for the rest of their lives and we kept in touch with annual letters, holiday cards, gifts and photographs. It would be more than two decades before I returned to The Netherlands for a visit.

I often thought about these young ladies whose lives ended abruptly, heartbroken by their tragedies. In the prime of their lives on both sides of the ocean, who I knew personally, they looked down on me like angels.

Motherhood Begins (mid 1980s)

During all the excitement of our first five years of marriage, I discovered that I could not bear children due to infertility. I experienced anxiety remembering the accident when Alberto and I first met. I thought about adoption while Alberto imagined a glamourous life without children. After six months of trying, my family physician suggested, I come back after a year if nothing happens. After that time, he referred me to an obstetrician / gynecologist (OB/GYN) in Bloor West Village with admitting privileges to St. Joseph's Health Centre. Endometriosis was a painful condition; tissue grew outside the uterus affected my reproductive organs. I endured terrible menstrual cramps for years. It was a long five-year struggle of doctor appointments, procedures, and medications to treat the disease.

The devastating losses of Gineke, Jeannet, and Kelly gave me the strength, courage, and determination to conquer this disease. In February 1985, I had surgery to open my blocked tubes and became pregnant three months later. I was forever grateful to my OB/GYN physician, Dr. Stone, a pioneer infertility specialist in Toronto who performed the surgery, and monitored my pregnancies, deliveries, and post-partum care during the 1980s.

Surprisingly, it was an easy pregnancy without morning sickness, and I worked at the insurance company in downtown Toronto until a week before my due date. However, I endured forty hours of labor before giving birth to my baby girl. A year later, he recommended we try again, and on my daughter's second birthday, I learned that I was pregnant.

I raked leaves one afternoon outside my home in early November while my daughter napped. As soon as I relaxed with a cup of tea, I felt the first contraction when Alberto came home from work. He summoned his parents to babysit the big sister while we rushed to the hospital. A more difficult and exhausting pregnancy, my son came into the world three weeks early on a Friday evening after eight hours of labor at 11 p.m. that evening.

Although it was customary practice for women to learn the gender of their babies during their pregnancy journey, my babies' sexes were not revealed during my ultrasounds. I watched the screen and imagined the sex but couldn't confirm it, keeping it a surprise. I noticed a difference in how I felt and carried each baby, which led me to believe they were different sexes. Both times, I gave birth naturally without a caesarian section. I stayed in hospital for five days of rest. I connected with a local La Leche League group for breastfeeding coaching and social support that met monthly for moms and babies to share stories of our childrearing journeys. I attended these meetings for four years.

My children automatically became dual citizens at birth of the USA and Canada with parents from both countries. I registered their births at the American Consulate in Toronto. They possessed two passports, one from each country, for their use when traveling across the border while they were in school.

I pursued my passion for handmade crafts while I was home with my young children. I asked my mother-in-law to babysit on Wednesdays so that I could attend a weaving class at the local community center. My mother gave me a twenty-inch floor loom to make placemats and other small household items. She had a larger loom in Rochester and enjoyed weaving household items and wanted to pass her passion on to me.

I joined a weavers' guild to get acquainted with local weavers and learn more about the craft. The leader of the guild asked their youngest and newest member to join their executive committee; they needed fresh ideas for programs at their monthly meetings.

New to the craft, volunteering, and non-profit organization leadership, I welcomed the challenge. I networked with artists who specialized in a variety of handicrafts to join our meetings and shared their passions in lectures and demonstrations. The guild members learned basket weaving, spinning, macrame, and viewed slide shows of weaving and crafts in countries around the world that members visited. The ladies enjoyed cuddling with my baby when I brought one to the monthly meetings. I became fond of handmade items I bought at craft shows to decorate my future homes because I appreciated the creativity, patience, time, and effort to produce a masterpiece.

It was tough adjusting to a single income household, but we made it work. We did not travel anywhere with our young children except to visit their grandparents in Rochester. As a stay-at-home mother, I could visit anytime, for as long as I wished, without work commitments. I enjoyed reconnecting with my Rochester friends who were also young parents, a nice social environment for our toddlers.

The Canadian government had a generous baby bonus benefit to supplement our income as new parents. The government issued a monthly check for each child until they reached age eighteen. It was deposited into separate accounts for the children that were later transferred to them after they finished school to create their own nest egg when they embarked on their careers.

I joined a few moms and tots' groups in the community to bridge the gap until school started. The children and I enjoyed a toy lending library, story time at the public library, and Gymboree, a physical activity program for toddlers. They attended nursery school a few mornings per week to prepare them for kindergarten and baby swimming lessons to get them used to the water for future vacations. I really enjoyed my new role as a stay-at-home mother, totally involved in their childhood development and introduced them to social situations designed for toddlers. I nurtured friendships with other mothers during that time and we often exchanged babysitting so that the children could play together at our homes.

As the children approached kindergarten, we had to decide on their school enrollment. After much discussion about the schools nearby our home, we chose to move to a bigger newer house in another city bordering Toronto. The sale of our current home and search for a new one became an exciting challenge factoring in the cost, the location, the amenities, and the children's activities. We moved to Mississauga, west of Toronto on the other side of the airport that was developing into a bedroom community for Toronto commuters and offered many opportunities for families with young children.

Chapter 11

Mississauga Beckons (1990 – 2010)

New Home, New School

After nine years living in a small bungalow in an older neighborhood, it was time to relocate to a new neighborhood where we were more comfortable raising our young family. In Canada, there were two years of half day kindergarten starting at age four, while I had one year of half day kindergarten at age five in the USA. There were two school boards, a public and separate (Catholic) to direct your tax support defined by law dating back to Confederation in 1867. Proof of baptism in the Catholic Church and one Catholic parent were requirements for elementary students to attend the separate school board. We chose to raise the children in the Catholic religion at their births to respect their paternal lineage. They were both baptized as infants at St. Gregory Church in Etobicoke and Alberto's cousins stood as godparents.

Mississauga was rapidly developing from a farm community with the lowest tax base in Metropolitan Toronto in the 1990s into a bedroom community for commuters who worked in Toronto. The location on the west side of the airport was ideal for Alberto's commute to work and for my commute to Rochester to visit my family. At that time, we bought a two-storey home, double the size of our bungalow, for the same price that we sold it, so we could make this move without an additional mortgage.

We moved in with Alberto's parents for three months from the closing of our bungalow until the closing of our new home. His parents gave us the second floor for sleeping and they moved to their basement family room. We ate all meals together. Out of respect and their generosity, I adapted to their daily routines and did not interfere with meal preparation. They babysat a few days per week when I drove to Mississauga to monitor the progress, chose design elements, and bought furnishings for the new home. It was fun but challenging to decorate a larger home.

There was 2,500 square feet of living space on the inside curve of a crescent with a fenced backyard on the south side facing the kitchen and the large front yard facing the street with the driveway and garage on the north side of the home. The back of the home was set close to the property line adjacent to the neighbor's home. There were six homes on the outside curve across the street. Our home had four large bedrooms on the second floor with two bathrooms. The fourth bedroom, the smallest above the front foyer was used as a study where I had a desk and small closet for coats to move downstairs when the seasons changed. The basement remained unfinished while we lived there so the children could run, play, throw balls, and shoot pucks. The living room and dining room were separated by the front door foyer with large dome windows facing east to catch the sunlight throughout the day. We installed a basketball net on the driveway to shoot hoops.

The builder laid the grass after completing all the homes in the new subdivision, two years after we moved into our new home. During that time, we explored the city, looking for parks, playgrounds, malls, and libraries. We enjoyed our weekly visit to the library to exchange books and attend story time. Listening to the librarians enthusiastically read out loud to children, engaging them in songs and simple crafts, sparked my interest to consider a future career working with children, reviving my dream that I abandoned in college.

I enrolled them in a nursery school program for a year at a local church in the morning a few days per week to prepare them for kindergarten receiving two hours of age-appropriate structured group activities. All parents were required to volunteer one morning each month and provide a group snack. I prepared the volunteer schedule, communicating with the parents to assign their duty. It was a nice way to meet and greet the nursery school community.

We discovered Streetsville Memorial Park, an ideal playground with swings, a slide, and climbing gym. Set against the Credit River, it had a walking path that extended for miles. A natural large rock formation along the path next to the river encouraged the children to climb and jump across the rocks. The river was renowned for a salmon run where we saw fishermen in high boots roam into the water to cast their poles. It was a peaceful environment to encourage my children to play together. I enjoyed the privilege and opportunity to stay home, nurtured them, and explored our new neighborhood.

This park was home to the Vic Johnson Community Centre with an outdoor pool in summer and an indoor skating rink, where Andy learned to skate and play hockey soon after he started walking. I enjoyed watching the toddlers skate around the ice and learn to shoot the puck, a Canadian sports tradition for all ages. House league hockey remained a part of his schedule until high school graduation. I saved his hockey jerseys with his name and number glued to the back and passed them on to his son.

He also pursued self-defense training while attending elementary school. He wore white pants and a robe to learn the Chinese Martial Art of Kung Fu progressing through the belt classes. I proudly watched his classes and observed his evaluations when he progressed to the next level. The instructor taught the young children how to fight without injuring their opponent.

He played house league soccer every summer through high school and later worked as a soccer referee for the younger teams. Accompanying Andy to his soccer and hockey games and practices, made me proud.

Jess joined a jazz dance class on Saturday mornings at a community center. At the end of the session, they performed a recital for the parents where they dressed in costumes made by community volunteers. At age five, all the girls dressed as Tigger and danced to Winnie the Pooh music. She also wore her orange and black striped body suit with a separate hood and tail for Halloween in the fall. She continued the dance lessons through grade eight wearing different costumes each year that I saved for future grandchildren.

She joined a gymnastics club after school. I enjoyed watching her perform aerial flips and cartwheels, without fear, more daring than my gymnastics class as a teenager. She continued gymnastics through high school, charting her community service hours, a graduation requirement in the 2000s.

At age eight, she joined a girls soccer league and progressed to a rep team where she played other teams across the region and weekend tournaments across the province. Alberto was the assistant coach of that team keeping them both involved at an elevated level of competition through her high school years.

These extracurricular activities kept the family busy throughout the year from the time they entered elementary school until they graduated high school. Often, we would eat an early dinner or take-out meals and proceed to separate activities. It not only gave the children exercise and training in sports, but also taught them self-confidence, discipline, and team-building skills that would follow them throughout life to college and their careers. We took turns alternating between the children's activities before Alberto started coaching, so that both parents could bond with the children separately in their activities.

Due to the hectic nature of their sports schedules and enrollment cost, we did not travel to faraway places. We introduced the children to Disneyland in California and Disneyworld in Florida and one summer we returned to my favorite ocean playground, Cape Cod. They enjoyed these vacations as school aged children. We connected with my cousins and their growing families on the California coast traveling the same route of our honeymoon twenty years earlier. In Florida, I introduced the family to Marvin and Carol and their daughter Dia when we met for breakfast one day. In Cape Cod, we explored the peninsula from one end to the other enjoying the sand dunes and swimming in the ocean. They were pleased to swim in both the Atlantic and Pacific Oceans on these holidays. Alberto also treated the children to major league baseball games in Los Angeles and Boston so they could experience the vibe of different ball parks across the country. We scheduled these vacations on school breaks following the Canadian school year calendar and I eventually worked for the school board so that I would be home with them during their school breaks.

We also enjoyed two more visitors from the Netherlands. I was pleased when Ankie wrote that she joined a camp in Algonquin Park in northern Ontario in the summer of 1999. Flying to and from Toronto, we arranged to meet before her adventure began. I welcomed her to my home in Mississauga, spoke Dutch, and showed her the community. She also accompanied me to the children's soccer games in the evenings. We took a day trip to Niagara Falls, a must see for all my out-of-town guests. We missed each other on my last trip to Europe twenty years earlier, so it was wonderful to connect again.

In 2005, Eva's daughter, Julia, pursued a student exchange in Batavia, New York, a small town between Rochester and Buffalo through the Rotary Club. Eva and her two sons, Sjoerd and Victor, arrived for a visit at the end of her stay to go camping in Algonquin Park. She rented a car, drove to Batavia to pick up Julia and borrowed camping equipment from her host family to embark on a wilderness road trip. They returned to my home in Mississauga three weeks later at the end of their vacation, camping in our basement. As Julia and Sjoerd were the same age as my children, everyone enjoyed a fun time together.

We moved to another home in Mississauga with an inground swimming pool the year before, a beautiful place to entertain our European family. I took Eva grocery shopping to an Asian grocery store, to make Bahmi (rice) and Nasi (noodles) Gorengs, Indonesian rijsttafels (rice table or stir-fry) to feed the hungry teenagers. At that time, I was not aware of any Dutch grocery stores in the region and could not find them on the Internet, so we improvised the recipes according to the ingredients we found in the grocery stores. When they returned to Europe, I packed the camping gear into my car to return it to Julia's host family in Batavia and visited my family in Rochester.

Re-enter the Workforce and Back to School

For five years, the children rode a bus to a temporary school. During that time, I worked as a lunchroom supervisor for one hour each day to monitor the children as they ate their homemade bagged lunches in the gym before proceeding outside for forty minutes of recess in the schoolyard. I volunteered in their classrooms, computer lab, and library for one period, or seventy-five minutes, every morning before the lunch period, and often stayed for another seventy-five-minute period after lunch if a teacher required my assistance.

I was thrilled to have a warm relationship with this school community, which trusted me to work with students individually and in small groups to improve their reading, writing, and computer skills. I loved getting back into the workforce, even though I was volunteering, after nearly a decade at home. It was a nice change of pace to get out of the house and interact with teachers and students. I also assisted the teacher-librarian with circulation and basic cataloguing duties, stimulating my mind. I truly enjoyed it, an early sign of where my career would eventually lead.

The library technician program evolved into online learning inspiring me to pursue additional college courses to complete my Bachelor of Science and Master of Library Science degrees online over the next decade, finishing what I had started three decades earlier. It was a rough start, but once I got into the groove of my education, I really enjoyed it. It challenged me both intellectually and technically, and I was extremely excited to finally have a degree in my hand that would make my mother proud. I was the only one in my family in my forties without a degree, and it felt like a significant accomplishment to finally achieve that goal.

My mother also returned to school in her fifties to pursue a Bachelor of Education and a Master of Library Science, after I moved to Canada. She worked in elementary school libraries in Irondequoit for more than a decade before retiring at the age of seventy. I often brought the children into her library when we visited so they could see where their grandmother worked. I didn't want to become a teacher, but observing my mother's workplace, I wanted to follow in her footsteps working in a library. She had a major influence on my entire life.

My parents showed me an advertisement in a Rochester newspaper of an innovative program at Empire State College, affiliated with the

State University of New York, where mature students could create their own degree plan using their work and volunteer experience as credits towards an undergraduate degree. The program was offered online to serve students around the world. My dad covered my tuition, a promise he made to me years earlier when I dropped out, to encourage me to return to school. I truly appreciated my parents' emotional and financial support, especially since my husband was non-committal. Computer technology was constantly changing. It was challenging to keep up with the technical aspects of online learning, an exciting adventure.

I discovered that my volunteer work on the executive committees of the Weavers Guild of Etobicoke, the Roseborough Residents Association, and Friends of the Library, Mississauga, during the 1990s, when I was a stay-at-home mother, demonstrated business management skills that qualified for credits towards a Bachelor of Science degree. I forwarded college transcripts from Elmira, Nazareth, and Sheridan Colleges to transfer lower-level college credits that were valid twenty years later. I needed thirty-two senior-level credits or eight senior-level courses in Business and Information Technology Management for graduation.

The terrorist attacks of September 11, 2001, delayed the start of the program for two weeks. I met online students who had family members directly affected by the World Trade Center explosions. It encouraged me to take an International News Perspectives course as a business elective, where I researched world news reports and discussed the impact they had on international foreign policies. The experience provided me with a broader perspective on the world as a whole and enabled me to continue expanding my understanding of global politics and America's role on the global stage. I completed this program in three years, taking two courses each semester.

In the summer of 2004, I picked up my mother in Rochester and we drove to Saratoga Springs, near Albany, New York, for the weekend to attend my graduation ceremony with one hundred other mature students who also designed their own degree programs. She was delighted that I graduated from college thirty years after I started, fulfilling a long-abandoned dream.

While working in the school libraries, I joined the Ontario Library Association (OLA) for professional development. I became involved with the Forest of Reading program that promoted reading to all age groups in the schools as a book selector and reviewer at the White Pine level for high school students, as well as an author representative at the annual Forest Festival in the spring in downtown Toronto, where students from all over Ontario gathered to vote on their favorite books.

At one of their annual conferences, I learned about an online Master of Library and Information Science (MLIS) Degree program for Teacher Librarians at San Jose State University (SJSU). I approached the school representative, a silver-haired middle-aged gentleman whose nametag shined on his lapel, and started a conversation, "Hi, Dan."

He noted my badge. "Nice to meet you, Margot."

"This program for Ontario Teachers," I asked, "is it open to all library staff?"

"The program targets teacher librarians to pursue a master's degree in library science," he explained. "We've advertised it for a year, and there hasn't been enough interest to run the program in Ontario."

Nancy, standing near us, who I would come to learn was a teacher librarian from Brantford (Wayne Gretzky's hometown near Hamilton, Ontario), tuned in: "I'm a teacher librarian who signed up for the course. Have there been other enrollments?"

Dan sighed. "Unfortunately, not. The school will refund your fees if you've paid them."

"No, I haven't been billed yet," she said. "I guess that's why I haven't heard anything from them."

Nancy and I became good friends over the five years that we pursued the online program together. We met for lunch in Burlington, Ontario, a few times, which was the halfway point between our homes.

Dan pivoted towards me and explained, "Margot, you don't have to be a teacher to enroll in the program. It's open to anyone who works in any school, public, or university library. What's your current position in the school?"

Smiling and recalling my successful meeting with the guidance counselor years ago, I said, "I'm a library technician in a high school, responsible for the catalogue, circulation, and system maintenance. I don't have the teaching certificate."

"Are you ready for a change?" he asked. "It's an intense program that would take a year or two full-time, longer if you pursue it part-time."

"I've heard there are residency requirements. What does that mean? California is far away, and I have a busy family life," I chuckled.

Dan laughed. "The residency was contingent on local enrollment and would occur in Ontario during the summer when teachers are off work. You can pursue the entire degree online and just show up for graduation, or we can mail you the degree."

"That is very appealing," I said, already sensing that I was going to pursue this regardless of my husband's approval. "How do I apply?"

He handed me the school brochure. "Have a look at our website, it tells you everything you need to know, and here's my business card. If you have any questions, call or email me anytime."

I put the brochure in my bag with the other paraphernalia I'd collected that day and excused myself to view the different exhibits. Over the next few months, I reviewed everything online and spoke with my parents during my spring break visit. They were ecstatic that I was finally taking my post-secondary education seriously and promised to pay for my tuition as a birthday gift.

Upon acceptance, I enrolled in my first two courses the following September. I met people from all over the USA online, working on group projects and chatting during office hours, a stimulating and rewarding experience for the next four years until I completed the graduation portfolio to earn that degree.

At the next OLA conference, I met Dan at the SJSU booth, re-introduced myself, and informed him of my pursuit. After chatting for an hour, he asked me, "Can you cover the booth while I take a lunch break?"

"Sure, I'd love to," I said, "but I'm not familiar with the program to answer questions."

"I trust that you'll be fine." He smiled. "Good Luck, I'll see you later."

I was nervous about whether I would be able to sell the program for him but felt proud that he trusted me to leave it in my hands. As it turned out, I secured a list of a dozen prospective students from all over Ontario in his absence. He packed his props to fly back to California, giving me the SJSU teddy bear and some promotional items like pens and bookmarks.

I met Dan a third time the following year at the Toronto conference, and he encouraged me to join the American Library Association (ALA) to attend their annual conference in June and volunteer with the Young Adult Library Staff Association (YALSA). I attended annual conferences in Philadelphia, Orlando, San Francisco, and Las Vegas, and volunteered on virtual committees for the next ten years. Although I never secured a professional librarian position during my career, I enjoyed the networking opportunities provided through my ALA and OLA memberships.

While pursuing my master's degree online, I researched, designed projects, and conducted interviews with librarians on various aspects of library operations at regional academic and public libraries for my graduation portfolio. I toured the University of Guelph and Brock University's libraries while my children attended those schools. I enjoyed discovering how libraries functioned in Ontario and how they related to the concepts taught in class while working full-time in high school libraries.

At the turn of the century, online learning was emerging into an innovative and immersive virtual technological learning environment. It was also nice to study at my own pace in my own space, as I had always struggled with weekly deadlines and classroom settings in the past. At that time, SJSU was the only graduate school offering an online format, where all classes, lectures, and office hours with professors took place virtually.

Projects involved both individual and group research studies. I worked with students across Canada and the USA, communicating through the school's online portal designing marketing plans, book trailers, and library programs for all age groups. I created case studies using local library data, which I gathered through observations and interviews with professional librarians. In the final course, I worked one-on-one with a faculty advisor, Debbie, an Associate Director of the library school, to create my portfolio that included assignments from all my classes encompassing the "Fourteen Competencies of Library Science." I received a perfect score and she wrote a glowing reference for my future endeavors. I appreciated that she recognized all my hard work and the progress that I had made.

Again, I embraced the technological demands of graduate school, same as I had at the undergrad level, determined to finish the program and attend my graduation in person. The school changed learning management platforms three times during my tenure. It was difficult to adapt to the new technology before classes resumed. At age fifty-five, I reached my goal and walked across the auditorium stage in San Jose, California, wearing a cap and gown. I went to the ceremony alone to meet classmates and professors whom I had worked with online. It was rewarding to finish my education and receive the degree in person.

I volunteered in various library-related projects and committees for professional development and networking purposes through my membership with the Ontario Library Association. I signed up as a selector and judge for the Forest of Reading Program that sent books to every school in the province. Representing the White Pine category for high school students, the committee read fifty young adult novels published by Canadian authors to choose the top ten books to present to every school in the province the following year.

One year, I hosted a children's author at the Festival of Trees, where children voted for their favorite book in each age category, an annual event at Harbourfront in downtown Toronto. Over the course of the school year before the festival, I received contact information of the author I was assigned to, a lady from Alberta, and we met over email. She sent me an autographed copy of her children's book and a promotional blurb to read when it was time to introduce her at the ceremony.

At Harborfront, we met in person at a coffee reception for the authors and spent the rest of the day together. She was pleased that her book was selected in the top ten for the White Pine category and I was pleased that my nomination of her book made it to the final round. At the end of the day, we walked around Harbourfront and celebrated over dinner. It was the fifth and final year that I volunteered in the Forest of Reading Program, a fabulous celebration to conclude my association with that program.

I learned about the Benjamin Franklin Award sponsored by the Independent Book Publishers Association (IBPA), in the exhibit hall at an ALA Conference. I applied to become a volunteer judge in one of 150 categories. This was an interesting assignment to read 50 books in a category and complete an assessment evaluating the format, design, and content of each book, selecting the top ten of the collection I received. I arranged for the books to be shipped to my parents in Rochester and retrieved them the weekend after they arrived to save on shipping costs and mailing delays by sending the books across the border to Canada. Two other judges were also assigned the same category anonymously. I was assigned to distinct categories each year, ranging from Children's to Self-Help and Young Adult Fiction. I was pleased that I always selected at least one of the top three books each year.

As this was a voluntary position with "free books," I could not sell them, so I donated most of the titles to my school and local public libraries, as public funding and operating budgets were declining at that time and saved the rest for my future grandchildren and my daughter's classroom. This initiative required a six-month commitment from September to March for two deliveries of books, one in September and the other in December. I devoted five years to this organization but found the timelines getting too tight to manage with later shipping dates and earlier judging deadlines. Being exposed to various genres and the debut writings of new authors, I appreciated their challenges and wondered if I could one day become a published author.

Reflections on my library career

For a quarter century, I worked in school libraries while my children attended school. The first five years were part-time and casual positions in elementary and secondary schools at the public-school board learning the trade in field placements for the Library Technician Diploma through Sheridan College. I networked with fellow librarians and support staff, forming genuine friendships. Upon graduation, I pursued a twenty-year career as a library technician in four secondary schools at the catholic or separate school board, commuting to the furthest corners of the district in Mississauga, Brampton, and Malton.

I initiated each transfer when vacancies became available either through retirements or maternity leaves. When I was hired by the school board, my first school was a forty-five-minute drive from home when the children were pre-teens and had a busy extra-curricular schedule with work and sports commitments. It was always a challenge to arrive home with the afternoon rush hour traffic. Less than two years later, as soon as a new school was built on the west side of Brampton where the students attended a "holding school" at a warehouse five minutes away in Streetsville for the first two years, I applied for that job and stayed for five years. When a technician moved out of a school in west Mississauga close to my residence, I requested a transfer and stayed for eight years. During that time, I pursued my divorce and bought a townhouse close by. However, relations with that teacher librarian soured. On my last transfer to a school in Malton, I had enough seniority to bump the lady on maternity leave where we switched schools and I stayed for six years through the Pandemic, working at home, and retired soon after the schools reopened.

As many of my library colleagues worked at one school their entire career, I preferred to move around to various locations, working in diverse environments with different administration and teaching staff. It was surprising to often reconnect with teachers I had met earlier in my career later in other schools. Some of these teachers also taught my children during their high school years and they inquired about their post-secondary progress. I often applied and interviewed for library positions in public and university libraries in the region without success. Having a unionized position at the school board secured my employment until retirement.

A proud accomplishment of my career was the opportunity to work with Library Support Services staff on a project to create Awards categories for over a million resources in all the schools in the district. I downloaded lists for several book awards at the elementary, middle, and secondary school levels and updated the online catalog accordingly. I had a glimpse of all the school libraries' collections. As schools closed for two years during the Pandemic, this project was managed from home.

The pandemic was a total shock to the system as school buildings closed, and learning went digital overnight for staff and students. I had remote access to my school account and library catalog, however, no physical access to the books on the shelf for collection development was a concern.

For ten years, I represented non-teaching staff on the School Council, also known as Parent Teacher Association (PTA) at three secondary schools. Monthly meetings were held in the evening to discuss school wide activities, budgets, student achievement and discipline between school administrators, teacher representatives, non-teaching representatives (me) and parents. My role reported on library activities, specifically the success of the Accelerated Reader Program. I also coordinated and assembled items for the School Newsletter that I edited and published quarterly. This position was eventually handed over to business teachers to encourage their students to create the newsletters embellished with illustrations, photographs, and graphic arts skills that I lacked.

I voluntarily participated in the extra-curricular school-wide activities. Along with attending school plays and concerts performed by students, I enjoyed the annual Multi-cultural Festival where staff and students set up tables of treats and souvenirs from their homeland. One year, I created a Dutch table displaying Dutch treats such as Kroketten, Edam and Gouda Cheeses, Dropjes (licorice) and Stroopwafels (waffle cookies stuffed with honey). Samples for consumption were given to attendees, and they admired my books about The Netherlands, wooden shoes, embroidery, delft blue tablecloth, and a windmill. Parents, students and staff were excited to hear about my European adventure during my senior year of high school many decades earlier. I enjoyed speaking about my year abroad and the lifelong friendships I developed. Many of these families had not traveled to Europe or only visited their homeland. I hope I inspired students to consider opportunities to travel and study abroad.

At the end of September, the annual Terry Fox Run / Walk honored the memory of Terry Fox who ran a marathon across Canada in 1980 to raise funds for cancer research. He ran forty kilometers each day from the east coast to Thunder Bay, Ontario, where he had to abandon his campaign when his cancer returned. An amputee with one leg, twenty-one years old, his determination to cross the country was reported daily on the evening news when I first arrived in Canada and raised millions of dollars for the Canadian Cancer Society charity. A five-kilometer walk / run became an annual tradition for schools and communities across the country in his honor. It was bittersweet conversation with colleagues tracking his progress. I always recalled his campaign that happened simultaneously with my relocation to Canada in those conversations.

I enjoyed a great rapport with students and teachers in school libraries. When I started at a new school early in my career, the teacher librarian introduced the Accelerated Reader Program to students and asked me to administer it. It was a literacy program to assess students' comprehension of books they read outside of class that counted as a percentage of their grade in English class. I set up the database each semester of all the students in the English classes and purchased books that had tests in the program. This program ran outside the curriculum and required the support of School Administration, English Department, and Library to succeed. I became the "resident" tech expert in my school as well as a consult for library technicians in other schools coordinating the resources, quizzes, and class lists. In the initial stages it ran on a server but eventually was administered online making it easier for downloading class lists and books that reflected the school library collection.

This program was successful under my mentorship which led to its introduction at other secondary schools across the district. I engaged in this initiative for fifteen years. A highlight of my career, that I cherished with pride. This initiative connected to the Forest of Reading Program offered by the Ontario Library Association where I assisted with the book launch each year.

After working for two decades in high school libraries, it was time to retire. As a library technician, I never enjoyed the perks of a professional librarian, but I created challenges throughout my career to promote literacy to aspire students to excel in literacy programs. In the library I worked with all students in all grades, so I witnessed their progress as they advanced from one grade level to the next. It gave me great pride to acknowledge that I was making a difference in many students' lives.

PART V

INNER PEACE AT LAST

Life after Divorce

2010 - 2025

Chapter 12

Marriage Collapse

Separation, Mediation, Divorce

After the children graduated high school, both children resided on or near campus at their universities. Jess came home every other weekend to work at her grocery store job and for the summer to work at the City of Toronto delivering calendars to residential homes around the city. Andy stayed at school, working at a grocery store near his residence. He lived in a home with six friends off campus where the rent was paid for the year, so he picked up more hours at the store in the summer and came home occasionally on weekends.

As empty nesters, the marriage drifted apart while we pursued our own interests. The memory of that 911 call fifteen years earlier was swirling in my brain. I asked myself, "Is it time?" I made a promise back then that if the relationship didn't improve, I would consider leaving him. I never recovered physically, emotionally, or mentally when he hit me on the neck while I was a stay-at-home mother with two young children. That argument stemmed from running out of propane while barbequing steaks for a Sunday night dinner. The steak was thrown out. The Peel Police arrived within minutes to separate us, took him away, and gave me a business card with a brochure to contact Victim Services. At that time, I had endured more than a decade of physical abuse whenever his rage burst before gathering the courage to make that phone call.

I often secluded myself and the children when I sensed an episode erupting. I don't know what caused these outbursts, but it was wrong to direct his anger towards me, swearing, hitting, and throwing things at me. The next day, I dropped the charges and allowed him back home on the premise he would attend anger management counselling, but the emotional abuse never stopped. The children needed a father, the family relied on his income, and being a landed immigrant without Canadian citizenship, I felt trapped. I knew that the children and I couldn't return to the USA without being accused of kidnapping or abduction.

After that call, I decided it was time to resume my education that I abandoned in my teens and re-entered the workforce as soon as both children started elementary school full time. My jobs, courses, and volunteer work kept me focused on my career. The children's extra-curricular sports activities ensured separate agendas for both parents in the evenings and weekends to drive them to their commitments. I hid my feelings of resentment for many years to keep my children engaged in their activities and education.

For several years, I confided my frustrations to a few girlfriends who experienced difficult divorces; I hesitated to proceed but living in misery was increasingly more difficult. I visited my parents and friends in Rochester alone with the children more often to remove myself from potentially dangerous confrontations. After the children graduated from college, I finally had the courage to leave and announced my intention to divorce after my graduation at San Jose State University.

A week later, I attended an information session at a local grocery store advertised in a Public Service Announcement (PSA) of the "*Mississauga News*" for anyone thinking about or pursuing separation and divorce. It was a crowded "cooking class" with fifty men and women in attendance eager to learn about the new law requiring all couples to pursue mediation to avoid court proceedings. Jess was surprised when she noticed my arrival at the class on her shift.

A few weeks later, after contacting a mediator advertised in the brochure, I started the conversation, "Alberto, I want a divorce!".

Alberto startled, "What? You've threatened me before and never followed through."

"I'm serious this time. I don't love you anymore," I replied. "We have grown apart while the children were away at school, instead of trying to fix our relationship."

"I don't understand," he remarked.

"My mind is made up; nothing will change it. I have already contacted a mediator to start the proceedings," I said. "You will be contacted as well for a consultation."

"Are you kicking me out?" he yelled, "On what grounds?".

"No, I will sleep in Andy's room as he prefers the basement in the summer and I will leave in the fall when I am back to work," I answered. "My parents and our children are aware of my intentions." I had been hinting at the possibility for a few months prior to the announcement.

The children were in shock but I assured them I would stay close and they were welcome to see me anytime. I would always be their mother. Communication with them became guarded because I needed to protect my privacy. They promised to keep separate relationships with both parents.

I visited my parents the weekend before the announcement. They were disappointed, but I reminded them that they had separated years earlier at the same age and time in their marriage. They agreed to respect my wishes and not have any further contact with Alberto. They had already endured three divorces of their five adult children, only one marriage in our family remained intact.

Mediation, performed by legal teams with mediators and marriage counselors in their offices, alleviated the stress on the court system. I contacted a lawyer specializing in family law that I found through the Peel Law Society website. I went to his office for a free consultation to confirm the procedure presented at the public meeting. I also met a marriage counselor and mediator who would preside over the process. Then Alberto went for a separate session and hired his own lawyer. He was surprised that I was informed on the process and initiated the proceedings independently. Like my approach to immigration three decades ago, I researched the process to ensure I navigated the legal proceedings with a clear and informed perspective, rather than acting without proper guidance.

We submitted all our financial records for review to calculate our net worth and discussed how to divide it equitably. These weekly meetings were frustrating, arguing about who would get what. The alimony was calculated on a formula that lawyers used to balance out our separate incomes. This amount never changed to reflect inflation and I never complained, fearing retaliation. It represented my contributions as the lower income partner throughout the marriage. The calculation, performed by an actuary, determined three calculations, and we agreed on the middle one. As the payee, I was taxed on that income while he, the payor, could claim a tax deduction.

After five months of deliberations, I packed my small red suitcase and met Ronald at his office before leaving the city for the weekend. We met monthly to update each other on the mediation proceedings and the legal consultations he had with Alberto's lawyer. He welcomed me into his office at 4 p.m., on a crisp November Thursday afternoon; it was the American Thanksgiving holiday.

"Ronald, I am heading home for a turkey feast, so I can't stay long," I announced.

He agreed and asked, "How are you doing? What is the progress with your negotiations?"

Tears were forming and he passed the box of tissues across his desk to me, "He is objecting to every detail the mediator presents. I am getting frustrated."

Ronald looked surprised, "It has been five months, and you have an easy case to divide your combined assets equitably," he remarked. "There is no child custody, no cottage or rental property, no adultery, and he agreed to the principal residence assessment." He paused and admitted, "Your no-fault divorce based on irreconcilable differences is one of my simplest cases."

I wiped my tears and said, "I really can't afford it, but I want to start court proceedings in the new year if an agreement is not reached by Christmas." I had no desire to waste our combined equity on an expensive court case and sensed he wouldn't like that either.

"Six months is fair and I will present that to his lawyer," Ronald agreed. "It might entice a settlement. It is getting late, have a safe drive to your parents. Happy Thanksgiving."

He walked me out to the car, and I started the long drive to Rochester. I called my dad that I would be late, and he said, "Take your time, there will be plenty of leftovers." I arrived at 7:30 p.m., enjoyed a delicious turkey dinner, and updated him on the negotiations.

Alberto signed the agreement before Christmas and started the alimony also known as spousal support payments in the new year. A fair and equitable settlement was reached enduring six months of heart-wrenching negotiations. Legally separated in June 2011 after thirty-one years of marriage, I filed for divorce exactly twelve months later.

As there were no custody arrangements for the children, they were independent adults in their early twenties, there was no desire for Alberto and I to remain friends. He gave the children an envelope with twelve postdated checks during the holidays to pass to me for the following year's alimony.

Upon receipt of the divorce decree the following summer, I legally changed my name back to my family name, as an act of closure. My birth name was easier to spell and pronounce. I needed a new identity to compliment my new status as a divorcee. As the children graduated from university and embarked on new careers, we no longer needed to share the same last name. Since I worked in the same district where the children graduated from secondary school, it was beneficial not to appear related.

I was also considering returning to the USA, so reverting to my family surname might trigger name recognition while searching for jobs in or near Rochester. I was often asked, "Are you the doctor's daughter?" and responded with a smile; they knew we were related. My parents supported my decision to divorce once I admitted what was happening in private. It was the first time in two decades that I revealed physical abuse and the 911 call. My mother remarked that he never answered the phone when she called and I always had to check the caller ID and answering machine as he never gave her messages to me.

When Alberto and I attended social events, we did not speak to each other, acting like strangers in a crowded room. Our children had separate relationships with both of us and I trusted them not to share my information. After a period of adjustment, I was at peace living alone.

Becoming Single Again

I was fifty-five years old, when I became single again after thirty-four years in a relationship with one man. It was a different feeling from being widowed where you are lonely and grieving the eternal loss of your spouse. I was not grieving a loss; but liberated from the constraints of an unhappy marriage.

I moved into a two-bedroom, two-bath apartment near the school I worked at in Mississauga, arranged by the real estate agent who assessed the house during the separation. It felt strange downsizing after thirty years of large homes but necessary living alone. There was extra space for the children who were living with their father in their childhood home but stayed with me occasionally. Whenever I went on a vacation, one moved in to "house sit." They had a spare key to my apartment to welcome them in my home at any time. We went for dinner at local restaurants most weekends. My apartment kitchen was too small to cook and entertain guests.

Two years later when the divorce settlement was distributed, I bought a three-bedroom townhouse in a neighborhood close to work, malls, and the highways. I gave both children a key to my home. I furnished their bedrooms so they could sleep there whenever they wished. They took the bedroom furniture with them when they moved into their first apartment. The finished basement with a family room had a sofa and television for their entertainment while I used the living and dining room on the main floor.

They were eager to move in after I bought the townhouse. Living with my adult children when they moved back home after university was vastly different from the times I lived with Alberto's parents when I moved to Canada and ten years later in between house moves. In their home, his mother did all the cooking, cleaning, shopping, and laundry, and his father did all the yard work and maintenance. We did not overstep their boundaries. It often felt like we were guests overstaying our welcome. Twenty years later, switching roles as the parent, my adult children wanted to maintain the independence that they enjoyed at university. I allowed it as long as they respected my property and shared the responsibility to maintain their living space.

Andy moved in for a year until it was time to live with his girlfriend, future wife. Michelle did not move into my home because she worked at a health care facility close to her parents' home. I also did not have space for a third vehicle in my complex. When I arrived home from a holiday, she was baking Christmas cookies for a gift exchange in my kitchen.

I walked into the entry, smelled the fresh baked goods, "Hmm, it smells good in here," I mused. "Getting ready for the holidays?"

"I should have asked but Andy said you wouldn't mind," she laughed. "I am using my mother's baking supplies because I couldn't find yours."

"Make yourself at home here," I replied, "Just clean up the mess when you finish."

I emptied the car and went upstairs to unpack while she finished baking and cleaned up her mess. When she was done, and I came back downstairs, she thanked me and gave me a plate of cookies from her baker's dozen.

I was glad that she felt comfortable using my kitchen in my absence. On another occasion, she cleaned up a flood around the furnace in my basement, calling her father for assistance when I was away and Andy was working. I commended her for taking responsibility to resolve the problem. Her parents gave me a desk that they no longer needed and helped Andy put it together to use in the spare bedroom. I sensed that Andy made an excellent choice for a future bride. A friend leased an apartment to them before they purchased their first home.

When he moved out, Jess moved in for three years before buying a condominium with her boyfriend, future husband. I was on a birthday vacation with my mother when I arrived home and found a tall young man cooking in my kitchen.

He welcomed me with a "Happy birthday, Margot" and told me to relax while he finished preparing my birthday meal of roast chicken, rice and beans, and grilled vegetables.

Jess appeared and said, "By the way, Mom, Zane moved in while you were gone. We are looking into renting an apartment."

I laughed, "This is his new home. Welcome aboard."

They smiled, excited, and in unison, "Really?"

We discussed rules, boundaries, and expectations over dinner. They lived together in my home for a year before purchasing a condominium. It was wonderful to have their company and watch their relationship flourish. I was happy to have a housemate who could fix things, and he painted the interior of my home on weekends when he was not working. Both of my children had happy marriages and families that made their mother proud.

As we followed different schedules, living with my adult children resembled a "roommate" arrangement, living independent lives. This arrangement helped their transition from school to careers as they were responsible for their own groceries, meal preparation, laundry, cleaning their rooms and bathroom, and car maintenance. I provided a roof over their heads rent-free that included utilities and cable television. They also parked their car in the garage since I left for work early in the morning. We shared a Costco membership to purchase common household items.

The townhouse complex had an outdoor pool, opened when schools closed for the summer, that was supervised by student lifeguards. This provided a relaxing atmosphere, an enjoyable way to meet the neighbors. As the complex was thirty years old, it underwent a massive building restoration project charged back to the residents. I lived there for five years but after two costly restoration payments and emerging health issues, I moved across town to a single floor condominium that was close to my daughter's new home.

I became friends with senior ladies at an aquafit class. We enjoyed social outings together on Saturday mornings after class, a new social network for me. One thing we had in common was the love of travel. I took salsa dancing lessons and accompanied two friends to dance halls on weekends. Those dance nights reminded me of the disco era of the seventies. Everyone was dressed up and the older guys were no longer shy, asking ladies to dance to show off their waltzing skills.

I wanted to revisit my favorite places in the USA and explore parts of Canada that I had never seen before. Maria and I ambitiously mapped out a road trip to the east coast. We spent twelve days traveling along the Trans-Canada Highway staying overnight in air bnb homes near Ottawa, Ontario, Quebec City, Quebec, and Moncton, New Brunswick, before reaching our destination on Prince Edward Island. We enjoyed four days exploring the island's beaches, Anne of Green Gables Historic Site, and Charlottetown.

On the return trip, we visited Manon, in Halifax, who I had met at a mom 'n tots' group in Mississauga decades earlier. When her husband transferred to Halifax, we stayed in touch, one of my best long time Canadian friendships. We visited each other's homes a few times over the years. I looked forward to the fresh seafood and lobster each time I flew to Halifax for a few days. From Halifax, we took a ferry to St. Johns, New Brunswick and drove through the northern part of Maine to Montreal for a fun day of sightseeing before returning home. It reminded me of my family road trips as a child, driving six to seven hours each day. We enjoyed each other's company and shared the driving, eager to explore unfamiliar places.

Two years later, Nina joined Maria and I on a road trip to Cape Cod, my childhood favorite beach holiday. We rented a cottage in

Dennisport exploring the beaches and Provincetown. It had been close to twenty years since my last trip to the Cape with my husband and children. This time, we enjoyed a whale watching tour on the Atlantic Ocean, where we wore ponchos to protect ourselves from the waves caused by the frolicking whales, a new and exciting adventure.

My friend, Joanne, and I yearned for a trip to the Big Apple. Memories of my dilemma with Marisa swirled in my head. We chose a four-day weekend bus trip with Comfort Tours, two days to travel each way and two days of touring the city. We invited two friends, Ruth and Maria, to join us, and enjoyed an exciting senior women's weekend retreat together.

The package included transportation in an air-conditioned coach bus, a hotel in a New Jersey suburb, and day tours of the city. We toured the Statue of Liberty, Ellis Island where I looked up Pop's name, the 911 memorial, Central Park, and other famous landmarks.

We also enjoyed free time in the afternoon to shop, eat, and browse before meeting the bus at Times Square to take us back to our hotel in the evening. We did not attend any Broadway shows so we would not miss the evening bus pickup. We were not comfortable navigating the subway to find our way back to the hotel by ourselves. The all-day bus route included rest stops at a prime outlet mall and a souvenir store that sold baked goods and deli sandwiches near the New York State Thruway. We enjoyed buying wine at the duty-free shop to have in our hotel room.

When I was not working, I traveled on weekdays to Rochester to avoid the traffic jams of weekend tourists, especially during summer weekends and holidays. Recalling the airport closure on my Christmas vacation to Veendam, winter storms around Buffalo were always risky. Thanksgiving became my final trip of the year until spring break in March around my birthday. I tuned into the Buffalo traffic and weather reports whenever I planned a weekend visit. Thanksgiving, my favorite holiday, was always a busy travel weekend, and I returned home on Saturday to avoid the traffic on Sunday. In the fall, the highway and borders were always congested when the Buffalo Bills football team played a home game. There were three border crossings between Buffalo and Niagara Falls, so it was always a gamble which one to enter.

One of my favorite social events was attending live theatre events. Southern Ontario had a vibrant performing arts community. I attended performances throughout my life at the Shaw Festival in Niagara on the Lake, the Stratford Festival west of Kitchener-Waterloo, and the Mirvish Theatres in downtown Toronto. Many times, I met my mother for lunch and a matinee performance in Niagara on the Lake near the New York and Ontario borders where the Niagara River flows between Lake Ontario and Lake Erie, a ninety-minute drive for both of us in opposite directions to meet in the middle.

She took chartered bus trips from Rochester to the performances. The Shaw Festival was famous for presenting plays by George Bernard Shaw, an Irish playwright of the early twentieth century, but also expanded into other dramas of twentieth century playwrights and musicals.

We enjoyed a nice meal at the Prince of Wales Hotel a block away from the Festival Theatre, a five-star restaurant serving theatre patrons throughout the day. Occasionally, we saw shows at the Courthouse and Fort George Theatres in the middle of the village on the main street, smaller venues with smaller stages perfect for dramas with few actors and one set designed for the entire performance. American tourists filled the theatres during the summer months. The village offered various restaurants and shops for visitors to stroll along the main street before and after a show. The festival season lasted from May to October annually. At the time of writing, the Shaw Festival celebrated its sixtieth anniversary, entertaining audiences for more than half a century.

The Stratford Festival was also a popular spot for live theatre performances, a two-hour drive from Buffalo, NY to the east and Detroit, Michigan to the west, open from April to October. It was centrally located in southern Ontario serving Canadians from Windsor and London to Toronto and Barrie, a two-hour drive in either direction.

Famous for Shakespeare productions, the Stratford Festival also presented musicals and drama productions on four stages in the town. There were bed and breakfast homes to house tourists for overnight stays, an enjoyable way to meet people globally. I often stayed overnight to attend two plays in one weekend. A beautiful boardwalk along Lake Victoria ran through the center of the village where stores and restaurants amused theatre patrons before and after the show. I often attended performances alone or with girlfriends.

The Mirvish Theatre, in the heart of downtown Toronto, had four venues along Yonge and King Streets, a fifteen-minute walk from

Union Station. I loved going to those performances by myself or with girlfriends, via GO Bus / Train to Union Station and walking to the theatre. Many times, my friend Jan, who I met at Sheridan College in the nineties, hopped on the bus or train in Milton and I met her in Meadowvale to attend performances together and enjoyed lunch in a restaurant downtown before the show. We often met Val, another Sheridan grad, for lunch circulating between venues in Burlington, Milton, and Mississauga until our retirements and relocations outside of the Halton Peel Region.

Founded by Ed Mirvish and passed down to his son, David, the company existed for over a century entertaining Torontonians with all kinds of theatrical performances from London's East End and New York's Broadway productions. I always treated myself to lunch or dinner downtown before or after the show, as it was usually the only time I traveled to Toronto after moving to Mississauga in the nineties. My passion for theatre arts began as a young child with the musicals that debuted in the 1960s and carried through to my adult and senior years, always seeking a new production at one of these venues annually, an enjoyable day trip close to home.

Another challenge of becoming single again, was dating and reconnecting with a teenage sweetheart.

Chapter 13

Rekindled First Love

The SJSU online program introduced me to social media. Nervous to join Facebook, one of my professors convinced me it was a wonderful way to reconnect with old friends and distant family members. With her reassurance I plunged into the online world with no regrets. During this online chat on a Saturday afternoon, she challenged all the women in the class to "google" their birth name, an interesting exercise as I had not used that name in thirty years. I found friends from high school and cousins who were already familiar with the platform, I rekindled old friendships and connected with my cousins in the social media environment.

At that time, there were Italian references to my family name, a singer in Italy, but no references to Rochester. Toronto links used my married name. As I scrolled further down the page of search results, there was a faded link stating, "Greg is looking for Margot." My heart dropped. I was devastated when I received that "return to sender letter" in Belgium more than thirty-five years earlier. My first love during my last year of high school; only my family and a few close friends knew about him. It was my first long distance romance at the tender age of sweet sixteen, an experience I would never forget with promises that were never kept.

I clicked on the link to set up a profile with my personal contact information. To read his message, I had to pay a fee to access it for a week, month, or longer. I called the website owner, listed at the bottom of the page and agreed to three months' access, which was enough time to contact him and get a response if he wanted to reconnect with me. When I was granted access, the message read, "Please contact me at xxxx address," no phone number or email address. After much deliberation and discussion with a colleague, I sent a brief note on a telephone message pad with my work phone number. I informed him to call after the bell at quarter past two in the afternoon, when students were dismissed and I had another hour to tidy up the library before quitting time. Few students used the library after school, and the teacher librarian attended meetings. Two weeks later, we connected. I called the website owner again after we exchanged phone numbers to cancel the remaining payment and delete that link in any search results for my name.

It was the end of the school year after the divorce when the first call came through at half past two on a Friday afternoon. I saw the caller ID and realized it was a California number. "Hello, Library, Margot speaking."

A deep voice on the other end of the line said, "Hello Margot, how are you, do you know who this is?"

"Hi Greg, long time no hear. What is going on?" I said, curious as to his interest to reconnect with me.

"I have been thinking about you for years, wondering what happened to you," he replied, "I put that search on the internet a long time ago. You never saw it until now?"

"I noticed that it was dated several years ago. I changed my name when I got married, and the Internet did not exist then," I sighed. "I found your inquiry when I googled my family name out of curiosity."

"Yes, it's been fourteen thousand days since we last spoke," he calculated back to the time when I left for Europe. "This is a good time to talk, while my wife is at work, and I will come home for lunch every day to call you if that's ok." He was self-employed and still lived in California, a three-hour time difference.

Smiling with a wide grin, "Yes, this is the only time I can talk to you during the day, while I am at work and there are no classes."

"Do you have a direct line or a cell phone, so I don't have to go through the school switchboard?" He wanted more information.

"This is the only way to reach me," I replied. I was not prepared to give him my home or cell phone number at that time.

He ended the call, "OK, I will call you on Monday, same time. Have a wonderful day."

We talked on the phone at the end of the school day for a year before we arranged to meet in person. It had been close to four decades since we last met in Rochester during the Christmas break of my last year of high school. We talked about what happened during our lives, our families, and our careers. We were falling in love again. We scheduled our first reunion after my divorce was finalized.

We met twice a year in California at New Years, the second week of my two-week break and for a week in the summer. He arranged for his wife to visit her family in Arizona when I arrived in California. We drove to Ensenada, Mexico on the Baja California peninsula, an hour's drive south of San Diego, California where a community of retired Americans resided and rented a room from his friend who owned an Air-bnb on the coast. A beautiful setting where we walked along the beach of the Pacific Ocean and ate authentic Mexican cuisine in roadside diners.

I became acquainted with the ladies in this retirement community and saw them at New Years Eve parties. I developed a friendship with one lady on Facebook, who informed me of all the gossip in the community whenever he visited.

Greg and I bought a trailer in this community on my third visit and parked it on a shared property with one of his friends who was the "caretaker" when he was not there.

He insisted, "It would be our hideaway, that his wife would not be comfortable in the trailer."

The following summer when I returned, she had decorated it and left some of her personal belongings there. During their Easter visit, they attended a BBQ in the community and one of the ladies noticed that Greg was with a different woman, not me.

I confirmed via a private message on Facebook that, "She was his wife who was not supposed to have any interest in this vacation home."

I confronted him on the phone, and he denied any wrongdoing insisting it would not happen again. During our next visit that summer, I requested reimbursement for the cost of the trailer.

He responded, "You paid cash, and the title was under my name, there was no proof of your payment."

I continued to see him for a few more years. I had accumulated thousands of Air Miles Rewards Points on a credit card to pay for these trips that I had to use before they expired. He introduced me to another female friend in California, under the guise that this couple would look after me if his wife came home unexpectedly before my scheduled departure flight. The two women met for lunch a week after my visit and the mask dropped.

He told me, "I assured my wife that you were an old school friend who looked me up when you came home for the holidays."

Although I knew it was wrong, reconnecting with an old boyfriend brought comfort to me during my transition to single life after thirty years in a relationship; it was not true love. A nice vacation in a warm, dry climate away from cold winters and humid summers during school breaks, it relieved my tension in the workplace.

Surrounded by secrecy to avoid detection from his wife on his phone, he liked old fashioned handwritten letters. I wrote and mailed letters to his business post office box; we did not communicate via email. For texting, we used code names that his wife would not question or recognize. I was listed as one of his customers or clients. There were no pictures of me fearing she would question it. She replied to a few of my messages so I had to be discreet.

This relationship gave me a renewed sense of peace and boosted my self-confidence. My adult children were living with their father while transitioning from college to the workforce. I was always on the job hunt in both the USA and Ontario, attended interviews but failed to secure a new position outside the school board since graduating with the master's degree.

The friendship lasted five years. I had a tough time letting go. I always traveled to California; he never came to my home or met me halfway. His early promises proved unreliable, leaving me uncertain about a future with him and hesitant to move away from my family. He consistently maintained control over our interactions, often disregarding my preferences during our relationship. He bragged about his affairs; I was not his first infidelity. At times when we visited Mexico together, I was frightened for my safety and potential abandonment. I asked my children to call, rather than text, the evening before my flight home to confirm my arrival time at the airport to pick me up the next day. As much as I loved his attention, I lost faith in him and knew he could not be trusted.

At the five-year anniversary, I confronted him about his intentions. I was free, and he was still married. He finally admitted that he would not divorce a second time, so we went our separate ways. I refused to be the other woman any longer. Wiser and stronger, I ended the relationship and blocked him.

Two girlfriends who did not know each other, one in Mexico and one in California, stayed in touch with me after the breakup but I was no longer interested in talking about him. They acknowledged separately that wildfire destroyed the trailer and all the homes in that community were lost. It was both a relief and a stroke of luck that an act of God rendered the trailer unusable.

During our courtship, he asked about my year abroad and if I stayed in contact with anyone in Europe. I told him about the friendships I had maintained, my Christmas trip in the late seventies, and my friends visits to Canada. He suggested it was time to return now that I was single with my children. I agreed it was time to show them my favorite place on earth.

Chapter 14

Return to Europe

In the summer of 2013, after the divorce, I yearned for a trip to Europe. It had been more than thirty-five years since I last visited before the marriage. The children had never been to Europe; our family vacations always took place in North America centered around my family's reunions and one visit to Cancun with the children when they were teenagers. I often hinted to Alberto that we should visit his birthplace, Italy, as a family but those requests were ignored. It would have been an ideal summer holiday while they were teenagers to see the country of their parents' heritage, as Alberto was born there before his parents immigrated to Canada when he was a toddler, and I was third generation Italian on my father's side of the family.

I emailed Eva, Elly, and Ankie to coordinate dates and booked flights for a two-week journey in the middle of August. I had to return home before the school year started in September. I asked the children to join me. Andy was on the job hunt and dating Michelle, who would later become his future wife. Jess had transitioned from working at the grocery store to teaching. I wanted to visit my friends in the Netherlands at least one more time in my life and show my children where I lived in Europe for a year as a teenager forty years ago.

Jess traveled with me but could not leave the day I had booked. Friday evening, August 9, 2013, I flew to Amsterdam, arriving Saturday morning. At Schiphol, I collected my bag and walked downstairs to catch the train for Utrecht. The train station was connected to the airport, an easy transfer after a long overnight flight. When I exited the station in Utrecht, I was amazed at the piles of bicycles parked outside the station, an obvious sign that cycling was the preferred mode of transportation over automobiles in this country where the land was flat and the roads were safe.

I stayed with Eva for three days in Maastricht. When she picked me up at the train station, we drove to Mama's nursing home and took her out for lunch. It was a sweet reunion, however, Papa and Jeannet passed away, and Hans was traveling overseas. Mama, in her eighties, was aging gracefully like my mother in America. I always referred to my Dutch parents as Mama and Papa, and my American parents as Mom and Dad to distinguish the relationships I had with them. I maintained contact with Mama and Papa through annual Christmas and birthday greetings, marriage and birth announcements, and photographs as our families expanded. I grieved the tragic loss of her daughter / my sister and her husband / my Papa, like they were my family. I cherished the memories of my life with them and subsequent visit before Jeannet's death. I was happy that Papa retired soon after her death to enjoy his retirement and final years with Mama. It was heartwarming when Mama and Eva visited me in Canada and my mother in America, sharing the familial bond. She passed away peacefully three years after this visit, at the age of ninety years.

We spoke a bit of Dutch, but mostly English. I was amazed that they continued to speak English as a second language whereas I had lost my ability to speak Dutch. I could read and translate their mail with dual-language paperback dictionaries, but I had not practiced speaking the language.

Arriving at the nursing home, I went into the lobby to greet Mama with a hug and three kisses on each cheek. Twenty-five years after I last saw her at my home in Toronto when my children were babies, she looked the same, aging gracefully.

"Mama, so nice to see you again," I smiled. "You look wonderful. How are you feeling?"

"I'm good," she replied, "A little tired now that I am older. It has been a long time since our last visit. How are the children?"

"I know, I wanted to return years ago but couldn't while I was married," I sighed. "Jess will meet me in Amsterdam next week; she couldn't travel this weekend due to a previous commitment and I couldn't change the flight."

"I'm glad she will join you," Mama remarked, "It's too bad I couldn't see her again, all grown up!"

"She and Andy enjoyed the visit with Eva and your grandchildren at our home eight years ago," I smiled, "and she will meet Elly and her family later this week."

"Mama, you remember when I went to America with the boys to meet Julia and her American family," Eva smiled. "We also visited Margot and June at their homes before we went camping in Algonquin Park in Canada."

"I remember Elly," Mama said, "her family also moved to our neighborhood."

"Yes," I winked, "I visited her family at the new house on Borgerspaark during my Christmas visit when they first moved in. Lovely homes on that street."

After lunch, we brought Mama back to her apartment. We stayed for a cup of tea before leaving for Eva's home near Maastricht, on the southern border of the country, near Belgium and Germany. We crossed the border into Belgium to get gas and groceries. We went for long walks in the village and visited outdoor cafes in town. On Sunday morning, we went to her yoga class which was taught outdoors on the top of a hill. It was fun stretching to music outside in the bright sun.

The next day we visited a farm situated behind a tall cement wall and gate in the middle of town. It was surreal, like entering the gated grounds of a castle. The locals scooped up fresh produce and baked goods to take home. It was different from the farmer's markets I was used to back home in Ontario and added to the ambiance and uniqueness of this European village.

On Tuesday, I took the train back to Schiphol to meet Jess when her flight arrived at 10 a.m. It was her first night flight overseas. We took a bus downtown and walked to our hotel, *Intel Amsterdam Centrum*. Was this the same hotel where I stayed for a month transitioning from Belgium to the Netherlands? It felt strangely familiar. Forty years later, the building looked the same but the inside was renovated and modernized with large windows allowing the sun to shine through, brightening my mood. I put on a brave face as my daughter was unaware of that part of my journey.

We booked one night and visited the Ann Frank Huis and Heineken (Dutch beer) Museum. Her home was a narrow tall building on the *Prinsengracht* where her family lived in a secret annex to hide from the Germans in 1942 for two years. Her diary became required reading in high school English classes as it depicted the horrors of the Jewish Holocaust during the war. We waited two hours outside for tickets, because we didn't book our tour in advance. The weather was perfect and like so many European cities, there was a central square nearby filled with restaurants, tables and chairs. We found a table to have a beverage and Dutch treats while hundreds of tourists buzzed all around us.

Checking the map, Jess found the Heineken Museum and there was time to get there for their last tour of the day. We stayed for a happy hour of beer tasting that was a lot of fun. It reminded me of the field trip to a winery many years ago during that chemistry class in college.

On Wednesday, we took the train from Amsterdam to Assen, a two-hour ride through tulips and windmills fields. We were amazed at the beautiful countryside away from the hustle and bustle of the city. I remembered the same journey four decades earlier when I traveled to the monthly YFU retreats. Jessica was amazed at the landscape, all flat, the fields filled with a rainbow of colorful tulips, and the massive windmills that were operating along the route. The fields were maintained and remained untouched, unlike the massive development of homes and businesses that occurred along the QEW in Southern Ontario over the years. My trips to Toronto in the seventies viewed miles of greenspace and farmland that had transformed into residential and commercial development along with widened highways in the last three decades traveling the route back and forth to visit my family in New York state.

Elly, Peter, and their daughter, Manouk, met us in two small fiats. Their son, Victor, was on a vacation with the family car. I rode with Elly and Peter while Jess and Manouk drove separately. The girls enjoyed their time together, speaking English and getting to know each other. It was wonderful to see Elly and Peter again and introduce our daughters for the first time as it had been thirty years since they visited me in Toronto before our children were born.

Their home sat on a court surrounded by beautiful flower gardens. Inside their home a steep spiral staircase led to the bedrooms, but they gave me a guest room on the main floor. A massive map of the world on their kitchen wall decorated with colorful thumb tacks represented all the places they visited over the years. I always enjoyed reading her annual Christmas letters about their travels, and here was visual proof of all the places they had visited. I had a collection of beautiful souvenirs that she sent me over the years. Her gifts always arrived on time for my birthday, which I reciprocated immediately as her birthday was two weeks later.

We spent two days and two nights together, touring the central part of the country, visiting a monastery, and eating at a medieval castle. Peter took us on a drive across the border into Germany, with no border checkpoint to stop at.

The second day we drove to Veendam where we visited Stationstraat 2, Winkler Prins School and the village centrum. The home and bank transformed into a plumbing business; I didn't recognize it as the beautiful, landscaped gardens were replaced by a cement parking lot. Peter found the owner behind the house and explained in Dutch that I had lived there forty years earlier, so we were allowed to explore the property for a few minutes. I showed Jess the bedroom I slept in on the second floor and Jeannet's room in the attic on the third floor.

It was strangely peculiar to find this beautiful stately home completely renovated into a commercial business, not an office building. The formal living and dining rooms on the main floor were gone with construction and plumbing materials scattered everywhere. Jess was surprised that I spent a year living in this small village in the "middle of nowhere," unlike our hometown in Canada and my hometown in America.

In the evening, Jess and Manouk mapped out the rest of our vacation and booked trains and hotels for two days each in Brussels and Paris and our last night in Amsterdam before flying home. Jess arranged the itinerary for the second week, including the hotels, restaurants, tourist attractions, and transportation. Each day had a good balance of activities at every city we visited. The hotels were centrally located surrounded by decent restaurants. We agreed on everything we planned to see.

The next day, Elly and Manouk drove us to Groningen to stay with Ankie. We spent two nights in her apartment surrounded by a beautiful city park. She did not own a car, so we took a bus to a Renaissance festival and visited her trailer where she spent weekends and summers. We also walked to the nursing home to visit her mother, Tante Trees, who like Mama, was aging gracefully in her eighties. I was pleased to see her one last time before she passed away a few years later. She remembered me and enjoyed meeting my daughter. She recalled the tree of life that she embroidered for Jess's birth and antique car she crafted for Andy's birth. I embraced this art form, and hand stitched several pieces of embroidery for a few years after I left Europe, creating scenes of Dutch culture that my mother framed to hang on her walls and eventually returned to me which will be passed down to my children. At the end of the first week, Jess was happy to see where her mother spent her senior year abroad as a teenager, meeting her friends that she has retained all her life, and contemplated living there to teach, as English was the second language that everyone spoke. I was delighted that this adventure impressed my daughter.

After two nights with Ankie, her brother Lex drove us to the train station to continue our journey. The train station in Groningen was a large, beautiful castle with glass ceilings so the light shone through the building. It was a busy station in the northern part of the country, with a large university population. We said goodbye to our Dutch friends, found the route for Brussels, and boarded a high-speed train to begin the second week of our journey.

As the first week was a reunion with my friends, Jess planned our second week as tourists. Our first stop was Brussels, in the southern part of Belgium where French was spoken. We checked into our hotel and dropped our luggage in our room near the Grand Place, a huge outdoor square. A UNESCO World Heritage site, it had a beautiful garden surrounded by cobblestones. The square housed restaurants, pubs, and boutiques that sold everything from souvenirs to clothing, cheese, chocolate, and tobacco; something for everyone. A famous statue, Manneken Pis, a bronze sculpture of a little boy sitting on a turtle, urinating into a pond at one end of the Grand Place, was originally a fountain used to distribute drinking water for hundreds of years before modern plumbing existed.

The political capital of Europe, Brussels was home to the European Parliament and other EU organizations. The next day, we toured the Atomium, a structure representing a molecule of iron, built as the centerpiece of the 1958 Brussels World's Fair (Expo 58). I had never been to Brussels on past European vacations, so it was a pleasure to tour this international city, the capital of the EU. It was the city I had in mind as a French speaking destination for my senior year abroad; however, I didn't specify the city, just the country on my application, not knowing at that time that the country had two separate French and Dutch speaking cultures.

Then we took the express train to Paris. This metropolitan city had a complicated underground train system, that Jess navigated with ease. We checked into our hotel, left our luggage, and headed out for dinner. We enjoyed Monsieur and Madame Croissants that resembled grilled cheese sandwiches.

In the evening, we walked along La Seine, the river that flows through the heart of the city to the Arc de Triomphe situated on the Place de L'Étoile, and climbed the circular staircase of two hundred eighty steps to the observation deck where we viewed the Eiffel Tower across the river all lit up, a beautiful evening to see a spectacular light show. It was crowded waiting in line to view the tower from across the river, one of the most famous towers in the world. Constructed in the early nineteenth century, the walls of the staircase were carved with lists of all the generals and battles fought in France, a history lesson as one climbed the stairs. As Jess ran ahead to view the light show at the top of the observation deck, I became short of breath and started wheezing as I slowly ascended the stairs arriving a few minutes later. It was my first time experiencing asthma, and I was later seen by a cardiologist for treatment; a beautiful sight, well worth the agony to see it in person.

I anticipated a relaxing holiday visiting my friends and touring a few famous cities with my daughter. I was not prepared for any medical emergencies that could occur while we were traveling together. I always carried travel insurance as a precaution but never needed to use it. At that time, I was proud of my level of fitness as I enjoyed long walks back home, so this asthma episode was a bit scary. It made me realize that I had to be more conscious of my health when traveling in the future.

The following day, we went to the Louvre, a beautiful art museum housed in a castle with a huge cobblestone square in front of the building for crowds to gather. The building evolved from a medieval fortress to a royal palace and finally, a world-renowned museum at the end of the eighteenth century during the French Revolution. Throughout its history, the museum represented French power, culture, and art.

Although we had tickets for the entire museum, the lines were long and moving slowly to enter the building. We were only interested in viewing Leonardo da Vinci's Mona Lisa, which was in a special viewing room, displayed behind a protective, temperature and humidity-controlled glass case for preservation.

Security guards throughout the complex were guarding the exhibits and monitoring tourists. It was the most beautiful art gallery I have ever visited. I recalled visiting various museums in Toronto, throughout the USA, and across Europe during childhood trips with my parents. Having reached an older age, I found great appreciation for the beauty of this painting, which has been carefully maintained over centuries.

We traveled back to Amsterdam by train for one more day before flying home. We booked the same hotel, found our room, and then stepped out for dinner. After dinner, Jess explored the Red-Light District famous for prostitution and drugs while I stayed at the hotel. As a young independent woman in her mid-twenties, I trusted her to be safe and gave her some freedom. She felt comfortable exploring the district as it was close to our hotel and we could communicate by cell phone. On the last day, Friday, August 23, 2013, we took the bus to Schiphol to catch our flight back to Toronto where Andy drove us home. He was happy to reunite with his sister and hear about our adventures.

It would have been nice to include Andy and have an extra week exploring more places, like London, Berlin or Rome, but we had to prepare our classrooms at the end of August before school opened after Labor Day. With the six-hour time difference, we also needed a week to adjust to the time change. I arranged this vacation in the beginning of the summer, relying on the availability of my friends in the Netherlands, it was the only time where I could visit them during the same week. I booked my flights before I asked the children to join me so it would have been impossible to leave earlier in August to gain more time for more destinations.

Jess was impressed with my friends in The Netherlands and enjoyed visiting my former home and school. There were no language barriers as everyone spoke English. I was happy to give her the opportunity to visit Europe. It opened her eyes to the world beyond North America, a privilege of a lifetime. She met the daughter of my friends, Elly and Peter, and knew Eva's children from their previous visit to Canada, to keep that connection flowing from one generation to the next.

I enjoyed travelling with my daughter; she was interested in every aspect of the vacation. I loved visiting Amsterdam, Paris, and Brussels, international cities that I vaguely remembered from decades ago. It was refreshing to see these cities through the eyes of an older adult, much different from my memories as a child and teenager. I became more familiar with these cities having learned about them through media sources not available years ago and being in control of my itinerary, I visited places I was interested in.

My big red suitcase is filled with memories from decades of travel and will continue to guide me on more adventures for the rest of my life.

THE END

Epilogue

Finally, Canadian Citizenship – Wednesday, April 5, 2017

A permanent resident card was issued to all landed immigrants after the September 11th attacks. It replaced the tattered yellow immigration document I carried every time I crossed the border since my entry two decades earlier. I also retained my American citizenship in case I returned to the USA for temporary residency.

Canada is a land of immigrants; you never lose your heritage, accent or language of your country of birth. Many of my friends came from different countries, spoke English with foreign accents, and communicated in their native language with their families.

Holding onto my American citizenship, I retained the right to vote in the Presidential elections every four years with an absentee ballot from 1980 onward. I applied for the ballot online and sent it to the Monroe County Board of Elections stating my childhood address in Irondequoit as my last USA residence. Not giving up my right to vote in the federal elections, was a citizenship right that I practiced every four years as a tie to my heritage that I cherished.

Retention of my American citizenship meant filing income tax in both countries annually, requiring the expertise of a tax accountant qualified to calculate both USA and Canadian taxes simultaneously as foreign income was reported to both the CRA (Canada Revenue Agency) and the IRS (Internal Revenue Service). I filed forms for marriage, divorce, name changes, address changes, the children as dependents, along with a list of my foreign bank accounts and investments annually. American citizens who relocated abroad were subjected to taxation on their worldwide income by the IRS for their entire lives. I never paid taxes to the IRS, but securing the services of a cross-border accountant became expensive and necessary when audits were conducted.

Apparently, the USA is the only country in the world that requires ex-pats to continue filing income tax once they relocate outside its borders with stiff penalties when it's forgotten. Inquiries I made to renounce my American citizenship would be costly and not worth the effort that could affect travel to visit my family and friends. I became a dual citizen like my children who enjoyed that status since birth.

When Donald Trump won the USA election on November 8, 2016, I anxiously considered my thirty-seven years as an "ex-patriot" when crossing the border; he campaigned that he would deport illegal immigrants. That evening, I downloaded the application for Canadian citizenship from the Canadian Immigration and Citizenship (CIC) website. My wrinkled and tattered immigration document, marriage and divorce certificates, name change documents, and Permanent

Resident card were included with the application along with payment of applicable fees. In the new year, I took the citizenship test on a specific date and time at the local courthouse along with one hundred other landed immigrants from around the world seeking Canadian citizenship. I found mock tests online, studied them, and learned the correct answers.

The test contained fifty multiple choice questions about Canadian government, history, geography, and culture. Canadian history was never taught in American schools, except for the fur trade when the continent was explored and discovered five hundred years ago. I learned about Canada from my children's school assignments and assisting students' research questions when I worked in school libraries. All students learned Canadian history, geography, and civics in secondary school. There were eight versions of the test handed out ensuring no cheating. The timer was set for one hour. Confident and happy, I recognized the questions and responses from my vigorous review of the mock tests online and finished the examination before the timer signaled the end of the examination. Everyone remained quiet and seated until all examinations were collected to respect those who needed the entire hour to complete the test.

I received notification to attend a citizenship ceremony six weeks later. On the fifth of April 2017, I was sworn in as a Canadian citizen by an Ontario Provincial Court Justice, alongside one hundred new citizens. I applied for a Canadian passport and carried both passports when I traveled across the border stating "American" when I entered the

USA and "Canadian" when I returned home. Becoming a Canadian citizen was the best decision of my life.

In 2025, as the world endured another term with President Trump threatening to "annex Canada as a fifty-first state," I was thankful that I became a Canadian citizen during his first term in office. I exercised my right to vote at all levels of government in Canada during my first decade of citizenship. I proudly supported the "Buy Canadian" initiatives and only traveled to the USA to visit family. Prime Minister Carney was the perfect choice to lead Canada against Trump's threats on his northern neighbor.

The fourth of May 2025 marked the eightieth anniversary of Liberation Day where the Canadian Armed Forces along with American and British soldiers, freed The Netherlands from German occupation in 1945, the end of World War II in Europe. I attended a photography exhibit with my Dutch Canadian girlfriend, Dini, entitled "Eighty Faces of Liberation," a remarkable display of photographs of eighty survivors who courageously shared their stories as children displaced by the destruction of the war. We became close friends over 25 years after working together at my first school job and sharing our love of Dutch culture.

Dutch immigrants settled throughout Canada after the war. The Dutch government sent tulips to Ottawa each year as a tribute for hosting the Dutch Royal Family in exile during World War II. Canadian soldiers brought their Dutch girlfriends, also known as "War Brides," to Canada. As the Dutch were one of many explorers to North America five hundred years ago, their influence is notable throughout the continent. I always cherished the memories of my year abroad, the family and friendships that evolved throughout my life.

Writing this memoir was challenging, recalling all the memories of my life. It has been an exciting trip down memory lane, searching photographs, letters, and diaries to create this narrative as well as print and online research to clarify people, places, and events mentioned throughout this story. I immersed myself into the language and cultural uniqueness in four countries on two continents. I have retained friendships for life on both sides of the ocean since childhood. There have been gaps in my travels throughout my life but the memories have never disappeared and the desire to see the world in my retirement despite health issues continues to inspire me...

Follow your dreams   **Embrace the unknown**

Conquer your fears   **Enjoy life**

Acknowledgements

This book was created with the love of many people who passed through my life. My sincere gratitude and heartfelt thanks to:

- Jessica and Andrew and their families for their love and support. Watching my grandchildren thrive is my greatest joy.
- June and Leo, for raising me in a home built on love, tolerance and respect for all races and religions as it forged my path throughout my life. They gave me the privilege to experience life in a foreign country in my youth, which gave me the courage to immigrate across the border as an adult.
- Mark, Jan, Paul, and David for making our family a beautiful home sharing wonderful experiences growing up together that continues as we procreate the next generation of our lineage.
- Marvin and his family who opened my eyes to living with diversity.
- My cousins and their families who celebrated birthdays, weddings, memorials, and holidays together strengthening our family bonds across the continent.
- Staff and students in Irondequoit for making it the best place to learn and grow maintaining ties through frequent high school reunions.
- My Dutch family and friends for welcoming me into their homes, forging lifelong relationships across the Atlantic Ocean.
- My Canadian friends for helping me adapt to life across the border.

- Colleagues at Empire State College and San Jose State University I-School for introducing me to the world of online learning to pursue my post secondary education as a mature student in the new millennium while technology was evolving.
- My writing coaches, Kevin, Joel, Leslie, and fellow classmates for encouraging me to author this memoir gluing all those pieces together in the puzzle called life.

Back Cover Summary

When Margot returns home after her senior year abroad and finds love in Canada, will she relocate and live happily ever after?

Her memoir debuts with the flight across the pond on her high school graduation day, then flashbacks to her childhood where she develops the love of travel. She embraces the European lifestyle in a fairytale far away from the hustle and bustle of city life on a student exchange program. A shock to her system when she returns home to face the reality of continuing her education, embarking on a career, and then a weekend adventure in Canada changes everything; finding love, a permanent international relocation, and a new life.

"The big red suitcase: How a love for travel led to adventure, culture shock, and diverse learning experiences," is a stunning debut memoir from Margot who grew up in America and Europe and ended up in Canada. A novel of self-discovery based on real life events adapting to different cultures, nurturing lifelong friendships, enduring hardships, and maintaining family ties across the border. A teenage adventure of a lifetime across the pond opened her eyes to a world of love, diversity, and endless possibilities.

About the Author

Retired and living a peaceful life in the Niagara Region of Ontario, Canada, Margot enjoys watching her grandchildren thrive. An enthusiastic librarian, she visits the local public library reading memoirs and historical fiction. She has volumes of family photos, films, and videotapes to convert to digital formats to preserve her family heritage. She enjoys day trips to view live theatre performances of classics, musicals, and dramas. She is looking forward to knocking more places off her travel bucket list, discovering new places when the time is right.

Bibliography

Books

1956: Remember When. Millersville, TN: Seek Publishing, [n.d.].

Docalavich, Heather. The Netherlands. Broomall, PA: Mason Crest, 2013.

Frank, Anne. Diary of a Young Girl. New York: Bantam, 1993.

Frommer, Arthur (1929-2024). Europe on $5 a Day. c.1957.

Halverhout, Heleen A.M. Dutch Cooking. Amsterdam: De Driehoek, [n.d.].

Hill, Clint (1932-2025). Five Days in November: In Commemoration of the 60th Anniversary of JFK's Assassination. New York: Gallery Books, 2023.

Jacobsen, Karen. The Netherlands. Chicago, Children's Press, 1992.

Landis, Paul. The Final Witness: A Kennedy Secret Service Agent Breaks His Silence After Sixty Years. Chicago: Chicago Review Press, 2023.

Loftis, Larry. Watchmaker's Daughter: True story of WWII heroine, Corrie Ten Boom. New York: William Morrow, 2023.

McCrae, John (1872-1918). In Flanders Fields. c. 1915.

Reynolds, Simon. Welcome to the Netherlands. Milwaukee, WI: Gareth Stevens Publishing, 2002.

Internet Resources (date accessed)

Accelerated Reader. https://www.renaissance.com/products/practice-instruction/accelerated- reader. March 30, 2025.

American Library Association. https://www.ala.org. March 30, 2025.

Amsterdam. https://www.britannica.com/place/Amsterdam. April 6, 2025.

Ben Franklin Award. https://www.ibpabookaward.org/. March 30, 2025.

Brussels, Belgium. https://en.wikipedia.org/wiki/Brussels. April 6, 2025.

Canada Immigration & Citizenship. https://www.canada.ca/en/services/immigration- citizenship.html. March 20, 2025.

Cape Cod. https://www.capecod.com/. March 30, 2025

Dufferin-Peel District School Board. https://www.dpcdsb.org. March 30, 2025.

Eastman Kodak. https://www.kodak.com, March 1, 2025.

Elmira College. https://www.elmira.edu. March 3,2025.

Empire State College (SUNY) Center for Distance Learning. https://sunyempire.edu/index.html. March 30, 2025.

Etobicoke Handweavers Guild. https://www.neilsonparkcreativecentre.com/learn/resident- groups/etobicoke-handweavers-and-spinners-2/. March 30, 2025.

European Union. https://en.wikipedia.org/wiki/European_Union. March 20, 2025.

Highland Hospital. https://www.urmc.rochester.edu/highland. March 3, 2025.

Hike for Hope. https://www.democratandchronicle.com/story/news/local/2013/11/08/whatever- happened-to-hike-for-hope/3479103/. April 6, 2025.

The Holocaust. https://en.wikipedia.org/wiki/The_Holocaust. May 13, 2025.

House of Guitars. https://houseofguitars.com/history/. March 22, 2025.

Hunt Hollow Ski Club. https://www.hunthollow.com/ March 30, 2025.

IBPA Independent Book Publishers Association. https://www.ibpabookaward.org/ March 30, 2025. (formerly Ben Franklin Award).

Irondequoit High School. https://ihs.westirondequoit.org. March 6, 2025.

Liberation Day. https://en.wikipedia.org/wiki/Liberation_Day_(Netherlands). May 13, 2025.

Maltman International. http://www.maltmans.com/. March 20, 2025.

Mirvish Theatre. https://www.mirvish.com. April 6, 2025.

Mississauga Public Library. https://www.mississauga.ca/library. March 30, 2025

Monroe Community College. https://www.monroecc.edu/, March 20, 2025.

Nazareth College. https://www2.naz.edu. March 3, 2025.

Netherlands. https://en.wikipedia.org/wiki/Netherlands. May 13, 2025

Netherlands in World War II. https://en.wikipedia.org/wiki/Netherlands_in_World_War_II. May 13, 2025.

North American Life Assurance Company. https://www.northamericancompany.com/. March 20, 2025.

Ontario Association for Family Mediation. https://www.oafm.on.ca/family-mediation/family- mediation-process/. April 6,2025.

Ontario Library Association. https://accessola.com. March 30, 2025.

Paris Je t'aime. https://parisjetaime.com/eng/. April 6, 2025.

Paul Bernardo murder conviction. https://en.wikipedia.org/wiki/Paul_Bernardo. March 30, 2025.

Roe vs Wade. https://www.elle.com/culture/career-politics/a39894580/roe-v-wade-summary. March 30, 2025.

San Jose State University I-School. https://ischool.sjsu.edu. March 30, 2025.

September 11th Attacks. https://en.wikipedia.org/wiki/September_11_attacks. March 30, 2025.

Shaw Frestival, Niagara on the Lake, Ontario. https://www.shawfest.com/ April 6, 2025.

Sheridan College. https://www.sheridancollege.ca. March 30, 2025

Steve Martin. https://en.wikipedia.org/wiki/Steve_Martin, April 6, 2025.

Stratford Festival. https://www.stratfordfestival.ca/ April 6, 2025.

Terry Fox Run. https://terryfox.org/, March 30, 2025

United Parcel Service. https://www.ups.com/ca/en/home. February 12, 2025.

Visit Rochester, New York. https://www.visitrochester.com/ April 6, 2025.

The Way International. https://www.theway.org/. March 30, 2025.

Welcome to Rochester, New York. https://www.cityofrochester.gov/ April 6, 2025.

White Mountains. https://www.visitwhitemountains.com/things-to-do/outdoors/hiking-trails. February 12, 2025.

Youth for Understanding Student Exchange Program (YFU). https://yfu.org. February 12, 2025.

Music Resources

Audrey Hepburn. Breakfast at Tiffany's – Moon River. https://www.youtube.com/watch?v=uirBWk-qd9A. c. 1961.

The Beatles. Hey Jude. https://www.youtube.com/watch?v=A_MjCqQoLLA. c.1968.

Don Potter. Over the Rainbow. https://www.youtube.com/watch?v=UU62fa9IkQ0&list=RDUU62fa9IkQ0&start_radio=1. c.1978.

Elton John. Daniel. https://www.youtube.com/watch?v=0f0TMfQNRk8&list=RD0f0TMfQNRk8&start_radio=1. c.1973.

Simon and Garfunkel. Sounds of Silence. https://www.youtube.com/watch?v=l0q7MLPo-u8. c.1964.

Stevie Wonder. I Just Called To Say I Love You. https://www.youtube.com/watch?v=58RgLQ_0Ars&list=RD58RgLQ_0Ars&start_radio=1. c.1984.

TIMELINE SUMMARY

DATE	LOCATION	PERSONAL EVENT	WORLD EVENT	AGE (YRS)
1956	Rochester	Birth March 20	USA vs USSR Cold War	0
1960	Irondequoit	Childhood Home	JFK wins Presidency	4
1961	Irondequoit	Listwood School	Breakfast At Tiffany's	5
1962	Irondequoit	Marvin attends IHS	Cuban Missile Crisis	6
1963	Italy	Parents 2nd Honeymoon	JFK Assassination	7
1964	Irondequoit	Love the Beatles	Civil Rights Act	8
1965	Road Trip - Southwest	Family Vacation	Sound of Music	9
1966	Irondequoit	Dake Middle School	Vietnam War Escalates	10
1967	Europe	Family Vacation	Vietnam War Protests	11
1968	Canadian Rockies	Family Vacation	MLK & RFK Assassinations	12
1969	Europe	Family Vacation	First Man on the Moon	13
1970	Irondequoit	IHS Begins, Pop Dies	Voting lowered to age 18, Earth Day	14
1971	California	Solo vacation – cousins	Greenpeace (environmental)	15
1972	California	Solo vacation – cousins	Munich Olympics Massacre	16
1973	Irondequoit	IHS Graduation	Roe vs Wade (Abortion legal)	17
1973	Belgium, Netherlands	YFU Program	Arab Oil Embargo (pro Israel)	17
1974	Netherlands	YFU Program	Nixon Resignation	18
1974	New York	Elmira College	Stephen King "Carrie" best seller	18
1975	New York	Nazareth College	Vietnam War Ends, "Jaws" movie	19
1976	Connecticut	Family Wedding	Nadia Comaneci Gymnast *10	20
1976	Rochester	Highland Hospital	Jimmy Carter Election	20
1977	Netherlands	Return Veendam	Saturday Night Fever (J. Travolta)	21
1978	Rochester, Toronto	Long Distance Romance	Star Wars, Video Games Debut	22
1979	Toronto, CANADA	Immigration	American Embassy Iran hostages	23
1980	Rochester	Wedding	Terry Fox run, Canada goes Metric	24
1981	Toronto	First Home	Canada frees American hostages Iran	25

1982	Toronto	Jeannet (summer camp)	Vietnam War Memorial Wash, DC	26
1983	Toronto	Elly and Jeanet visit	Sally Ride, first woman in space	27
1984	Netherlands	Jeannet Suicide	Michael Jackson Moonwalk	28
1985	Toronto	First Pregnancy	Live Aid Concert for famine relief	29
1986	Toronto	Childbirth - daughter	Space Shuttle Challenger Disaster	30
1987	Toronto	Motherhood	Canadian loonie replaces $1 bill	31
1988	Toronto	Childbirth - son	Pan AM Terrorist Bomb Scotland	32
1989	Toronto	Mama Nel visits Canada	NAFTA begins - Canada, Mexico, USA	33
1990	Mississauga	Second Home	Hubble Space Telescope orbit earth	34
1991	Mississauga, Wisconsin	Family Wedding	USSR collapses – Cold War ends	35
1992	Mississauga	School Volunteer	Bill Clinton elected President	36
1993	Mississauga	Lunchroom Supervisor	Paul Bernardo murders in Ontario	37
1994	Irondequoit	IHS 20th Reunion	Baseball strike cancels world series	38
1995	Florida	First Family Vacation	OJ Simpson accused of murder	39
1995	Rochester	Family Wedding	Uncle dies	39
1996	Oakville	Sheridan College begins	Canadian toonie replaces $2 bill	40
1997	Cape Cod, MA	Second Family Vacation	JK Rowling Harry Potter debut	41
1997	Mississauga	St Paul CSS	Princess Diana death in Paris crash	41
1998	Oakville	Sheridan College	Google launched, Clinton impeached	42
1999	Mississauga	Ankie Visit	Columbine School Shooting Colorado	43
1999	California	Third Family Vacation	Global Scare Y2K Bug	43
2000	Oakville	Sheridan Graduation	International Space Station opens	44
2000	Mississauga	Clarkson SS	Survivor - Reality Television debut	44
2001	Mississauga	Records Clerk, FOL	September 11 Attacks	45
2001	Online	ESC begins	War in Afghanistan	45
2002	Cancun, Mexico	Fourth family vacation	Euro currency debut	46
2003	Streetsville	Campion CSS, FOL	Columbia Shuttle disaster, Iraq war	47
2004	Saratoga Springs, NY	ESC Graduation	Aunt dies	48
2004	Mississauga	Third Home	Social Media debut	48
2005	Mississauga	Eva Visits	Hurricane Katrina New Orleans	49
2006	Online	SJSU MLIS begins	Twitter launched	50
2007	Brampton	Campion CSS	Internet Streaming, Amazon Kindle	51
2008	Mississauga	Loyola CSS	Castro resigns, Stock Market crash	52
2009	Irondequoit	IHS 35th Reunion	Obama Presidency	53
2010	Mississauga	Loyola CSS	Vancouver Winter Olympics	54
2011	California	SJSU Graduation	Osama Bin Laden Murdered	55
2012	Mississauga	Separation / Divorce	Sandy Hook School Massacre	56
2012	Prince Edward Island	Road Trip girlfriend	Canadian pennies eliminated	56
2013	Europe	NDL, Brussels, Paris	Obama 2ndTerm, King Willem NDL	57

2014	Cape Cod	Road Trip girlfriends	H McCallion Mississauga Mayor retire	58
2015	Malton	Ascension CSS	Justin Trudeau – Canada PM	59
2016	New Orleans	Birthday Vacation Mom	Bastille Day Massacre - France	60
2016	Chicago, Sedona	Family Weddings	Family Deaths – Aunt, Uncle, FIL	60
2017	Mississauga	Canadian Citizenship	First Trump Presidency	61
2017	Montana, Maine	Family Weddings	Canada 150 yrs anniversary	61
2017	Milton	1st Grandson birth	Brexit – UK leaves EU	61
2018	Ontario, Canada	Children's Weddings	Doug Ford Premier Ontario	62
2019	Irondequoit	IHS 45th Reunion	Zelenskyy elected President Ukraine	63
2020	World Shuts Down	Work From Home	COVID closed borders	64
2021	Mississauga	Retired DPCDSB	Biden – Harris Presidency	65
2022	Antigua (winter)	Caribbean Vacation	World Reopens / MIL dies	66
2023	Mississauga, Milton	2 Granddaughters born	King Charles III Coronation	67
2024	Hamilton	2nd Grandson birth	Sweden in NATO, Israel / Gaza War	68
2024	Irondequoit	IHS 50th Reunion	Trump won Second Presidency	68
2025	Mississauga	Liberation Day 80 yrs	Mark Carney – Canada PM	69